# CONSUMPTION
# AND IDENTITY
# AT WORK

# CONSUMPTION AND IDENTITY AT WORK

Paul du Gay

SAGE Publications
London • Thousand Oaks • New Delhi

SAGE Publications Ltd
6 Bonhill Street
London EC2A 4PU

SAGE Publications Inc
2455 Teller Road
Thousand Oaks, California 91320

SAGE Publications India Pvt Ltd
32, M-Block Market
Greater Kailash – I
New Delhi 110 048

**British Library Cataloguing in Publication data**

A catalogue record for this book is available from the British Library.

ISBN 0 8039 7927 4
ISBN 0 8039 7928 2 (pbk)

**Library of Congress catalog record available**

Typeset by Mayhew Typesetting, Rhayader, Powys
Printed in Great Britain by Redwood Books, Trowbridge, Wiltshire

# Contents

# Acknowledgements

This book has been a long time in the making and as a result the debts accumulated are vast. Where to begin? Well, thanks first to John Allen and Graeme Salaman who supervised the doctoral research project upon which this book is based and with whom I am glad to say I still enjoy a close working relationship.

A significant part of this book resonates with the voices of women and men who work in retail. I would like to thank all those people in the various organizations I visited who gave up their time to talk to me about their work and lives.

I am also pleased at last to be able to thank publicly my friends and family for their emotional and (let's face it) financial support during the PhD process; in particular, I would like to thank my parents, Pat and Peter du Gay, for their love and other forms of assistance, and Celia Lidchi, for allowing me to use her house as if it were my own.

Another debt is owed to those who have discussed ideas with me, or allowed me to steal them. Among the many I would like to thank especially: Huw Beynon, Frances Bonner, Richard Brown, Julie Charlesworth, John Clarke, Gill Court, James Donald, Stuart Hall, Stephen Hill, Peter Miller, Beverley Mullings, Keith Negus and Nikolas Rose. I would also like to thank the ESRC (Grant No. R00428824061) and the Social Science Faculty Research Committee at the Open University for providing the financial support which enabled my research to take place.

During the long period of preparing this text I have received considerable encouragement and support from Sue Jones at Sage. I would like to thank her for helping me to develop some implicit themes from earlier drafts.

Henrie Lidchi read the entire text in draft and it has benefited greatly from her wise counsel. My greatest thanks, as ever, are to her.

Some of the material contained in this book has appeared elsewhere in modified form: parts of Chapter 3 have appeared as 'Enterprise culture and the ideology of excellence', *New Formations*, 13, 1991; and 'The enterprising subjects of excellence', in J. Child, M. Crozier, R. Mayntz, P. du Gay et al., 1993, *Societal Change between Market and Organization* (Aldershot: Avebury). An earlier version of Chapter 5 appeared as 'Numbers and souls: retailing and the de-differentiation of economy and culture', in *British Journal of Sociology*, 44(1), 1993.

# Introduction

The death of God left the angels in a strange position. They were
overtaken suddenly by a fundamental question. . . . The question was,
'What are angels?'

(Donald Bartheleme, 'On Angels')

The question of 'identity' has become a central theme in a variety of
debates within the social and human sciences. Within the field of international relations, for example, the identity of the modern 'nation-state' as
an ostensibly 'sovereign' entity has been put into question in the light of an
intensification in patterns of global interconnectedness. Similarly, within
certain forms of sociological analysis, the dominance of 'class' as the
'master identity' of the social – that category through which all social
identities are mediated – has been problematized by, for example, the
growth of various new social movements: 'feminisms', black struggles, the
ecological movement, among others. Although the term 'identity' has taken
on different connotations depending upon the context within which it is
deployed, one thing appears clear, 'identity only becomes as issue when it is
in crisis, when something assumed to be fixed, coherent and stable is
displaced by the experience of doubt and uncertainty' (Mercer, 1991: 43).

The world of paid work, employment and organization has not been
exempt from this 'identity crisis'. For example, recent changes in the
industrial and occupational structures of modern Western societies have
posed questions about the 'identity' of a modern economy conceived of
both in terms of the dominance of large-scale manufacturing industry and
in terms of a national system of interdependent sectors, and about the
identity of 'the modern industrial worker' defined as a white, male breadwinner working full time (Pateman, 1989; Allen, 1992b). In other words,
such developments as the expansion of services, the increasingly global
organization of production and exchange, and the 'feminization' of the
labour force have revealed the 'constructed' character of ostensibly stable,
unified and 'natural' economic identities. In so doing they have served to
indicate that rather than being some original, unchanging 'base' –
remaining identical with itself throughout all the changes it undergoes – the
'economic' is a culturally and historically malleable category, and, thus,
that any established economic identity is in essence a *contingent* identity.

Let me explain what I mean by this. At a simple level, to suggest that
something is contingent amounts to saying that the conditions of existence
of an entity are exterior to it and not interior to it. In other words, a

contingent identity can never manage to constitute itself fully because it relies upon something 'outside' of itself for its very existence. Thus, a contingent identity only constitutes itself *in relation to that which it is not*. However, because that identity would not be what it is outside of the relationship with the force antagonizing it, the latter is also part of the conditions of existence of that identity. Following some suggestive remarks by Laclau (1990), it is therefore possible to say that any social identity is basically *dislocated*. According to Laclau (1990: 39), every identity is *dislocated* in so far as it 'depends upon an outside which both denies that identity and provides its condition of possibility at one and the same time'. In this reading, 'identity' becomes an extremely ambiguous achievement, dependent upon its ability to define difference and 'vulnerable to the entities it would so define to counter, resist, overturn, or subvert definitions applied to them' (Connolly, 1991: 64).

However, as Laclau (1990: 45) goes on to suggest, if any identity is basically a contingent identity then power is always inscribed in the relation an established identity bears to the differences it constitutes. Laclau explains this affirmation in two ways. First, he suggests that, if a contingent identity is a threatened identity, it can only establish itself through repressing that which antagonizes it. Thus, to study the conditions of existence of any established identity is to delineate the power mechanisms making it possible. Secondly, he argues that, because an established identity is not a homogeneous point but an articulated set of elements, there can be no identity without the exercise of power. As this articulation is not a necessary articulation, 'its characteristic structure, its "essence" depends entirely on that which it denies' (Laclau, 1990: 32).

To return briefly to the examples cited above. In her discussion of the 'patriarchal welfare state', Pateman (1989: 186–7) draws attention to the contingent character of the identity of the 'modern industrial worker' and the power relations inscribed within that particular creation. Rather than being a universal, gender-free 'individual', she argues, the 'modern worker' is a male breadwinner who has an economically dependent wife to take care of his daily needs and look after his home and children. In other words, the identity of the 'modern worker' is established in large part through the power and status afforded to men as husbands, and the constitution of women as their economic dependents or 'housewives' relegated to the private sphere of the home. The stable, public identity of the 'modern worker' is therefore established through the positioning of women as 'other' within the domestic sphere.

However, as Pateman (1989: 196) has indicated, the historically contingent character of this breadwinner/dependant dichotomy has been dramatically revealed as the conditions of its existence have been quite substantially undermined in the 1980s and 1990s. Changes in the social position of women, technological and structural transformations within the global economy, and the persistence of high levels of unemployment have served to problematize the 'violent hierarchies' through which the fixed, stable identity of the 'modern worker' was established. As a result, what it means to be a worker is no longer as certain as it once was.

Similarly, as Allen (1992a), for example, has indicated, the identity of a modern national economy, conceived of both in terms of a system of internally related sectors with links out to the wider international economy, and in terms of the dominance of manufacturing industry as its 'engine of growth' and provider of 'real jobs', has been made problematic by a number of developments. For example, the organization of production and exchange on an increasingly global scale has led to the 'dislocation' of national economies. Rather than systems of interconnected sectors whose boundaries correspond with those of a nation-state, national economies are fast becoming sites across which international forces move at varying rates.

At the same time, the predominance of service industries within contemporary Western societies has put into question the identity of a modern economy structured in the image of manufacturing industry (Allen and du Gay, 1994). If, for example, the identity of 'real work' is associated with employment in manufacturing and established in relation to the 'unproductive' labour of services, what is the status of that identity when the overwhelming bulk of employment in Western societies is now located in so-called 'services'? Once again the contingency and 'constructed nature' of an apparently 'given' identity is revealed as the conditions of its existence are negated.

If every identity is dislocated to the extent that it relies upon a constitutive 'outside' which simultaneously affirms and denies that identity, then it follows that the effects of dislocation will never be unambiguous. If, on the one hand, they threaten established identities, on the other, they are the foundations upon which new identities are established (Haraway, 1990; Laclau, 1990; Connolly, 1991). As Pateman's (1989: 196) analysis suggests, the displacement of the identity of the 'worker' is not the universal disaster that some have maintained. Because this identity was largely constituted in relation to the subordination of women within the domestic sphere, its demise is more disturbing for some than for others. In other words, to the extent that the 'modern worker' is basically a male character, his passing may be considered more a gendered tragedy than an totally unambiguous one. If dislocation unhinges stable identities, it also opens up the possibility of new articulations: the construction of new identities and the production of different social subjects.

This book is an attempt to explore some of the new articulations that are emerging within the world of paid work and organizations. In particular, it is concerned with delineating and examining the construction of new work identities and the production of different work-based subjects.

## Dislocation and the subject of work

Following Laclau (1990: 39), therefore, it could be argued that the world of paid work and organizations has not been immune from 'the generalization of dislocatory relations'. However, while it has been generally accepted that contemporary economic life is increasingly dislocated, there has been vociferous disagreement as to how the effects of this dislocation should be interpreted (Sabel, 1982; Lash and Urry, 1987, 1993; Beynon, 1992).

For some, the growth of service work, for example, involves a change in the relationship between different spheres of social activity, and establishes the possibility of new forms of work-based identity. According to Urry (1990), because an important feature of much service work is the more or less direct relationship between one or more service providers and one or more service consumers, the traditional separation between 'production' and 'consumption' characteristic of manufacturing employment no longer holds. The inherently 'social' nature of much service work could therefore involve a distinct change in the cultural relations of the workplace, and the production of novel, 'hybrid', work-based subjects.

On the other hand, Beynon (1992: 177), for example, acknowledges that enormous changes have taken place 'in the organization of work, in its content and distribution between people and places', yet he feels that the distinction made between the nature of manufacturing work and most service work is highly exaggerated. For Beynon, the content and organization of most service jobs involves the extension rather than the erosion of manual industrial labour. In other words, most contemporary service work entails the continuity of industrial labour 'maintained within different sets of relationships and contexts' (Beynon, 1992: 182).

Thus, whereas for Urry (1990) contemporary service work can be seen to involve new articulations between work and consumption and the creation of complex work identities, for Beynon (1992) contemporary service work involves the extension of industrial labour into different areas of work and forms of work relationship, with a consequent diminution in the possibility of that work affording any positive meaning or identity to those performing it. According to Beynon (1992: 182), the service employee, just as much as the traditional industrial worker, is subjected to 'the onward march of capital', whether the latter is conceived of as 'organized' or 'disorganized' in character.

Although both Urry and Beynon stress the dislocated nature of contemporary economic life, they operate with very different conceptions of 'dislocation'. For Beynon, economic dislocation seems to have an objective meaning and appears to be part of a process that is predetermined. The subject of change is therefore internal to that process and is determined by it. For Urry, on the other hand, the effects of dislocation are more ambiguous. Rather than maintaining some definitive essence outside of its dominant articulation, the identity of 'work' is seen to be actively transformed by changes in its organization. If, for example, the worker's relationship with non-work activity is modified by the shift to service employment then there is no longer the same identity – the worker – in a new situation, *but a new identity*. In other words, given that every social identity is a contingent construction, and given that any contingent identity is essentially relational in its conditions of existence, any changes in the latter cannot fail to affect the former.

For Urry, therefore, what it means to be a worker is not set in stone, once and for all, but is dependent upon historical and cultural conditions. Urry suggests that the idea that 'work' has some essential 'real' meaning which precedes or evades its dominant discursive articulation in any historical or cultural context cannot be substantiated. Rather, he argues that the 'truth' about the being of any activity is only constituted within a particular discursive context. In other words, what economic activity means cannot be deduced simply from the existential materiality of its constitutive elements, but only from its situation within a determinate system of social relations.

At the same time, Urry (1990: 271–4) also suggests that if the shift to services is in the process of dissolving certain established divisions between work and consumption and of producing more complex, 'hybrid', work-based subjects, then analysis of these developments will need to reflect this increased complexity. For example, if knowledge of the dynamics of contemporary consumer culture is essential to understanding the construction of work identities then an examination of work organization and conduct is no longer amenable to a purely 'productionist' analysis. Because an important part of the production and consumption of a service is the 'quality of the service interaction' then service work cannot be conceptualized only as an economic phenomenon but must also be understood in terms of cultural relations (Allen and du Gay, 1994). Thus, if the growth of services establishes a new identity for 'work' as an object of analysis, it simultaneously requires different, possibly new, approaches to understanding that object.

In keeping with the spirit of the latter argument, this book can be read as an attempt to examine the production of novel work identities utilizing theoretical tools derived from sources not traditionally associated with the study of work and organization. While there are obviously interpretative risks to be borne in adopting an approach which breaks with more conventional forms of analysis, there are times, as Foucault (1987: 8) suggests, 'when knowing if one can think differently than one thinks, and perceive differently than one sees, is absolutely necessary if one is to go on looking and reflecting at all'.

## Content and organization

This book, then, examines how contemporary changes in the government of organizational life have impacted upon organizational and personal identity. In particular, it explores the ways in which new modes of organizational conduct have blurred traditional differences between production and consumption identities.

The book is divided into two parts. Part I (Chapters 1–4) explores certain limitations in traditional approaches to the analysis of work identity

within the social sciences and attempts to construct an alternative framework for analysing the *discursive* construction of work-based subjectivity
and identity. The concept of 'discourse', it is argued, provides a means of
overcoming the debilitating 'binary oppositions' – between 'action' and
'structure', 'individual' and 'productive apparatus' and 'ideology' and
'truth' – that have characterized analyses of work identity.

Chapter 1 begins by discussing the historically privileged role that has
been accorded to 'work' in the formation of identity by the social sciences.
It then goes on to outline and evaluate critically the major approaches to
the study of work-based identity and subjectivity within the social sciences,
particularly those derived from (different versions of) Marxism, neo-
Weberian sociology and symbolic interactionism. Chapter 2 indicates how
the debilitating essentialisms characterizing these theories can best be
overcome. The chapter focuses upon the contemporary turn to culture
within the human and social sciences and argues that it is within cultural
theory that the most productive theoretical tools can found for analysing
the construction of work-based subjectivity and identity. Of particular
importance here is the assertion that identity and subjectivity are constituted discursively and hence that all forms of work-based identity and
subjectivity are fundamentally contingent. Chapter 3 builds upon the
theoretical arguments outlined in Chapter 2 by tracing the ways in which
the categories of 'worker' and 'manager' have been constituted at different
historical junctures through their positioning within a variety of discourses
of work reform. A central argument of the chapter is that changes in the
ways of conceptualizing, documenting and acting upon – in other words,
governing – the internal world of organizations actively transform the
meaning and hence 'reality' of work. The chapter is concerned with
delineating the ways in which different categories of person are 'made up'
at work through a focus upon contemporary discourses of organizational
reform (particularly as these have developed in Britain and the United
States). In the chapter I argue that a key feature of these new modes of
governing organizational life is the way they problematize traditional
separations between production and consumption identities – between what
is properly thought of as inside and what is properly thought of as outside
the domain of organizational existence. I suggest that, by re-imagining
organizational life through the language of consumer culture, these new
discourses of work reform brook no opposition between the mode of self-
presentation and self-understanding required of people as consumers and
that required of people as employees.

If the primary image informing representations of organizational life
today is that of the 'sovereign consumer', and if organizational practices
and technologies are increasingly structured around 'staying close to the
customer', then it is apparent that interpreting the production and regulation of work-based identity and subjectivity necessitates an understanding
of the dynamics of contemporary consumer culture. Chapter 4 is concerned
with providing just such an understanding through delineating and

critically examining the main conceptualizations of consumption and consumer culture developed within the social sciences. The chapter argues that the representations of consumption circulating within the social sciences have tended to veer between the two extremes of 'structural pessimism', on the one hand, where consumer culture is entirely determined by the forces of production, and a 'heady romanticism', on the other, where consumption is seen as an inherently creative activity entirely divorced from that of production. The chapter outlines an approach to contemporary production/consumption relations which seeks to avoid these twin pitfalls of determinism and voluntarism. It argues that rather than representing consumption and production as two fully constituted objectivities, they should be conceptualized as inherently dislocated, as relational semi-identities involved in unstable, overlapping relations.

In Part II of the book, the main themes introduced in Part I are developed through an examination of contemporary changes in the government of organizational life in an industry where the blurring of the boundaries between production and consumption identities is perhaps most pronounced – retailing. Chapter 5 provides a rationale for focusing upon retailing as a crucial site in the current dislocation of production and consumption relations. The chapter begins by examining the cultural contours of retailing and stresses, in particular, the importance of the retail sector to the mode of existence and reproduction of contemporary consumer culture. It then proceeds to outline some of the major logistical developments occurring within the sector and indicates how these signal the shift to a more flexible system of accumulation within retailing. The chapter concludes by focusing upon some of the subjectivizing aspects of contemporary programmes of organizational reform within retailing, both for consumers and increasingly for retail employees.

Drawing on original research in the retail sector, Chapters 6 and 7 explore the processes through which shifts in the government of organizational life make up new ways for people to conduct themselves at work. In particular, these chapters build a picture of how contemporary discourses of organizational reform take hold in particular contexts, how the dreams and schemes they advocate and articulate are operationalized, how these discourses construct particular identities for employees and how the latter negotiate these identities in their everyday working lives.

In the concluding chapter I summarize the main themes developed in the book and offer some parting comments concerning the relationship between contemporary discourses of organizational governance and the domination of individuals as work-based subjects. In particular, I attempt to show how it might be possible to gain some critical purchase on these discourses of organizational reform and the regime of subjectification to which they are inextricably linked.

# PART I

# 1

# The Subjects of Production

Throughout this century the relationship between a person's sense of who they are – their personal identity – and the paid work they perform for a living has been a source of regular, if almost always implicit, concern to nearly all those engaged in theorizing about modern work organization and behaviour. Indeed, such concerns can be traced in the work of authors as seemingly diverse as Elton Mayo (1933) and Harry Braverman (1974). Mayo, for example, was keen to encourage the creation of an effective, scientifically informed managerial élite who would ensure that the modern industrial worker's innate need for belonging was met through the active construction of a strong sense of work-group identification. For Mayo, the creation of distinctive forms of work-based identification was an essential antidote to the potential pathologies of modern industrial civilization.

While deploying a very different theoretical schema, Braverman was also concerned with the effects of modern economic organization upon traditional forms of work-based identity. Although he deliberately avoided any explicit discussion of the possible effects of 'deskilling' on workers' consciousness, Braverman clearly believed that the process he described had profound consequences for people's experience of work. For at the same time as the logic of capital marched inexorably onwards, destroying craft-based knowledge and organization, it also eradicated the possibility of craft-based identity.

For Braverman, this process of transformation is tinged with nostalgia. His text is permeated with a sense of mourning for 'the world we have lost'. Again, this is something the Marxist also shares with the managerialist. For both writers, modern work is problematic. The focus of this problem is the question of meaning. Both Mayo and Braverman represent work as the crucial source of meaning in people's lives. As a fundamental human category, work is represented not only as livelihood, but also as a stable, consistent source of self-identity. However, as Berger (1964) has indicated, the process of differentiation integral to the advent of modernity involves the disarticulation of this 'essential' link between a person's sense of who they are and the work they perform. Thus the great divides of modern existence – between the public and the private, between work and leisure – bring into being 'the problem of work'.

Because Mayo and Braverman define what it means to be human primarily through work, it is unsurprising that they should represent the dynamics of modernity in pathological terms, as undermining people's essential 'real' identity. For both writers, modern work is *alienating*; it is held to estrange or separate people from one another and from their own self-identity. In turn, the link they posit between work and humanity leads them to advocate a similar solution to this problem of alienation: the creation of a work-based 'dream home'.

Mayo's solution to the anomie of industrialism takes the form of training managers how to create conditions at work that will satisfy workers' 'innate' needs for 'belonging'. Meanwhile, the more radically inclined Braverman indicates that alienation will only be overcome through the destruction of capitalism and its replacement by a social system where people can once again be at one with each other and themselves through their work: namely communism/socialism. What unites these two writers is a belief that the dynamics of modernity make it no longer possible for people to identify humanly with the work they perform, coupled with a desire to transcend this fundamental antagonism by creating a 'dream home' that will somehow fix a person's place in the world once more and hence re-establish his or her essential 'real' identity and personal authenticity.

As Anthony (1977: 34–5) has suggested, through the vehicle of an essentialist representation of work as the key to human self-actualization and self-fulfilment, both managerialist discourse and radical Marxist and sociological critiques of capitalist work forms can be seen to share remarkably similar assumptions. He goes on to argue that 'the essential paradox of alienation is that it emerges with any meaning only as a result of an over-emphasis on a work ethic and work-based values.' However, it is not simply certain managerialist and Marxist accounts that are framed within the discourse of alienation. Nearly all sociological analyses of work-based subjectivity and identity have been cast within the shadow of this modern problematic. 'Alienation' has acted as a nodal point around which discussion of the proper place of paid work in people's lives has been conducted (Mills, 1953; Goldthorpe et al., 1968; Thompson and McHugh, 1990).

In this chapter I propose to examine critically three major social scientific – predominantly sociological – approaches to the study of work-based subjectivity and identity, indicating, among other things, their formative relation to this modern problematic of alienation. Although these three approaches constitute the sites where the 'problem' of work-based subjectivity and identity has received most explicit attention within the social sciences, it is still rare for subjectivity and identity to be the main focus of analysis. Rather, they normally form a part of some alternative project, such as an attempt to explain changing forms of working-class consciousness.[1]

I begin by focusing upon Marxist understandings of subjectivity at work, and the fundamental role that the concept of alienation has played, and continues to play, in such analyses. I then move on to explore neo-Weberian approaches to the study of work identity, indicating how these were constructed in part in reaction to Marxist notions of alienation. Lastly, I examine the tradition of symbolic interactionism concentrating, in particular, upon the relationship between 'communicative interaction', 'self' and 'work' forged within this paradigm. I show how the analysis of work identity advocated by the interactionists is formed in apposition to the 'architectonic constructions' of orthodox Marxism – with its problematic of alienation – and other 'structural' sociologies (Rock, 1979).

Having outlined and critically examined these three approaches to the analysis of work-based subjectivity and identity, I will then go on to assess their explanatory reach. In particular, I will focus upon the theory of the subject residing within each of these traditions.

## Marx, alienation and the work-based subject

Marxist understandings of subjectivity at work 'begin with the concept of alienation' (Thompson and McHugh, 1990: 308). As with many of Marx's formulations 'alienation' is imbued with different meanings in different contexts (Ollman, 1971). However, two main uses of the term can be distinguished in his work. First, there is 'social alienation': the power that human products and processes may come to acquire over their creators. In this sense, alienation is closely linked to the notion of 'reification' – for if social phenomena cease to be recognizable as the products of human action then it is understandable to perceive them as material things, and thus to accept them as inevitable. Secondly, there is what is sometimes referred to as 'spiritual alienation' or 'lack of self-actualization' (Elster, 1985). In the latter use of the term, the alienation generated by capitalism is represented as a lack of a sense of meaning. Marx's interest in the nature of work and its role in constituting human personhood is mainly revealed in his discussions of this version of alienation. In the *Economic and Political Manuscripts*, for example, he asks

> In what does this alienation of labour consist? First that the work is *external* to the worker, that it is not part of his nature, that consequently he does not fulfil himself in his work but denies himself, has a feeling of misery, not of well being, does not develop freely a physical and mental energy, but is physically exhausted and mentally debased. The worker therefore only feels at home in his leisure, whereas at work he feels homeless. His work is not voluntary but imposed, *forced labour*. It is not the satisfaction of a need, but only a means for satisfying other needs. Its alien character is clearly shown by the fact that as soon as there is no physical or other compulsion it is avoided like the plague. Finally, the alienated character of work for the worker appears in the fact that it is not his work but work for someone else, that in work he does not belong to himself but to another person. (Bottomore and Rubel, 1963: 177–8)

As this passage suggests, under the capitalist regime of production workers are alienated from the product of their labour since what they produce is appropriated by others and consequently they have no control over its fate. At the same time, they are also alienated from the very *act of production*. Working becomes an alien activity because it offers no intrinsic satisfaction. However, these two facets of alienation really only serve to highlight the ultimate crime: that under the capitalist mode of production workers are alienated from their human nature or 'species being'. According to Marx, if workers are alienated both from the act of production and from the products of their labour, then their productive activity is systematically deprived of those specifically human qualities which distinguish it from the activity of animals and thus define what it means to be a person.

While Marx frequently suggested that human nature and needs were a product of history and culture, thus appearing to endorse an anti-essentialist position, it is also apparent throughout his work that one capacity in particular is deemed to define humanity: namely, the capacity for creative labour.[2] As Gaukroger (1986: 306–7) has indicated, Marx claimed that the alienation of labour formed the basis of all other forms of alienation, and that with the overcoming of alienated labour all other forms of alienation would be eradicated. While 'conscious life activity distinguishes man immediately from animal activity', for Marx the conditions of emergence, or 'origins', of human consciousness are linked inextricably to production. 'Man' becomes aware of himself, he argues, 'in a world that he has created.'

> It is just in his work upon the objective world, therefore, that man really proves himself to be a species being. This production is his active species life. Through this production, nature appears as *his* work and his reality. The object of labour is therefore the *objectification of man's species life*: for he duplicates himself not only, as in consciousness, intellectually, but also actively in reality, and therefore he sees himself in a world that he has created. In tearing away from man the object of his production, therefore, estranged labour tears him from his species life, his real objectivity as a member of the species, and transforms his advantage over animals into the disadvantage that his inorganic body, nature, is taken away from him. (quoted in Gaukroger, 1986: 303–4)

Simply stated, Marx sees it as 'Man's nature' to be 'his' own creator. Humans are deemed to form and develop themselves and their capacities by working on and transforming the natural world outside of themselves in association with their fellow human beings. In this progressive relation between humans and the world, it is in humankind's nature to be in control of this process, to be the initiator, the subject in which the process originates.

Thus the conception of human nature articulated by Marx is one in which it is assumed that people realize their identity as human persons, as a 'species', only through creative labour that is carried out for their own purposes and not under the control and exploitation of others. This implies that alienation is essentially an *objective* condition; it is not necessarily reflected in felt job dissatisfaction or frustration. Indeed, it is quite possible for alienation to grow increasingly more widespread throughout the social body without any growing feeling of discontent among those subjected to it. To put it bluntly, the analysis of alienation appears to require no consideration of the subjective experience of its effects.

Rather than being concerned with whether people's conscious desires are satisfied or how people think about themselves and their lives, alienation refers to the question of whether people's lives in fact actualize the potentialities which are objectively present in their human essence (Elster, 1985). In this reading, people are alienated when they are not being what they could possibly be in the best of all possible worlds. In order for them to become what they could be – to fulfil their human potential, or achieve 'self-actualization' – a different type of social formation is required. For Marx, the victory of communism/socialism over capitalism was to provide the central generating mechanism through which people would become human once more; that is, fully realize their potential as all-round creators. In other words, because complete human persons could never exist under conditions of alienation, subjectivity could have no force or effect. It could only await its activation/fulfilment in the destruction of capitalism and the building of socialism/communism.

Until that transformation was achieved, individual human agents living under the 'real conditions' of capitalism were to be represented simply as bearers of economic categories such as labour and capital. The later Marx insisted that 'only the people is a concrete fact', and allowed himself to consider people only 'in so far as they are the personifications of economic categories, embodiments of particular class relations and class interests' (quoted in P. Smith, 1988: 4). Thus, when Marx claimed that 'men make their own history' it was only the plural (and, needless to say, the masculine) form of the noun which was of importance.

Clearly, what is missing from Marx's account is any discussion of how individual human agents as bearers of class traits come to reconcile their existence as individual subjects with their existence as a 'collective subject', or to convert from one to another. In other words, the dynamics of alienation rely upon a certain neglect of 'what goes on in people's heads' (P. Smith, 1988: 4–5). Rather than attempting to explain the processes through which the social gets folded into the psychical, Marx instead suggests that the objective condition of alienation by its very nature prevents workers from being able to perceive their own situation (Elster, 1985: 107).

At this point it becomes apparent how closely related the concept of 'spiritual alienation' is to the notions of 'ideology' and 'false consciousness' in Marxist theory (Eagleton, 1991: 70). As Bottomore and Rubel (1963: 21) have indicated, 'false consciousness of individuals is a condition of alienation, and ideology is the system of beliefs produced by such a false consciousness.' For Marx, becoming a complete human being implies a release for the 'subject' from its alienation in the social, *and*, more generally, from the obfuscations and distortions of ideology. 'Man' is only able to emerge from 'the people' and become a 'concrete individual' in the realm of 'real freedom' where ideology no longer exists to alienate 'him'. As Gaukroger (1986: 311–12) suggests, some kind of imaginary wholeness of the human being can thus be seen to reside at the end of Marx's theoretical trajectory. Similarly, P. Smith (1988: 7) argues that 'If the goal of a socialist revolution is to be the development of "complete individuals" this surely marks an appeal to either a pre- or post-ideological condition where the subject/individual is again a plenitude.' The passage from 'really existing' conditions to those that would allow the 'complete individual' to flourish clearly involves the eradication of mystification, and it is around the notion of the 'real' that Marx attempts to conduct his argument for that dissolution.

In his work there appear to be two levels of reality at work. First, there are the 'real conditions' under which human agents live their lives in the here and now: the everyday realm of lived experience. This is the 'real' that Marx posits in opposition to the Hegelian idealist dialectic (Bottomore and Rubel, 1963: 22). At one and the same time, however, Marx also proposes a second and more truthful level of reality – a 'real' that is hidden within and by the representations that constitute ideological appearances. In other words, the second 'real' is contained within the first 'real', waiting to be activated. As P. Smith (1988: 11) suggests, although the language Marx deploys tends to obfuscate the differences between these two levels of reality, 'it seems that the one (the one shot through with "illusions" and the "appearance of simplicity") is merely the false representation of the other (the one which will become "simple and transparent" and in which the fully developed "individual" will live).'

As Hall (1984: 66; 1988) among others has argued, this proposition that 'real men' somehow live on the cusp of another reality that is only susceptible through the gaze of scientific Marxism is preposterous; merely an objectivist fantasy which presumes that real life conditions can be known independently of language, culture and history, by a few (Marxist) individuals 'armed with properly formed concepts' and lucky enough to enjoy a 'God's eye view'. The notion of false consciousness, which this idea of a double reality brings into being, implies that a strict separation can somehow be maintained between material social life and consciousness and its products. However, as Raymond Williams (1977: 60) has indicated, 'consciousness and its products are always, through variable forms, parts of the material social process itself.'

This double-decker notion of the real has led to a view of ideology – that which distorts a more truthful reality – as always a negative force; as one which is never enabling for those human subjects inhabiting ideologically constituted social space (Hall, 1988; Eagleton, 1991). If ideology is viewed in this way, and if the subject of history is always represented as subjected to social formations, then this appears to diminish significantly any impulse towards social change on the part of the individual human agent. As Laclau (1990), for example, has suggested, the only transformatory force available to such a view would appear to be a 'subjectless' automatic history.

Such a 'take' on the historical process inevitably foresees the eradication of ideology, and issues a demand for the unveiling of history's real truth. The desire to establish a transparent relationship between the socially active signifier and the real relations to which it might refer is thus expressed in a vocabulary of truth and falsity, clarity and misrecognition. This negative conception of ideology is most clearly articulated in *The German Ideology* where Marx refers to the realm of consciousness in which 'men and their relations appear upside down as in a *camera obscura*'. Thus ideology entails misperception and an incomplete knowledge of reality. It constitutes the dark realm of falsity in relation to which the light of objective Marxist 'science' will prevail.

What is important here is the idea that a fundamental 'real' object takes precedence over the sense of ideology as reality. The simple and transparent social organization that Marx envisages communism/socialism as constituting will involve the righting of the lines of light in the camera obscura so as to produce an undistorted image. It is in the perception of this undistorted image that the complete labouring individual that Marx talks of will participate (P. Smith, 1988: 12–13).

However, if the site of the subject continues to be seen as a matter of false consciousness, some argument must be put forward to indicate the conditions of possibility for the passage into the realm of light, and the 'raising of the subjective blinds' (P. Smith, 1988: 13). Traditionally within Marxism this argument has been advanced around the duality of theory and practice, and around the question of a possible distinction between ideology and science. However, these debates have tended to gravitate towards the same truth/falsity distinction which had authorized the contention that ideology can be represented as a distortion mechanism, preventing the establishment of true knowledge (Beechey and Donald, 1986). To this extent traditional Marxism has had no real choice but to predicate the possibility of new social relations upon the disappearance of ideology.

## Braverman and beyond

While Marx's conception of alienation has been shown to be a dubious explanatory device, it has also proved to be an extremely enduring one. Virtually all industrial sociology of a Marxist variant has some, if often unacknowledged, recourse to the problematic of alienation as an explanatory mechanism. One of the most influential post war Marxist texts in the sociology of work and employment, Braverman's (1974) *Labour and Monopoly Capital*, is centred around the objectivist concept of alienation.

Braverman (1974: 27) defended an exclusive focus upon the objective construct of class, and a deliberate avoidance of the subjective aspects of deskilling, on the grounds that it provided a radical riposte to 'bourgeois' accounts of changes in the labour process, in which, he argued, 'alienation' only existed in the consciousness of workers. In other words, Braverman objected to influential accounts, such as those of Blauner (1964), because he felt that they assumed and implied that workers could be liberated from alienation through specific mechanisms such as job-enrichment programmes and technologies, while, to his mind, the exploitative and oppressive structure of capitalist relations of production remain unaltered. While Braverman's thesis came in for wide-ranging criticism from within the Marxist tradition (Edwards, 1979; Storey, 1985), as well as from outside, most significant attempts to extend Braverman's analysis from within the field of Marxism have continued to deploy, if only implicitly, the concept of alienation.

One overwhelming theoretical weakness in Braverman's text has been identified by a number of critics within the Marxist tradition (Burawoy, 1979, 1985; Thompson, 1990; Thompson and McHugh, 1990): namely, that the 'objective' and 'subjective' aspects of the labour process can somehow be separated out and examined independently of one another. Reacting to Braverman's objectivist stance, Burawoy (1985: 24) argues that an understanding of the capitalist labour process cannot proceed without due attention being paid to the 'subjective' experience of work. Just as Marx's original conceptualization of alienation eradicated the subject from history, so, following in his footsteps, does Braverman.

As Thompson (1990: 114) has argued, 'the construction of a full theory of the missing subject is probably the greatest task facing labour process theory.' However, attempts to provide just such a theory from within the Marxist tradition have remained problematic. This has been due, in large part, to the continued presence of unacknowledged traces of the alienation hypothesis within these projects.

One of the earliest, and still possibly the most significant, of post-Braverman attempts to insert the subject into Marxist analyses of the labour process is Burawoy's (1979) *Manufacturing Consent*. Shaped in large part as a reaction to Braverman's thesis (1979: xiii–xiv), Burawoy sets out to examine how 'capitalism' has managed continuously to secure increasing volumes of surplus value at one and the same time as it obscures the seemingly exploitative nature of its control of the labour process. His arguments revolve around an account that deploys ethnographic evidence to counter Braverman's thesis of labour intensification resulting from an increase in management control and the separation of conception and execution. For Burawoy (1979: 72), the major generating mechanism in the simultaneous obscuring and securing of surplus value is an 'expansion of the "self-organisation" of workers as they pursue their daily activities.' In other words, it was the relaxation of management control within the context of the development of an elaborate shopfloor-induced 'game' of 'working out' that ensured the simultaneous generation and obscuring of surplus value. As a result of 'playing the game', Burawoy noted a sharp fall in management–worker conflict as antagonisms were deflected horizontally across the organization and away from the (for him) essential arena of class struggle. For Burawoy (1979: 89), the active involvement of the workforce in 'making out' generated a particular sense of work-based identity which compensated for the negative features of wage labour. In his eyes, what guaranteed the securing of surplus value, while obscuring the consciousness of its extraction among workers, was absorption in the 'game' and the subjective sense of autonomy and freedom it generated in workers involved in playing it. As Burawoy suggests, the pressures of 'making out' came more from fellow workers than from management, because 'playing the game' brought psychological and social rewards to those involved in it.

> when one is trying to make out, time passes more quickly – in fact, too quickly – and one is less aware of being tired. The difference between making out and not making out was thus not measured in the few pennies of bonus we earned but in our prestige, sense of accomplishment, and pride. Playing the game eliminated much of the drudgery and boredom associated with industrial work. (Burawoy, 1979: 89)

While Burawoy's discussion of the 'production of consent' at work does indicate how a sense of identity was created by workers in the practice of 'making out', his analysis has proved somewhat controversial (Knights and Willmott, 1989; Davies, 1990). For one thing, Burawoy's theory of consent is predicated on a fundamental division between work and non-work consciousness. He argues that shopfloor culture tends to be produced independently of any external influences (1979: 156). In other words, for Burawoy, consent is 'manufactured' relatively independently of a particular individual's biography or social attributes: gender, race, age etc. According to him, while particular social attributes may determine the placement of particular people into particular labour processes, it is their positions within production that determine their workplace 'consciousness' and behaviour. Accordingly, 'internal factors' are most likely to account for the production of consent.

Thus Burawoy's account suggests that shopfloor behaviours and satisfactions can be understood in terms of gender, age or 'race' free motivations and are shaped entirely in relation to positions within production. This suggests that once people arrive at the workplace they are no longer recognizable as black, old, female, or whatever, but simply assume a gender-, age- or race-evacuated identity as 'workers'.

This weakness in Burawoy's study is clearly related to the ontological priority he affords to the category of labour. Following Marx, Burawoy represents labour as humankind's fundamental constitutive activity. Consequently, the place and weight accorded to ethnicity, gender and the rest is determined by labour, because labour is *the* category through which all other aspects of existence are mediated. As Knights (1990: 311), for example, has indicated, Burawoy shares with Marx 'a tendency to fall back upon an essentialist theory of human nature . . . he assumes that the absence of conditions through which to express "the potentiality of the human species" is experienced as a deprivation for which compensation must be sought by constituting "work as a game".' In other words, he defines what it means to be a person, first and foremost, through the activity of 'creative labour'.

It transpires that the 'turn of the subject' in Burawoy's analysis is predicated upon Marx's objectivist fantasy of alienation. That workers 'play the game' is deemed to have less to do with anything else – such as the maintenance of their identity as particular sorts of male persons (Knights and Willmott, 1989; Davies, 1990) – than their desire to compensate for a thwarted human essence. By elevating labour to the status of 'essence', Burawoy effectively negates any further analysis of subjectivity at work.

Although Burawoy's attempt to insert the subject into the labour process is formed in reaction to Braverman's objectivist project, in the end it simply reiterates many of the problems inherent in Braverman's account. In particular, a common dependence upon the problematic of alienation in both projects ensures that the multiplicity of social relations positioning the subject – whether of gender, of ethnicity, of generation and so forth – disappear into the amorphous category of 'labour/worker'.

## Neo-Weberian approaches

In their different ways, both Braverman and Burawoy conceive of their respective projects as attempting to remedy a major deficiency in postwar sociological approaches to the study of work and employment. Braverman (1974: 27) described *Labour and Monopoly Capital* as a corrective to a focus among postwar industrial sociologists upon action and consciousness at the expense of the structures which condition their expression. While criticizing Braverman for his strong objectivism, Burawoy (1979: 136–40) also makes it clear that he has no truck with the middle-range 'actionalist' approaches of 'bourgeois' sociologists. In particular he singles out for criticism the neo-Weberian studies of Goldthorpe and Lockwood (Goldthorpe et al., 1968, 1969) for what he considers to be their exclusive focus upon external 'orientations' to work and their consequent neglect of the fundamental role of the relations of production in constituting workers' consciousness. As indicated earlier, for Burawoy (1979: 135) 'whatever consent is necessary for the obscuring and securing of surplus value is generated at the point of production rather than imported into the workplace from outside.'

In other words, for both Braverman and Burawoy, the 'action frame of reference',[3] articulated most keenly by *The Affluent Worker* project (Goldthorpe et al., 1968, 1969), represents a major blot on the sociological landscape because it attempts to deny the validity of alienation. It does so, they argue, by focusing upon subjective consciousness to the detriment of structural context, and by highlighting external 'orientations to work' at the expense of analysing the relations of production, and the dynamics of the capitalist labour process. However, for the authors of *The Affluent Worker*, the neo-Weberian 'action frame of reference' provided a refreshing antidote to extreme objectivist accounts – such as those of orthodox Marxism – of changes in working-class consciousness (Lockwood, 1988). In many respects, as Goldthorpe et al. (1969: 183–5) suggest, their approach was shaped in reaction to contemporary Marxist analyses, and, in particular, to the problematic of alienation.[4] For Goldthorpe, Lockwood and colleagues, the analysis of work identity contained within *The Affluent Worker*, and especially the explanatory device of 'orientations to work', was basically an unanticipated by-product of a much grander project (Goldthorpe et al., 1969: vii). It is to the wider context of this project that I now turn.

### The 'affluent worker' and the 'embourgeoisiement' hypothesis

The main aim of *The Affluent Worker* project was to examine empirically the claim that the British working classes of the late 1950s and early 1960s were becoming increasingly middle class. In other words, the study sought to explore the issue of *embourgeoisiement*. During the late 1950s many commentators were concluding that growing affluence in many Western economies was leading to the incorporation of prosperous manual workers into the middle classes. In Britain, a third consecutive Conservative victory at the polls in 1959 seemed to confirm the validity of the *embourgeoisiement* hypothesis, by indicating that the traditional class basis of party politics was being eroded.

Goldthorpe, Lockwood and their fellow researchers identified three main developments which were alleged to be of crucial significance to the progressive *embourgeoisiement* of the British working class. There were changes in economic circumstances (increased incomes and access to mass-produced consumer goods, with consequent changes in lifestyles); changes in the technology and organization of work (the decline of manual labour; developments in technology 'beyond conventional mass production methods', making work both more intrinsically satisfying, and thus creating a greater identification between workers and the companies employing them); and changes in the urban landscape (increased owner-occupation, suburbanization, and the redevelopment of the inner city). However, it was not the authors' objective to assess critically the evidence of these changes but rather to discover whether, in those contexts where most of these factors were to be located, they exhibited the effects attributed to them.

Having identified the main elements of the *embourgeoisiement* thesis, the empirical approach taken by the researchers proved quite straightforward: to find a prototypically affluent working-class population and discover how middle class it had become. In the event, sample populations of manual workers from a small number of factories in Luton became the subjects/ objects of the research programme.

Six years after initiating the project, and literally hundreds of interviews later, the authors were in a position to formulate their conclusions. They uncovered a portrait of the affluent worker which was unlike either of their posited ideal typical models: the 'traditional' (or 'solidaristic' model) and the 'bureaucratic' model inferred from the *embourgeoisiement* theorists.[5] Instead, they 'discovered' that the Luton workers did not adopt a 'them' and 'us' attitude to work; nor did they see their union as part of a wider labour movement. However, this coexisted with a lack of identification between worker and firm: the workers didn't see themselves as part of a team with the same objectives. These workers experienced little intrinsic satisfaction in their jobs. The lifestyle of the affluent worker was also most evidently not of a 'traditional' kind, involving neither networks of kinship nor those of neighbourhood. Moreover, the affluent worker didn't participate in the mutual entertaining or club membership which might be expected of those aspiring to middle-class status. Finally, in their 'images of society' the affluent workers adhered neither to the dichotomies of class power essential to 'solidaristic' working-class consciousness, nor to the hierarchies of status and prestige perceived by those with a 'bureaucratic' middle-class image set.

In each case, then, the affluent worker assumed a set of attitudes related to but qualitatively different from those associated with the ideal-typical complexes of work and social relations contained in the 'traditional/ solidaristic' and 'bureaucratic' models of consciousness. In their attitude to employment, the affluent workers appeared to believe a contract existed between themselves and their employer: they agreed to undertake arduous and boring work in return for which they expected a high wage. The contract was subject to continuous negotiation and here, though they rarely attended a branch meeting, the affluent workers expected their union to represent them. In their leisure time, they had withdrawn from group activity, preferring instead to spend all their time, money and energy within the confines of the nuclear family, to an extent which justified the use of the term 'privatized' to describe their outlook. As Lockwood (1975: 202–3) suggested:

> The social environment of the privatized worker is conducive to the development of what may be called a 'pecuniary' model of society. The essential feature of this ideology is that class divisions are seen mainly in terms of differences in income and material possessions. Basically, the pecuniary model of society is an ideological reflection of work attachments that are instrumental and of community relationships that are privatized. It is a model which is only possible when social relationships that might provide prototypical experiences for the construction of ideas of conflicting power classes, or of hierarchically independent status groups, are either absent or devoid of their significance.

The affluent workers' 'image of society' depended mainly on an assessment of income, so that, while they knew they were better off than some, they were equally conscious of being worse off than others. On the basis of these findings, the *embourgeoisiement* thesis was rejected.

## The affluent worker and work identity

As indicated above, the analysis of work behaviour and attitudes developed by Goldthorpe and his fellow researchers was largely an unanticipated by-product of the wider aims and objectives of the *embourgeoisiement* project. In particular, their major explanatory device of 'orientations to work' – the meaning attached by workers to their work which predisposes them to think and act in particular ways towards that work – arose from the adoption of an action frame of reference during the course of the Luton research, when the initial approach guiding the project – the 'technological effects' approach – proved inadequate. Having failed to find, as expected, marked dissimilarities between those in different occupational groupings – such as semi-skilled assemblers, process workers and machine operators – in their relationships with workmates, supervisors, employers and unions, the research team began to look for other explanatory principles. In so doing they arrived 'at the idea of the explanatory importance of the nature of workers' orientations to employment, this being considered as a factor influencing job choice, mediating the individual's experience of work tasks and roles, and thus necessarily influencing his definition of the work situation and his conduct within it' (Goldthorpe, quoted in Bulmer, 1975: 14).

The authors associated ideal-typical orientations to work with specific complexes of work and community social relations. Thus the action frame of reference was not treated as something outside of, or separate from, an analysis of social structure but conceived of as a necessary part of such an analysis. In other words, the orientations which workers were deemed to bring into the workplace were not randomly distributed in the population, but were themselves systematic products of extra-industrial structures (Bulmer, 1975: 14).

> We believe that in industrial sociology what may be termed an action frame of reference within which actors' own definitions of the situations in which they are engaged are taken as an initial basis for the explanation of their social behaviour and relationships ... An action frame of reference would direct attention systematically to the variety of meanings which work may come to have for industrial employees. And this in turn would then compel recognition of the fact that in modern society the members of the industrial labour force form a highly differentiated collectivity – in terms, for example, of the positions and roles they occupy in their non-working lives, in their sub-cultural characteristics, and in the pattern of their life histories and objectives for the future. (Goldthorpe et al., 1968: 184)

According to Goldthorpe et al., the privatized affluent worker exhibited an 'instrumental' orientation to work. As indicated above, privatized instrumentalists were the very embodiment of 'economic man'. They saw work merely as a means to a financial end and did not invest it with a group or communal meaning: they shared no sense of occupational identity or community. Their 'social imagery' exhibited a 'money model' of society which viewed differences in income as the basis of stratification and was unconcerned with 'class relations' as Marxists would understand them. In large part, Goldthorpe et al. (1969: 182) argued, this propensity among affluent workers to accept work as essentially a means to extrinsic ends was best understood as something that 'to an important degree existed independently of, and prior to, their involvement in their present work situations'. In other words, the typically privatized, family-centred and consumption-based lifestyle of the affluent worker was the main determinant of their attitude to and (lack of) identity with the work they performed for a living. While this 'instrumental orientation to work' of the affluent worker flew in the face of the expectations of the *embourgeoisiement* thesis, it also tended to negate the interpretations of work identity based upon the idea of latent alienation.

Although Goldthorpe et al. acknowledged that the *embourgeoisiement* thesis had come in for severe criticism from Marxist sociologists, they argued that the alternative explanations for 'working-class passivity' developed by the latter relied on an unverifiable claim concerning the 'objective' intensification of 'alienation'.

> That the increasing impoverishment of the working class has not occurred and that living standards have, in fact, substantially improved has to be recognised. But, it is claimed, although the immediate 'survival' needs of the worker may thus have been largely provided for, his fundamental needs as a human being – those essential to his human potentialities – remain unfulfilled and indeed deliberately frustrated, and at the same time the worker's awareness of this fact is systematically inhibited. For example, while affluence gives the worker increased possibilities as a consumer, his greater income is taken up merely in the satisfaction of the 'false' needs that are imposed upon him by prevailing institutions and interests – the need to live in the manner prescribed by advertisements and the mass media, the need to 'have fun', to 'relax', to 'escape', and so on. No matter how strongly these needs are actually felt, they are false in that they do not derive from real freedom in self-expression but are rather the result of indoctrination and manipulation . . . Furthermore, it is also stressed that, in the last analysis, the alienated consumer has to be understood in terms of the continuing alienation of labour in the organisation of production. (Goldthorpe et al., 1969: 15–16)

According to Goldthorpe et al. (1969: 179) alienation 'is not a specifically sociological concept: it is rather a notion expressive of a certain human and social philosophy which often figures crucially in a rhetoric of revolution. It is not intended to be tested against fact.' However, they go on to acknowledge that the idea of 'latent alienation' does have some resonance with many of the findings they reported on the attitudes and behaviours of the workers they studied. For example, the overriding concern exhibited by affluent workers with increasing their standards of domestic consumption, the extent to which their future objectives were defined in terms of those standards, their home-centred and typically privatized style of life – all these were features which could be regarded as aptly exemplifying what Marxist critics pejoratively called 'the civilization of individual consumers' where modern workers, or 'happy robots' (Mills, 1963), sought 'cheap fun' to make up for the lack in their human essence caused by the objective presence of alienation at work.

Most crucially, however, Goldthorpe et al. (1969) suggested that the idea of alienation appeared closely applicable to the affluent workers' experience of their work, and to the meaning and place that work typically held in their social lives. Indeed, Marx's comment that alienated labour was not the satisfaction of a need, but only 'a means for satisfying other needs' seemed to sum up the spirit of the authors' main conclusions.

For Goldthorpe et al. (1969: 180) the figure of the alienated worker was 'far more readily recognisable in our research data than the worker "on the move towards new middle-class values and middle-class existence"'. None the less, while suggesting that the descriptive picture of the objectively alienated worker painted by many Marxists offered a persuasive means of summing up some of their own findings, the *interpretation* of this picture proffered by Marxist sociologists was completely rejected by *The Affluent Worker* researchers. In other words, while the description of the alienated worker appeared salient, the underlying assumptions of the latent alienation thesis were considered to be erroneous.

One such assumption was that alienation, as exhibited in a preoccupation with 'false' consumer needs, derived fundamentally from the work situation. In this reading, it was precisely because the worker was not 'at home' in his work – because work deprived 'him' of 'his' necessary creative activity – that 'he' could only find power in 'his' non-work existence, specifically in the passive dream state of consumption. Such a position was considered fundamentally at odds with the research findings of *The Affluent Worker* project. For Goldthorpe et al. (1969: 181) there was no direct and uniform association between immediate, shopfloor work experience and employee attitudes and behaviour that were of wider reference. This was the case, they argued,

> because the effects of technologically determined conditions of work are always *mediated* through the meanings that men give to their work and through their own definitions of their work situation, and because these meanings and definitions in turn vary with the particular sets of wants and expectations that men bring to their employment. Thus, among the workers we studied, no systematic relationship was to be found between the degree to which their work might be considered as objectively 'alienating' and, say, the strength of their attachment to their jobs, the nature of their relationships with workmates, or their stance in regard to their employing organization. (Goldthorpe et al., 1969: 181)

According to the authors, rather than being a simple effect of their – often significantly differing – tasks and roles within the organization of production, the instrumental attitudes of their subject population appeared to originate outside of the workplace, prior to their involvement in the jobs they were doing when interviewed. This interpretation was confirmed, the authors argued, by the fact that many of their respondents had previously performed jobs of an intrinsically more rewarding, and objectively less alienating, nature, but had given these up to perform work of a more alienating character for a significantly increased wage.

> Rather than an overriding concern with consumption standards reflecting alienation in work, it could be claimed that precisely such a concern constituted the motivation for these men to take, and to retain, work of a particularly unrewarding and stressful kind which offered high pay in compensation for its inherent deprivations. It might indeed still be held that to devalue work rewards in this way for the sake of increasing consumer power is itself symptomatic of alienation – perhaps even of alienation in an extreme form. But in this case, of course, the idea of work as being invariably the prime source of alienation has to be abandoned and its origins must be sought elsewhere; specifically in whatever social-structure or cultural conditions generate 'consumption-mindedness' of the degree in question. (Goldthorpe et al., 1969: 182–3)

The authors suggested that, as consumption has assumed an increasingly important place in Marxist analyses of working-class passivity, the explanatory reach of alienation has also been expanded. For example, in the so-called 'mass culture critique' of the Frankfurt School sociologists (Marcuse, Adorno et al.) the influence of advertising and the mass media is cited as a major factor in the constitution of individuals as 'happy robots', and, thus, as a key component in the maintenance of working-class inertia. However, Goldthorpe et al. (1969: 183) suggested that the mass culture critique offered no guidance as to how, for example, 'individuals and groups are *differentially* exposed to and responsive to the models of con- sumption that the media present'. Instead, they indicated the importance of factors such as life-cycle phase and geographical and social mobility in determining the extent to which media influences will be countered, unopposed or reinforced by '*interpersonal influences*'. For the authors, 'if giving priority to "the passive needs of personal and domestic life" is to be taken as constitutive of alienation, then, one would suggest, serious analysis calls for the development of a new empirical sociology of consumption rather than for the refurbishing of an old philosophical anthropology of production.'[6]

According to Goldthorpe et al. (1969: 183–4), the objectivist fantasy of alienation could offer no assistance to sociological analysis. To analyse work identity and the meaning of consumption solely in terms of alienation was, in their view, to engage in a form of social diagnosis 'which in the end cannot be rejected by force of logic or evidence and which, by the same token, others are in no way constrained to accept'. It was not self-evident to the authors that the affluent worker's concern for comfortable housing and leisure goods such as televisions was a visible manifestation of 'false needs'. Rather, they considered the material possessions and amenities their respondents strove for as representing 'something like the minimum material base' on which the affluent worker and 'his' family 'might be able to develop a more individuated style of life, with a wider range of choices, than has hitherto been possible for the mass of the manual labour force'. In particular, they indicated that, given the quite painful dilemma that their respondents faced between less intrinsically satisfying work and greater economic rewards with which to carry out their lifestyle projects (a dilemma, they suggest, often not faced by those in a superior class position), they 'would not be inclined to talk *de haut en bas* of "stunted mass-produced humanity", "made-to-measure consumers" or "sublimated slaves"' (1969: 184). Rather than ascribing an ontological priority to the category of 'labour', Goldthorpe et al. (1969: 187) insist that the relative importance of production and consumption in the construction of subjectivity and identity is an issue for sociological enquiry.

### Some problems with the neo-Weberian approach

As one of the most substantial contributions to postwar British sociology, it is unsurprising that the claims contained within *The Affluent Worker* project have been the subject of considerable critical attention. Within the sociology of work and employment, attention has focused, in particular, upon the notion of 'orientations to work' (Westergaard, 1970; Beynon and Blackburn, 1972; Daniel, 1973; Critcher, 1979; Marshall, 1988).

While the notion of 'orientations to work' deployed by Goldthorpe et al. was designed to put an active subject at the heart of their project, much of the criticism aimed at *The Affluent Worker* has revolved around the place of the individual actor in their analysis. Although Goldthorpe et al. rightly criticize orthodox Marxism for treating people as 'cultural dopes', the status of the subject in their own study is far from clear (Critcher, 1979: 32–3).

According to Marshall (1988: 111), for example, there is just as much of an essentialist subject at the heart of *The Affluent Worker*, as there is in the worst excesses of the alienation hypothesis. For Marshall, the neo-Weberian authors of *The Affluent Worker* are guilty of decontextualizing subjective experiences and meanings, with the result that their attempt to impute a particular type of identity to their subjects remains unsubstantiated. The instrumental worker, he argues, appears to be nothing more than 'the result of a shallow arraying of data for each *individual* along a *single* dimension'.

Echoing the Marxist critique of Westergaard (1970), Marshall suggests that Goldthorpe et al.'s thesis concerning 'instrumental orientations' may be true but it is trivially so. In effect it does little more than reinvent the wheel: if the structural dictates of a modern market economy ensure that workers are interested in their wage packets then in these circumstances it should come as no surprise that ambitions and desires are often articulated in pecuniary terms; money, after all, is the generalized medium of exchange in Western market economies.

The main issue is not so much that people have 'instrumental orientations' but what these orientations might mean to the individuals concerned. However, this question is one the authors of *The Affluent Worker* have no answer to. In part, as Critcher (1979: 31–3) argues, this is actually a problem of methodology. Their interview schedule asked a lot of questions about workers' perceptions – of their jobs, of the role of their unions etc. – but very few were designed to elicit the workers' feelings about these topics. While Goldthorpe et al. talked about the importance of actors' own definitions of their situation, the attitude survey they deployed had the effect of separating 'orientations' from social action, thereby leading to a static model of an unchanging instrumentally orientated worker whose ability to pursue his or her 'essential' interest in pecuniary gain is governed entirely by changes in the social structure that are unrelated to workers' actions (Marshall, 1988: 111–14).

Rather than overcoming the structural determinism they deplored in orthodox Marxism and hence avoiding the strictures of essentialism, Goldthorpe et al. ended up repeating many of the same mistakes. Despite their eloquent testimony to the action frame of reference, the authors of *The Affluent Worker* adopted, in practice, the extreme Weberian position of distinguishing sociology from history and defining the purpose of sociological enquiry as the construction of ahistorical 'ideal types' (Marshall, 1988). The underlying premise of their approach is that there exist identifiable value-complexes, images of society and 'orientations to work' that can be directly related to highly visible factors in an actor's immediate social milieu. Thus types of 'identity', for example, can largely be read off from various structural factors. So the strong sense of occupational identity attributed to the 'traditional proletarian' worker is conceived of as a product of 'his' objective work and community situation. Similarly, the lack of work-based identification associated with the affluent worker can be explained by 'his' instrumental orientation to work.

In this way, identity becomes detached from social action. 'Identity' appears to be something static, 'unchangingly determined by the objective characteristics of which it is a reflection' (Marshall, 1988: 114). Such an outcome is obviously at odds with the professed aims of neo-Weberian sociology – to provide explanations which go beyond an emphasis on the structural constraints which condition action to include an attempt to understand the meaning of that action for those involved in it – and more in line with the sort of Marxist orthodoxy Goldthorpe et al. set out to counter.

As Marshall (1988: 119) suggests, the subjects of *The Affluent Worker* study appear to be completely devoid of biography. The limits imposed by conventional attitude surveys and structural interview schedules ensure that the affluent worker appears as a subject 'possessing constant wants and interests (originating in an unspecified source or sources)'. Apparent changes in workers' demands and behaviour 'can therefore only be explained by reference to changes in the present system of constraints holding them in check' (Marshall, 1988: 121). This form of historicism leaves 'orientations to work' devoid of historical context, detached from particular practices or action and, therefore, apparently unaffected by changes in these. In other words, unless 'instrumentalism' is located firmly within its contexts, and unless some attempt is made to go beyond the one-dimensional and predictable pecuniary responses generated by attitude surveys about 'orientations to work', the hypothesis imputing an economistic, privatized identity to affluent workers remains unsubstantiated (Critcher, 1979; Marshall, 1988). At the heart of the neo-Weberian approach to work identity lies a tautological argument: 'identity is referred to as part of the explanation of why an individual or group should pursue a particular course of action but that very choice of action is seen as evidence for the identity attributed to the individual or group' (Brown, 1986: 1).

For Marshall (1988: 120), the first step towards a more constructive approach to the study of work identity – one that avoids the pitfalls of both orthodox Marxism and neo-Weberianism – must involve the reintroduction of social action into the framework of sociological analysis. Attitude surveys and other large-scale quantitative methodologies simply cannot deal with action, he argues. They lead researchers to divorce identity from action, thereby effectively eradicating meaning from the research agenda through a process of decontextualization.

Rather than attempting to explore identity using highly structured attitude surveys and isolated interviews, it should be investigated as a component of everyday practices. According to Marshall (1988: 120), 'since there is no necessary correlation between speech and action, satisfactory explanations of either require independent evidence as to both the action and the subject's perception of it.' In other words, because language is not self-evidently meaningful – because its meaning is always a function of its use, its intended audience, the conditions of its deployment and so on – the analysis of action, identity or consciousness can only be conducted in the context of lived practices.

For Brown (1986: 1), one possible way out of the impasse into which neo-Weberian approaches to work identity have fallen is provided by symbolic interactionism. Within this sociological tradition identity has been conceptualized as created in and transformed by symbolic social action. Echoing Marshall's (1988: 121–2) call for deployment of the ethnographic imagination in the study of the lived practices within which identities are embedded, Brown points to the interactionist's utilization of participant observation in the analysis of identity construction and transformation over time.

## Symbolic interactionism, self and identity

Born in Chicago of a fusion between American pragmatist philosophy (C.H. Cooley, J. Dewey, G.H. Mead, C. Peirce, W.I. Thomas et al.) and German formalist sociology (in particular, the work of G. Simmel), 'symbolic interactionism'[7] has from its inception denied the utility of macro-sociological reasoning. In portraying the social as a fluid and changeable series of transformations, interactionists have effectively negated the language of structure and statics, transforming sociology into 'a limited abstracting discipline which was incapable of substantial gener-alisation, propositional thinking or metaphysical thinking. It must dwell on the world of the self and the grammar that sustained that world' (Rock, 1979: 236). Essentially, the notion of 'symbolic interactionism' derives from the work of G.H. Mead, and the distinction he developed between symbolic and non-symbolic interaction.

> In non-symbolic interaction human beings respond directly to one another's gestures or actions; in symbolic interaction they interpret each other's gestures and act on the basis of the meaning yielded by the interpretation . . . Mead's concern was predominantly with symbolic interaction. Symbolic interaction involves *interpretation*, or ascertaining the meaning of the actions or remarks of the other person, and *definition*, or conveying indications to another person as to how he is to act. Human association consists of a process of such interpretations and definitions. Through this process the participants fit their own acts to the ongoing acts of one another and guide others in doing so. (Blumer, 1966: 537–8)

As Stryker (1980: 33–4), for example, has suggested, 'of all the precursors of symbolic interactionism, none is more important or influential than George Herbert Mead. Indeed, to a considerable degree, Mead's concep-tualization remains central to all contemporary versions of the framework.'

Of crucial significance to Mead's thought, and hence to interactionism generally, are the notions of self and identity. Mead's 'social psychology' was aimed at breaking down the established Cartesian dualisms of mind and body, individual and society (Henriques et al., 1984: 13–25). The basic thesis that Mead propounded was that the 'mind' and the 'self' were formed within the social, communicative activity of the group. Thus, Mead was one of the first modern social theorists to explore the notion that identity develops within discourse. For him, discourse and language are social activities, and in no sense the personal property of individual human beings.

Like the later Wittgenstein, or de Saussure, Mead views language as a system of signification independent of the intentions of individuals con-sidered as singular entities. For Mead, language is always connected to the field of social interaction so that a word or gesture largely derives its meaning from its connection to social meanings. In turn, social meaning refers to the meaning that an act takes on from the place it occupies in the totality of interaction in the group. However, as Burkitt (1991: 37) has argued, for Mead, 'the original and primary function of language remains as a medium for the more successful mutual adjustment of individuals within their social activity.' In other words, language plays a key role in regulating social behaviour, which is seen as necessary for both social order and a harmonious existence.

According to Mead, the role of language is crucial to the process of social communication, and to the emergence of the self and the subjective attitude:

> The individual experiences himself, not directly, but only indirectly, from the particular standpoints of other individual members of the same social group, or from the general standpoint of the social group as a whole to which he belongs. For he enters his own experience as a self or individual, not directly or immediately, not by becoming a subject to himself, but only in so far as he becomes an object to himself just as other individuals are objects to him or in his experience; and he becomes an object to himself only by taking the attitudes of other individuals towards himself within a social environment or context of experience and behaviour in which both he and they are involved. (Mead, quoted in Burkitt, 1991: 36)

Language is the most significant element in this process because it is through language that people internalize the attitudes of the social group and, on the basis of this, form themselves as subjects. It is only through language that such a general, impersonal standpoint can be communicated against which individuals can react to their own selves and organize their responses accordingly. This is due to the status of language as an impersonal system of signification. Language provides individuals with a thoroughly objective standpoint through which they become objects to themselves.

Against the tenets of methodological individualism Mead is claiming that identities do not emerge through individuals' own private experiences but only in social life, where 'other selves in a social environment logically antedate the consciousness of self which introspection analyses' (Mead, quoted in Burkitt, 1991: 37). In other words, that seemingly most private of domains, the self, is not private after all: the self only emerges in social processes of interaction, communication and the use of language.

The 'social self' articulated by Mead has two constitutive elements, both involved in a constant dialogue: these are the 'me' and the 'I'. The former is defined as the individual as an object of consciousness, and the latter as the individual as having consciousness (Joas, 1987). As Rock (1979: 236) suggests, the social self of symbolic interactionism is 'grounded in an internal dialogue between consciousness as subject and consciousness as object. That dialogue is ordered by conversation, and discourse has become a model for all analysis of interaction.'

Thus both 'faces' of the self are social and only emerge together in discourse. Because the 'I' is the self as having consciousness, it is associated with the fundamental sense of who and what we are. However, the 'I' cannot function as such without the simultaneous presence of a 'me'. The subjective sense of identity could not develop without the simultaneous constitution of the self as a social object. According to Burkitt (1991: 40) Mead's 'I' is '"contemplated action-in-progress" while the "me" stands beside objectified past actions and is identified with them'.

> The 'me' on its own would be totally without unity as it breaks down into many different selves, each one associated with past social acts in different local

circumstances. The objective self will have many aspects to it, and possesses many capacities stored from past experiences which can be used in the future. And it is the active 'I' which draws on these resources as it moves into the future, its reflective function planning activity in accordance with the 'me' – or parts of the 'me' – of past acts, while its active function executes these plans in activity . . . The self, then, is only created and sustained as a mobile region of self-producing social activity. (Burkitt, 1991: 40)

For Mead, the fact that the self is constituted in discourse means that certain aspects of a person's sense of who he or she is are bound to mirror and incorporate the general morals or values of the wider group contained within discourse (Henriques et al., 1984: 16–22). The self takes on 'the values of the group' through the mechanism of the 'generalized other'. The latter is 'an abstract summation and embodiment of all the varied replies that have been elicited by different "me"s. It represents a kind of condensed general will which respond to the self's performances' (Rock, 1979: 143). As it is language that makes possible broad opportunities to participate in communication, then the use of language suggests the creation of 'the most diffuse of all generalized others – the community of speakers of which one is a member: the most inclusive social class of humans is the one defined by the logical universe of discourse (or system of universally significant symbols) determined by the participative communicative interaction of individuals' (Rock, 1979: 145).

According to Mead, therefore, the development of identity only takes place under social conditions. The construction of identity occurs in the social organization that arises from the mutual adaptation of conduct, or adaptation that is situated in current activity and which takes place through the medium of communication. It is in this communication, particularly through language, that individuals become self-reflexive and gain control over their own responses during social activity. The values and morals of the generalized group also enter consciousness through language and play a significant role in the control of behaviour, taken as necessary for both social order and a harmonious existence (Burrell and Morgan, 1979; Henriques et al., 1984: 209).

## Symbolic interactionism and work identity

In direct opposition to the aspirations of objectivist sociological projects, interactionism treats the self as the moving centre of social formations.[8] It alone is deemed to synthesize whatever order exists. Thus 'society' is represented as ceaselessly produced in myriad exchanges which can have little fixity of structure or definition. For interactionism, the 'God's eye view' inherent within Marxism and similarly disposed macro-sociological apparatuses appears to maintain that the world can be made to yield an unconditional and absolute logic, and that those who do not grasp this logic are blinded by mystification, by a disadvantaged structural position, by an unfortunate location in the flow of historical process, or by a lack of proper intellectual weaponry (Rock, 1979: 28–9). This position, interactionists argue, is untenable. There can be no Olympian plain from which to look down in judgement upon the social, because the social is only constructed in a continuing process of interaction. The social is animated by the everyday practices of people in interaction and not by an immanent and *sui generis* logic of its own.

This processual view of the self as the moving centre of 'society' has considerable consequences for the study of work identity. As Moorhouse (1989: 22) has indicated, interactionist studies such as those of Roy (1969, 1973), Gold (1964), Hughes (1971) and Becker (1963, 1971), for example, provide very powerful criticisms of 'any kind of alienation notions' by indicating how paid time in even the most routinized of environments can be given purpose and how meaning is generated in the interactions of shopfloor life.

The interactionists argued that no work situation – no matter how apparently autonomous or restrictive – can be understood without reference to the action and beliefs of those involved in it (Joas, 1987), and that even the most 'dirty' and 'lowly' of occupations could become a source of identity for those performing them (Becker, 1963; Hughes, 1971). Everett Hughes (1971), for example, argued that sociologists of work and employment need to ignore the 'normal' categorization of occupations (skilled, unskilled, professional etc.) and instead concentrate upon the processual 'career' of persons through their work lives; in other words, upon 'the moving perspective in which the person can see his life . . . and interpret the meaning of his various attributes, actions and the things that happen to him' (Hughes, 1971: 137). In this way the commonalities of modern working life would be revealed.

The interactionists propose that, as a subjectively meaningful account or narrative of one's biography, the notion of 'career' can be as usefully applied to a shop assistant as to a solicitor. In effect, they suggest that a much greater range of work experience can be deemed capable of providing meaning than the notion of 'alienation' seems to allow. However, while the concept of 'career' was not used to measure the degree to which a person's paid work was their 'central life interest', it was deployed to indicate that even the most restrictive of work situations could and did involve the symbolic construction, in interaction, of identity and community (Becker, 1963; Hughes, 1971; Roy, 1973).

For interactionists, the effective levelling function performed by a concept such as 'career' gave the lie to the structural determinism of orthodox Marxism and other objectivist sociologies. Rather than assuming that 'alienated labour' could not derive any 'real' sense of identity from routinized capitalist work, interactionists attempted to indicate that all 'careers' were progressions through 'identity bestowing situations' (Goffman, 1961; Gold, 1964; Salaman, 1974).

In his classic participant observation study of informal interaction at the workplace, Roy (1973) reports on his experiences of working a six-day week on unskilled, highly repetitive factory work, and how he and his fellow 'operatives' faced and dealt with 'a formidable "beast of monotony"'. At first the work in question was 'a grim process of fighting the clock . . . I had struggled with the minutes and hours during the various phases of my industrial experience, but never had I been confronted with such a dismal combination of working conditions on the extra long work-day, the infinitesimal cerebral excitation, and the extreme limitation of physical movement' (Roy, 1973: 208). Gradually, however, Roy became aware of the social interaction going on around him. What at first appeared to be 'just a stream of disconnected bits of communication which did not make much sense', and 'occasional flurries of horseplay so simple and so unvarying in pattern and so childish in quality they made no strong bid for attention' (1973: 209), soon took on a different complexion as Roy became more involved in shopfloor life. The more he familiarized himself with the communicative interaction about him the more 'the disconnected became connected, the nonsense made sense, the obscure became clear, and the silly actually funny. And as the content of the interaction took on more and more meaning, the interaction began to reveal structure. There were "times" and "themes", and roles to serve their enaction. The interaction had subtleties, and I began to savour and appreciate them' (1973: 210).

These initially meaningless events were 'revealed' to Roy as rituals, games with known and accepted rules, expectations, roles and routines – patterns of horseplay, joking and seriousness which succeeded in 'marking off the time', giving it content and hurrying it along. Once involved in these activities, Roy (1973: 214–15) allotted them an important function: 'they captured and held to make the long day pass. The twelve hours of repetitive work per day became "easy to endure" as the "beast of boredom" was gentled to the harmlessness of a kitten.' Through the medium of these patterns of informal interaction, Roy argued, a work-based culture and identity was forged among the operatives that proved a key source of 'job satisfaction', which he deemed to have a 'negative effect' on labour turnover (1973: 217–18).

In keeping with the interactionists' concern with a 'sociology of regulation' (Burrell and Morgan, 1979: 17) – in other words with providing an explanation of the *status quo*; of how the social is formed and maintained in interaction – Roy indicated that from the informal interactions he observed/participated in

> may also be abstracted a social structure of status and roles. This structure may be discerned in the carrying out of the various informal activities which provide the content of the subculture of the group. The times and themes were performed with a system of roles which formed a sort of pecking hierarchy . . . The fun went on with the participation of all, but within the controlling frame of status, a matter of who can say or do what to whom. (Roy, 1973: 218)

At the same time, 'in both the cultural content and social structure of . . . group interaction could be seen the permeation of influences which flowed from the various multiple group memberships of the participants.

Past and present "other group" experiences and/or anticipated "outside" social connections provided significant materials for the building of themes and for the establishment and maintenance of status and role relationships' (1973: 219). Here Roy indicates that the 'symbolic work' of social interaction permeates the paid employment/leisure divide. The struggle to make meaning at work involved the deployment and utilization of many of the forms, interests and communications of 'leisure' and 'free-time'. Without eliding the differences between work and leisure, Roy indicates that similar processes of 'meaning making' go on in both spheres, that they permeate one another, and that individual identities are produced as a result of all forms of symbolic work.

## The 'unexplicated context': criticisms of symbolic interactionism

For the interactionists, identity is both produced and transformed in a continuing process of symbolic social interaction: 'the student of identity must necessarily be deeply interested in interaction for it is in and because of . . . interaction that so much appraisal of self and others occurs' (Strauss, 1969: 44). This conceptualization of identity as an on-going socially accomplished process has a number of consequences for the practice of sociological analysis. For example, the embeddedness of identity in communicative social action means that its articulation by sociologists must of necessity involve them in attempting to understand the meaning of social action for those involved in it. Interactionists attempt to do this through the use of 'sensitizing concepts' and participant observation techniques. At the same time, because interactionists stress that all forms of symbolic social interaction involve identity construction, they have argued that no work situation, for example, can be assumed to be incapable of providing a sense of identity to those involved in it.

However, the theoretical and methodological trajectory of interactionism is not without its costs. Everett Hughes' (1971) levelling concept (or 'form') of the 'career', for example, can be seen to be a somewhat ambiguous achievement. On the one hand, as indicated above, the concept reiterates the interactionist claim that many different types of paid work involve similar symbolic processes of identity and community construction. However, at the same time, this 'levelling' also has the effect of eradicating *difference*: 'we need to rid ourselves of any concepts which keep us from seeing that the essential problems of men at work are the same whether they do their work in the laboratories of some famous institution or in the messiest vat room of a pickle factory' (Hughes, 1971: 300). By focusing exclusively upon the similarities between occupations and work experience in terms of 'forms' of symbolic interaction, important differences, particularly those relating to the question of power relations and 'structural' inequality, are consequently lost from view.

Burawoy (1979: 34), for example, blames Roy's reliance upon an exclusively interactionist methodology for his failure to delineate the broader environment within which his studies of workplace interaction were conducted: 'What he could not gather from participant observation is not to be found in his work.' As a consequence, the wider social relations within which the interaction he described is inscribed are ignored. Burawoy (1979: 34) notes that Roy tells his reader nothing about the company, 'the union, other departments, the state of various markets and so on'. The interactionist's 'insistence on being a closed (secret) participant observer imposed serious limitations on the material that could legitimately be deployed in analysis'.

Because of a pragmatist attachment to the exigencies of everyday interaction, the interactionists have not developed any consistent theory of the wider social formation. Even though interactionists identify language as an impersonal system, and therefore as a form of 'macro'-structure, they do not develop adequate explanations of the formation of processes at a macro-level. As Burkitt (1991: 51), for example, has argued, while Mead hinted that the division of labour was an important feature of modern social formations – because it was the objective basis for the differentiation of roles and therefore individual identities – he offered no explanation of the social processes that led to the greater complexity of this division. Instead, a unitary social domain is posited – the 'generalized other' – within which the individual subject is unproblematically located. In other words, a conformity is assumed between the individual and the values and social regulatory systems of the broader social formation (Henriques et al., 1984: 209).

In the division of labour, Mead argued, the individual

> always and necessarily assumes a definite relation to, and reflects in the structure of his self or personality, the general organized pattern of experience and activity exhibited in or characterizing the social life-process in which he is involved, and of which his self or personality is essentially a creative expression or embodiment. (Mead, quoted in Burkitt, 1991: 51)

As Giddens (1979: 254) has suggested, Mead's philosophy, and hence symbolic interactionism more generally, 'lacks an understanding of the broader society as a differentiated and historically located formation'. Interactionism is therefore unable to offer an adequate appreciation of the problems of institutional analysis and transformation.

According to Robertson (1980: 260), the failure of interactionist conceptions of identity to deal with the issues of power relations, ideology and 'institutional transformation' is largely a product of its development within 'the American context'.

> In *the American context* the notion of identity has often been used . . . to suggest that it is out of what we might call 'identity work' that 'society' (as a processual notion) is constructed (that is out of encounters with others, and *via* others with self . . . In general, it could be said that symbolic interactionists have conceived of identity formation as an ongoing activity relative to a posited but unexplicated context.

For Robertson, underpinning both traditional and modern variants of American pragmatist philosophy (Rorty, 1991), for example, as well as symbolic interactionism, is a 'cultural commitment to *equality*' which militates against consideration of the sorts of problematics – of 'ideology', social stratification, power inequality etc. – that have preoccupied many European sociological discussions of 'identity'.[9]

**The subject of work**

Having outlined and critically examined three of the most prominent approaches to the study of work-based subjectivity and identity within the social sciences, I now want to examine their explanatory reach. It is apparent that no unequivocal picture of the work-based subject emerges from an analysis of these approaches. As Knights and Willmott (1989: 537) have indicated, social scientific studies of work identity generally, and sociological studies in particular, have tended to gravitate, often despite their best intentions, to one or other pole of the dualism between action and structure, individual and society.

Dominating debates in this field has been the Marxist problematic of alienation, where the oppressive structure of capitalist relations of production is deemed to have alienated 'Man' from his 'species being' as a creative labourer. Because complete, unambiguous, human persons are recognized as coming into being only with the destruction of capitalism/ ideology and the building of communism/socialism, subjectivity is represented as having no force or weight under present conditions of alienation. As a consequence of this form of overdetermined analysis and explanation, no room is left for, and no weight assigned to, individual and/ or group experience, meaning and action: structure virtually eradicates agency. As Barrett (1991: 110) has suggested, the question of subjectivity 'is a massive lacuna in Marxism', one which has 'stood in the way of a broader consideration of experience, identity, sexuality, affect and so on', not only in paid work but in all other spheres of social existence.

In opposition to the objectivist stance of the Marxist problematic, the neo-Weberians deployed an 'action frame of reference' to the study of work identity. By focusing upon 'actors' own definitions of the situations in which they are engaged', the neo-Weberians argued that no systematic relationship could be found between the degree to which a worker's occupation could be described as 'objectively alienating', and the degree to which workers identified with the jobs they performed. However, while the neo-Weberians argued that they had installed an active subject at the heart of their analysis, thus overcoming the structural determinism they deplored in orthodox Marxism, the subject they delineated also appeared to be almost exclusively subjected to social formations. Despite their eloquent testimonies to the action frame of reference, the neo-Weberians adopted the extreme Weberian position of distinguishing sociology from history and defining the purpose of sociological enquiry as the construction of ahistorical 'ideal types'. Thus their 'subject' – whether the 'instrumental' worker, 'traditional proletarian' or whatever – was largely a product of the objective work and community situation which he or she inhabited. Different forms of identity were largely 'read off' from structural factors.

The underlying premise of this approach was that objectively identifiable value-complexes, images of society and 'orientations to work' – ideologies, if you like – could be revealed that were directly related to an actor's immediate social milieu, and which were unproblematically translated into the minds and behaviours of these actors. In this way, the subject was once again divorced from social action: a static creation, unchangingly determined by the objective characteristics of which it is a reflection.

In direct contrast to Marxist and neo-Weberian analyses, the symbolic interactionists placed the 'self' in social action at the centre of their project. In portraying the 'social' as a fluid and changeable achievement of human communicative interaction, the interactionists effectively negated the language of structure and statics. According to interactionism, the 'self' is the moving centre of social formations: an ongoing socially accomplished process. It alone is deemed to synthesize whatever order exists.

The self comes into being through taking on the attitudes of others towards it within communicative social interaction. Language is the most significant element in this process because it is only through language that people 'internalize' the attitudes of the social group and thus constitute themselves as subjects. However, as indicated earlier, this formulation, on the one hand, assumes both a local and unitary social domain, and, on the other hand, leaves unproblematized the content and take-up of these attitudes. A conformity is assumed between the individual subject and the values and morals of the 'generalized other'.

While interactionism has placed a great deal of emphasis upon regarding 'social life' as the active accomplishment of purposive, knowledgeable actors, and upon the 'social origins' of reflexive consciousness, the status of the 'social' itself in interactionist thought is extremely limited. Because the 'social' tends to be equated with small interactional groupings and the 'generalized other', interactionism offers no explanation of the broader society as a differentiated and historically located formation.

Similarly, although interactionists identified language as an impersonal system, and therefore, in some senses as a 'macro'-structure, they were unable to provide an adequate account of the formation of processes at a macro-level, or of the relation between such macro-structurings and the micro-processes of everyday interaction. The 'macro' is a posited but unexplicated context in interactionist thought. Therefore, while interactionism sets out to overcome traditional dualisms it ends up replicating them.

Because interactionism fails to engage with the language of structure and is unable consequently to explore the workings of structural power inequalities, of ideology and so on, it cannot begin to consider how social divisions and conflicts are inscribed in the self through social organization and how these limit the scope for consciously chosen actions by individuals in the social group. For interactionism, the unproblematic take-up of social values by the self in a unitary social domain leaves, for example, no place for a theory of the repressed unconscious and the truly 'split' subject of psychoanalysis, and flies in the face of anthropological and historical research which has indicated how varied and diverse are the ways in which 'the person' and 'selfhood' can be and have been categorized in different social formations and epochs (Beechey and Donald, 1986: ix–x).

If, as Giddens (1979: 255) has argued, the notion of human agency cannot be understood without the notion of structure, and vice versa, then this 'duality of structure' be conceptualized outside history. In consequence, 'the social totality cannot be best understood as in functionalist conceptions of the whole, as given "presence", but as relations of presence and absence recursively ordered.' According to Laclau (1990: 44), this paradox of social action indicates the centrality of the category of 'dislocation'. For Laclau, dislocation is the 'primary ontological level of constitution of the social' because to understand social reality 'is not to understand what 'society *is*, but what *prevents it from being*'. Thus any *identity* is dislocated in so far as it 'depends on an outside which both denies that identity and provides the conditions of its possibility at the same time' (Laclau, 1990: 39).

If subjects are simply the product of structures, for example, as in the Marxist and neo-Weberian conceptions of work identity considered above, then a total determinism would govern social action, and history would be reduced to the status of automaton; change, chance, contingency would be inconceivable. However, if the structure that 'makes up' the subject does not manage to constitute itself fully, if it can only constitute itself in relation to an 'outside', as Laclau suggests, then the structure will not be able fully to determine the subject.

> The structure will obviously not be able to determine me, not because I have an *essence* independent from the structure but because the structure has failed to constitute me as a subject as well. There is nothing in me which was oppressed by the structure or is freed by its dislocation; I am simply *thrown up* in my condition as a subject because I have not achieved constitution as an object . . . I am *condemned* to be free, not because I have no structural identity as the existentialists assert, but because I have a *failed* structural identity. This means that the subject is partially self-determined. However, as this self-determination is not the expression of what the subject already is but the result of its lack of being instead, self-determination can only proceed through processes of *identification*. (Laclau, 1990: 44)

Unsurprisingly, the emphasis on social action and processes of identification in symbolic interactionism provides an antidote to the structural determinism of both Marxist and neo-Weberian analyses of the subject. However, interactionism problematically asserts that the 'self' has *no* structural identity, and consequently that agency can be theorized without the notion of structure. None the less, despite this excessive reliance upon agency to the detriment of social structure, there is one common thread uniting interactionist analyses of the subject with those advocated by Laclau: that is, that discourse is an organizing principle of social life and subjectivity. However, for Laclau, as for other post-structuralists and post-Marxists, discourse is not equated with a 'local moral order', as in interactionism, but rather is understood as constitutive of social reality *in toto*.

In the next two chapters I shall explore the notion of discourse and examine the ways in which subjectivity and identity can be said to be constituted 'discursively'. In order to do so I begin by discussing the recent upsurge of interest in 'culture' within the social sciences, for it is only through examining the epistemological implications of the contemporary 'cultural turn' that the full importance of the concept of discourse can emerge.

## Notes

1 For those working in the neo-Weberian tradition, for example, the analysis of occupational identity and community was simply an aspect of this wider project (see, for example, Goldthorpe et al., 1969).

2 Marx's conception of creative labour is predicated upon the model of artistic activity. As Gaukroger (1986: 305–8; see also Hunter, 1987; Taylor, 1989), for example, has indicated, such a model was a familiar one in German Romanticism. In this model human development was conceived of in terms of an inner power which strived to realize and maintain its own shape and effectivity against outside forces. Without such striving or activity there could be no self-knowledge because a person only comes to know him or herself by expressing him or herself and recognizing him or herself in that expression. One comes to know oneself not through introspection but through the products of one's own activity.

3 The 'action frame of reference' is an approach to social research 'which attempts to explore the work–community nexus and to show how socially generated and distributed aims, attitudes and values can account for work behaviour' (Rose, 1988: 251). The approach derives most of its founding assumptions from the methodological recommendations of Max Weber. Simply put, the Weberian strategy of enquiry demands an attempt to distinguish *typical* social actors and *typical* patterns of action, but also the *meanings* actors typically attribute to their actions. The investigator deploying this approach therefore assumes that social action is produced partly by reference to a set of meanings the actor shares with others. Thus, Goldthorpe et al. (1969) constructed a typology of social action based on three kinds of 'orientation to work': the *instrumental orientation* of the 'privatized worker'; the *bureaucratic orientation* reflecting patterns the authors considered to be typical of those located among white-collar employees; and the *solidaristic orientation* inferred from the authors' understanding of 'traditional' working-class employment and community relations, such as those of coalmining and shipbuilding. Although there are many neo-Weberian studies of occupational identity and community (for example, Brown and Brannen, 1970a; Brown et al., 1972; Hill, 1976; Newby, 1977; Davis, 1979), I will concentrate here upon the most influential of all such studies, *The Affluent Worker* project.

4 This relationship between Marxist analyses and those of the neo-Weberians throws into stark relief the continual gravitation between one or other pole of the subject/object, action/structure dualisms within sociology in general, and industrial sociology in particular.

5 The 'traditional model' is constituted by a number of interlinking factors. First: an 'unrationalized' work situation which is deemed to provide interesting tasks, freedom from managerial and technical constraints, and teamwork. The important lifestyle elements concern

the structure of the family and community existence. 'Traditional' workers live in occupational communities of workmates who are also neighbours and friends, in single-class areas which are geographically and socially isolated from the mainstream of society, in stable and long-established communities. By contrast, in the 'bureaucratic' model employees are deemed to hold a 'hierarchical ideology' relating to expectations of upward mobility. However, they find work 'intrinsically satisfying' and are more highly involved in their jobs than most industrial workers, and identify with the aims and objectives of the firms for which they work. Because of this degree of job involvement they are also considered more likely to form occupational communities: 'this tendency should be more pronounced the more they are geographically mobile and thus the more they are dependent on friendships acquired through their occupational roles' (Lockwood, 1975: 29). 'Bureaucratic workers' are also more likely to live in occupationally mixed communities. Finally, these employees are likely to be involved in 'interactional status systems': whether social visiting or membership of and participation in voluntary associations is taken as a measure of communal (and hence status) interaction, the 'bureaucratic' worker ranks much higher than any of the other ideal types (Goldthorpe et al., 1969).

6 This is a point to which I shall be returning in Chapter 4.

7 The term 'symbolic interactionism' was coined by H. Blumer in 1937. Although the term is used to describe several schools of thought I will be referring to the work of the so-called Chicago School. I do not propose to examine the positivistic interactionism of M. Kuhn and the Iowa School.

8 This view of social action as being constructed through an interpretative process has, as its methodological consequence, the requirement that the process of construction be observed in order that the meaning of the social action can be analysed. The formation of action must be traced by viewing the situation as it is seen by the actor. Symbolic interactionists therefore stress the need for insightfully 'feeling one's way inside the experience of the actor'. This leads interactionists to reject the deployment of scientific method (in other words, to the prior formulation and testing of hypotheses); of cause and effect models; of goals of predicting behaviour; of the use of statistical techniques; and of a reverential attitude towards the ideal of scientific objectivity. Instead, they have tended to deploy the qualitative technique of participant observation whereby the sociologist inserts him or herself into the research setting, permitting him or her to record and experience events as they unfold. However, this technique is inherently problematic. On the one hand, as 'observer' the sociologist must survey social life from without, treating it in a manner which is unfamiliar and disturbing to ordinary experience. On the other, as a participant he or she must attempt to merge with the world around him or her. For the most part this tension is resolved in practice; in other words, by formulating ideas and explanations *in situ*. According to Blumer (quoted in Stryker, 1980: 95) such an approach is 'more valuable many times over than any representative sample'.

9 As Robertson (1980: 261) suggests, 'American conceptions of identity within the symbolic interactionist tradition are . . . typically individualistic in reference to *a diffuse notion of otherness* . . . This feature of American sociological conceptions of identity is of course bound-up with such attributes of American social theory (and, of course, American society) as the relative absence of attention to historically provided social niches. In this respect it is the absence of concern both sociologically and phenomenally with class stratification in the European sense which is very important. The cultural commitment to equality (with categories declared to be "fully American") has amounted to a commitment to the identity of all men (in the sense of their sameness in human terms). Against such a backdrop the search for personal and group identity is likely to be more intense than other societal circumstances where class stratification has been more crystallized.' It is also interesting to note that the contemporary pragmatist project of Richard Rorty (1982, 1991), firmly established as it is in 'the American context', has come in for much of the same criticism levelled at symbolic interactionism in the past: the neglect of power relations, failure to deal adequately with structural inequality and so on (see, for example, Bernstein, 1991).

# 2

# The Production of Subjects

These days it seems increasingly difficult to get away from 'culture'. Within the academy, for example, the concept of 'culture' has come to dominate debates in the social and human sciences. At the same time, the substantive concerns of other spheres of existence have increasingly come to be represented in cultural terms. In the domain of formal politics in the UK during the 1980s the ruling Conservative Party's radical programme of reform was represented in large part as a cultural crusade, concerned with the attitudes, values and forms of self-understanding embedded in both individual and institutional activities. In other words, the government's political project of reconstruction was defined as one of cultural reconstruction – as an attempt to transform Britain into an 'enterprise culture'.

One of the most interesting – indeed, remarkable – instances of the contemporary turn to culture has occurred within the world of work and employment. In recent years, people working in large organizations are likely to have found themselves exposed to 'culture change' programmes as part of managerial attempts to make enterprises more efficient, effective and profitable. Thus, even in the most 'material' of domains – that of business and organization – programmes of reform have come to be defined in cultural terms.

The first question that comes to mind is how do we explain this upsurge of interest in culture: what are its conditions of emergence and main constitutive characteristics? This is a very big question and not one susceptible to easy, off-the-peg answers. However, I want to make a start by suggesting that the current interest in 'culture' can be seen to have both an epistemological and a substantive slant and that social scientists taking the 'cultural turn' have invariably found themselves developing one or other of these slants and more often both at the same time.

What links both elements of this contemporary turn to culture is a renewed awareness of the importance of meaning in social life. In social theory, for example, this implies an increased concern with language and how it is used to produce meaning. In other words, in this manifestation the turn to culture involves an acknowledgement that social practices are invariably 'meaningful practices'; that in order to conduct a social practice human beings must give it a certain meaning, have a conception of it, be able to think meaningfully about it. The production of social meanings is therefore a necessary condition for the functioning of all social practices.

This concern with the production of meaning also lies at the heart of (the substantive) contemporary managerial interest in 'organizational culture'. As Peter Anthony (1994: 17–27), for example, has argued, the turn to culture within organizations is premised upon a belief that 'rationalist' systems of organizational management systematically destroyed meaning at work and that, in order to compete effectively in the turbulent modern global economic environment, the foremost necessity is to 'make meaning' for people at work. 'Culture' is accorded a privileged position in this endeavour because it is seen to structure the way people think, feel and act in organizations. The aim is to produce the sort of meanings that will enable people to make the right and necessary contribution to the success of the organization for which they work. To this end, managers are encouraged to view the most effective or 'excellent' organizations as those with the appropriate 'culture' – that ensemble of norms and techniques of conduct that enables the self-actualizing capacities of individuals to become aligned with the goals and objectives of the organization for which they work.

This focus upon culture as a means of producing a particular relationship to self among members of an organization suggests that its deployment as a managerial technique is intimately bound up with questions of identity. As Renato Rosaldo (1993: xi) has suggested, it is a pronounced feature of the present that 'questions of culture . . . quite quickly become . . . questions of identity' and developments along both the epistemological and substantive flanks of the 'cultural turn' seem to bear this out.

In this chapter I am primarily concerned with unpacking the epistemological strand of the 'cultural turn' and delineating its implications for our understanding of identity formation. In Chapter 3, I shift focus to concentrate upon the substantive turn to culture within organizations and seek to indicate the ways in which attempts to manage organizational culture have major implications for the sorts of work-based identities that can flourish within an enterprise.

## The cultural turn: epistemological questions

The explicitly philosophical or epistemological strand of contemporary cultural analysis refers to a development known as the 'linguistic turn'. It involves a reversal of the relationship that has traditionally been held to exist between the vocabularies we use to describe things and the things themselves. The usual, you could say common-sense, assumption is that objects exist 'objectively' as it were 'in the world' and as such are prior to and constraining of our descriptions of them. In other words, it seems normal to assume that molecules and genes exist prior to and independently of scientists' models of them. Or that society exists independently of sociologists' descriptions of it. What these examples serve to highlight is the way in which language is assumed to be subordinate to and in the service of the world of 'fact'. However, in recent years the relationship between language and the objects it describes has been the subject of a radical re-think. Language has been promoted to an altogether more important role. Theorists from many different fields – philosophy, literature, feminism, cultural anthropology, sociology – have declared language to bring facts into being and not simply to report on them. Let me explain the thinking behind this declaration.

At one level it is obvious that objects can be said to exist independently of language. A stone will still exist as a physical object regardless of our descriptions of it. However, that object we identify as a 'stone' only becomes recognizable as a 'stone' when it is named, when its physical presence is given meaning through language. In other words, the fact of a particular physical object being identifiable as a 'stone' depends on a way of classifying objects and making them meaningful. If there were no human beings on earth, those objects that we call stones would still be there none the less; but they would not be 'stones' because there would not be a language capable of classifying them and distinguishing them from other objects. If, as Richard Rorty (1982: xix) puts it, 'there is no way to think about . . . the world . . . except by using language', then the world as we find it will be a function of that language, and we won't alter the one without altering the other.

This idea that things only have meaning through their insertion within a particular classificatory system or 'language game', as Wittgenstein put it, has some pretty profound consequences. Taken-for-granted assumptions about the 'nature' and 'essence' of things are immediately open to question if one accepts that the meaning of any object resides not within that object itself but is a product of how that object is socially constructed through language and representation. Let's take an example.

One of the areas most troubled by the implications of the cultural turn has been the philosophy of science. Ever since the Enlightenment, 'science' has occupied an exceptionally important role in the life of modern societies through its claim to offer objective and impartial knowledge of the world. In modern Western cultures, the notions of 'science', 'rationality', 'objectivity' and 'truth' are intimately bound up with one another. Science is thought of as offering 'hard' truth: truth as correspondence to reality, the only real sort of truth worthy of our attention (Rorty, 1991: 35). This conviction that there are objective, theory-independent and language-independent 'facts' detectable by natural science – that science gets at the truth of an object – has made it the ultimate arbiter of claims to truth in many different areas of enquiry. Philosophers, theologians, sociologists, historians and literary critics have all had to worry about whether they are being 'scientific', whether they are entitled to think of their conclusions, no matter how carefully argued, as worthy of the term 'true'. Because the search for objective, hence unassailable, 'truth' is identified with 'using reason', the natural sciences have become thought of as the paradigms of rationality.

The association of science with 'real' knowledge and 'timeless' truth has made it a tempting target for theorists taking the linguistic turn. For, if science could be shown to be just one among many different 'language games', what would this do to its claims to be the ultimate arbiter of 'truth'? With so much at stake it will come as no surprise to learn that the battles over the status of scientific knowledge have been long and bloody. Let's take a look at how the protagonists line up. As indicated above, traditional thinking claims that objects exist prior to and independently of their insertion into scientific knowledge. So, in physics, for example, the assumption would be that the reality referred to by the term 'atom' was 'determinate' before the concept 'atom' came along. On this account, the reason why physicists have come to use the term 'atom' as they do is because there really are atoms 'out there' which have caused themselves to be represented more or less accurately – caused physicists to have words to refer to them and to engage in a social practice called micro-structural physical science.

Theorists taking the cultural turn are quite willing to agree with at least one element of this argument: that language is shaped by the environment within which we live. However, they regard the attempt to endow objects with an essence which precedes their linguistic articulation as a crucial error. In other words, they reject the argument that it is the essence of atoms themselves – their 'atomicity', if you will – which has caused physicists to have words to refer to them. In contrast to this position, they argue that natural facts are also discursive facts.

By the term 'discourse' they refer to a group of statements which provide a language for talking about a topic and a way of producing a particular kind of knowledge about a topic. Thus the term refers both to the production of knowledge through language and representation and the way that knowledge is institutionalized, shaping social practices and setting new practices into play. They argue that atoms are discursive objects because to call something an 'atom' is a way of conceiving of it that depends upon a classificatory practice. The classificatory or discursive practice therefore comes first and the 'atom' second. Again, this is not to deny the *existence* of something which physicists have come to term 'atom'. However, it is to assert that this object only achieves *being (or meaning)* through language, within discursive articulations, and that these discursive articulations are historic and contingent (Laclau and Mouffe, 1987: 104). Seen from this perspective, it would be absurd to ask whether, outside of all scientific theory, atomic structure is the true, objective nature of matter – for the point is that atomic theory is a way we have of classifying certain objects, of making them meaningful, but that these are open to different forms of conceptualization that may emerge in the future. In other words, the truth, factual or otherwise, about the meaning of objects is always constituted within a particular discursive context, and the idea of a truth outside of all context is nonsensical.

Merely to state this view is to see the problems it presents to traditional thinking. Notions of 'objectivity', 'accuracy' and 'verisimilitude' are immediately and profoundly problematized. They no longer seem able to provide the comfort and guidance they once did for they cannot be seen as absolute judgements emanating from 'on high', as it were, but as judgements made relative to differing and competing vocabularies. Similarly, a whole host of distinctions and oppositions – between fact and value, reason and rhetoric, truth and politics – become if not untenable then at least contestable and disputable.

As debates in the philosophy of science mentioned above hint at, the elaboration of the cultural turn by philosophers, sociologists, feminists and literary critics has met with considerable resistance. While some of this criticism has verged on the apocalyptic – the cultural turn being equated with the end of Western civilization as we know it – much of it has been serious and thoughtful. Many of the more thoughtful criticisms of the cultural turn are structured around two basic theses: (a) that denying a reality beyond discourse which can serve as a foundation or point of reference for debate is to fall into the bottomless pit of 'relativism'; (b) that affirming the discursive character of every object is to engage in a form of 'idealism'. Let's take a closer look at these two criticisms and see if we can begin to assess their explanatory reach.

## Criticizing the cultural turn

What do critics of the cultural turn mean when they accuse its proponents of 'relativism'? The first thing to note is that the term is not meant as a compliment. It invariably carries with it pejorative undertones. But why? Well, the term seems to emerge in debate whenever someone argues that judgements as to what is true, for example, flow from local contexts rather than from the identification of transcendent or general standards. The accusation of 'relativism' carries pejorative meaning because of the fear that if judgements are relative to particular contexts and there is no context of contexts – no point of origin or foundation which can act as a source of authority so compelling that everyone, no matter what his or her history, education, political situation etc., defers to it – then there is no way to tell the difference between right and wrong, to prefer one argument to another and so on (Fish, 1994: 10–11). Thus, being called a 'relativist' implies that you espouse the view that every belief on a certain topic, or perhaps about any topic, is as good as any other.

However, as Richard Rorty (1982: 166) has commented, 'no one holds this view' and certainly not practitioners of the cultural turn. According to Rorty, those feminists, sociologists and philosophers who get called relativists 'are those that say that the grounds for choosing between . . . opinions are less algorithmic [scientific] than had been thought'. He suggests that the main debate 'is not between people who think one view as good as another and people who do not. It is between those who think our culture, or purpose, or institutions cannot be supported except conversationally, and people who still hope for other sorts of support' (Rorty, 1982: 166).

As Rorty's comments suggest, 'relativism' is a bit of a false problem. A relativist position would appear to be one which imagines human agents as standing apart from all contexts of judgement and faced with the task of identifying the right and true ones. However, as we have already seen, no one is ever in that 'originary' position, unattached to any normative assumptions and waiting for external guidance; rather, we are always and already embedded in one or more social practices whose norms of conduct and habits of action make us who we are and therefore we are not only capable of making distinctions and passing judgements but cannot refrain from so doing.

However, stating this does not always see an end to the worry about relativism; often the debate takes another turn. The argument normally proceeds something like this: if there are multiple and competing vocabularies, each with its own claims to truth, how do we find a means of adjudicating between them? Isn't it here that the absence of independent standards becomes disabling, since in the event of competing and contradictory accounts of a particular matter, there is nowhere to go for an authoritative judgement?

In answer to this question, proponents of the cultural turn argue that authority is not something that exists in some timeless space, presiding over debates between competing vocabularies from a position *outside* of them. Rather, as Stanley Fish (1994: 10–11) has argued, *authority is the prize for which the competing vocabularies vie with one another*. That a closure is often reached with one vocabulary temporarily dominant is indicative less of that vocabulary's correspondence to an objective truth than to the fact that it has managed to fashion authority for itself in the course of debate. In other words, conversational authority and truth are *political achievements*. It is the outcome of the struggle between competing vocabularies that will decide what the truth of a particular matter will be; it is *power relations rather than facts about reality which make things 'true'*.

To turn to the second criticism: what do critics of the cultural turn mean when they charge it with 'idealism'? Within philosophy, the essence of 'idealism' is the reduction of the real to the concept: the affirmation of the ultimately conceptual character of reality. Simplifying greatly, we can say that for idealists the external world is either constructed by or dependent upon the mind.

It is not too difficult to guess why critics might conceive of the cultural turn as essentially idealist. By arguing that all objects are given meaning through language, proponents of the cultural turn appear to leave themselves open to the charge that they do not believe that there is any reality outside of the mind; that objects not spoken, written or thought about do not exist. The favourite target here is the concept of 'discourse'. How can everything be conceived of as discourse, the critics argue, when so much of human activity is extra-linguistic? If speech, writing and thought do not exhaust reality, they ask, why conceive of the world solely in terms of discourse? In trying to answer this question we need to be quite specific about identifying the status of the concept of discourse deployed by proponents of the cultural turn. I want to start by exploring the relationship between the *linguistic* and the *extra-linguistic* for this holds the key to understanding what discourse means for those taking the cultural turn. With apologies to Wittgenstein – for the example I use is his – let's think about building a wall.

Imagine you are building a wall with a colleague. At a particular moment you ask your colleague to pass you a brick and once she has done so you add the brick to the wall. We can conceive of two distinct acts taking place here. The first act – asking for the brick – is, of course, linguistic; the second – adding the brick to the wall – is extra-linguistic. The question is how much is to be gained from conceiving of these two acts as qualitatively different from one another in kind – the one linguistic, the other extra-linguistic? For proponents of the cultural turn, the two actions are not discrete or isolated because they are both part of a wider process – that of building the wall. Let me explain.

If we have an activity called 'building a wall', how should we characterize it? Can it be conceived of as purely linguistic? Obviously not because it involves material actions that are extra-linguistic. Similarly, though, we cannot conceive of building a wall as purely extra-linguistic, for the total process also involves linguistic activity. The sensible thing seems to be to admit that the total operation – building a wall – includes *both* linguistic and extra-linguistic elements and cannot be reduced to one or the other; rather *it has to be prior to this distinction.* This totality which includes both linguistic and extra-linguistic elements is what proponents of the cultural turn refer to as 'discourse' (Laclau and Mouffe, 1987). Seen in this way it becomes apparent that discourse cannot be conceived of as 'idealistic' because it does not exclude the 'extra-linguistic'; rather, it serves to undermine divisions between language and material practices by indicating the ways in which meaning and use are intimately connected. As indicated earlier, discourse is about the production of knowledge through language. However, as Stuart Hall (1992) has indicated, it is itself produced by a practice: 'discursive practice' – the practice of *producing meaning.* Since all social practices are meaningful practices, they are all discursive.

Let's quickly try to sum up the location of the term 'discourse' within the cultural turn. As we have seen, if the meaning of an object – as opposed to its mere existence prior to its insertion in language – is constituted within discourse, it becomes no longer possible to differentiate the discursive from any other area of reality. Because meaning and use are constitutive of one another, it makes no sense to differentiate between them in terms of a 'linguistic'/'extra-linguistic' distinction. The discursive is not therefore one object among many (although concrete discourses are) but rather, as Ernesto Laclau and Chantal Mouffe (1987: 105) have suggested, a *theoretical horizon.* In other words, *the discursive is the boundary of the meaningful.*

While this defence of the term 'discourse' counters the charge of 'idealism' made against it by critics of the cultural turn, it has at the same time generated a new line of attack. This involves a renewed concern with the essence of objects. The argument proceeds something like this. If all objects are discursively constructed, critics ask, why is it that their meanings are forever changing? Is it perhaps the case that what is involved in the battle over the meanings of objects is less the *construction* of those objects but rather their correct *apprehension*? In other words, the critics suggest, perhaps the discursive failure to stabilize the meanings of objects derives from an inability to discover the 'real' meaning of the object – its essence? The failure to stabilize the meaning of an object is thus the result of a failure correctly to apprehend its 'real', objective meaning.

For proponents of the cultural turn, the fact that the meanings of objects change is neither a source of surprise nor regret. As we have already seen, they do not think that an object has an essence that precedes or evades that object's articulation within discourse. Rather, they argue that the meaning that any object has at any given time is a contingent, historical achievement.

As I have indicated, theorists of discourse argue that the meaning of objects is different from their mere existence, and that people never confront objects as mere existences, in a primal manner; rather, these objects are always articulated within particular discursive contexts. However, they go on to argue that no discursive context is ever completely self-contained – that there is always an 'outside' which prevents it from constituting itself as an autonomous entity. But what do they mean by this and how do they reach this conclusion? Well, let's look at their reasoning more closely.

As we have already seen, the cultural turn breaks with what is known as the 'referential theory of language' and the 'mimetic theory of representation' – the idea that language stands in a transparent one-to-one relationship with objects. For theorists of discourse, words have no meaning in and of themselves but obtain meaning in relation to other words in a classificatory system. What theorists of discourse therefore stress is the *relational* character of language – that words only get to mean what they do in relation to something else which they are not. Thus the word, 'mother', for example, only means what it does because the words 'father', 'daughter', 'son' and so forth also exist. The totality of language is therefore a *system of differences* in which the identity of the various elements is purely relational. In this sense, difference is always constitutive of the identity of an object. Or, as Jacques Derrida might put it, the *presence* of something always carries with it the *traces* of something else which is *absent*. This relational or differential character is not exclusive to linguistic identities but holds for *all social relations*. Once again, this does not mean that everything is simply a linguistic phenomenon, but rather that, as Jacques Lacan (1987) would have put it, all social identities are 'structured like a language'.

If this is the case – that is, if all identity is differential, and if the system of differences is never completely closed – then *any identity* will never be totally secure and fixed for all time. In other words, it is basically impossible to attribute a fixed meaning to objects because the process of attributing meaning is by its very nature open-ended and contingent.

Let's try to clarify things a little by unpacking what it means to talk about a 'contingent' identity. As indicated in the Introduction, at a simple level, to suggest that something is contingent amounts to saying that the conditions of existence of any object are exterior to that object and not interior to it. In other words, a contingent identity is never fully autonomous because it relies for its existence upon something outside of itself. Thus, a contingent identity is only constituted in relation to that which it is not. None the less, because that identity would not be what it is without the relationship it has with this 'outside', the latter is also part of the conditions of existence of that identity. Let's take an example.

The identity categories of 'man' and 'woman' are often represented as fixed, stable and autonomous – in other words, as natural. They are normally interpreted as biological categories, and biological differences are commonly regarded as guarantors of the essential capacities and dispositions of women and men. However, if every identity is relational, then surely these categories will be contingent rather than 'natural' or 'essential'? As feminist scholars have indicated, the idea that biology underscores the unambiguous authenticity of femininity and masculinity is itself a historical invention. Not only this, it is a product of power relations, in which the category 'man' is synonymous with 'humanity' in general, whereas 'woman' is precisely defined as a specifically feminine and frequently sexual category.

In other words, the category 'man' only constructs its identity through excluding that which it is not and establishing a violent hierarchy between itself and its 'other' – 'woman'. In linguistic theory, a distinction is drawn between 'marked' and 'unmarked' terms (Laclau, 1990: 33). The latter convey the main or principal meaning of a term, while the marked term adds a supplement to it. Thus, we can say that the term 'man' differentiates the latter from 'woman' but is also equated with 'human being' which is the condition shared by both men and women. 'Woman' is therefore a 'mark', in contrast to the unmarked term of 'man'. Men's specific gender is thus ignored: men represent the universal and the human against which women are positioned as 'other'. At the same time, however, because the identity 'man' only establishes itself in relation to that which it is not, it would not be what it is without the presence of this 'other'. Furthermore, given that any contingent identity is relational in terms of its conditions of existence, it is important to note that any change in the latter is bound to affect the former.

What this amounts to saying is that every identity is *dislocated*. As we have seen, according to Ernesto Laclau (1990: 39), every identity is dislocated because it depends upon an outside which simultaneously denies and affirms that identity. Thus every identity is always an ambiguous achievement because its emergence is dependent upon its ability – power – to define difference. However, it is also important to note that revealing the contingent nature of an established identity does not automatically put into question the continued existence of that identity. To think that it does is to misread the lesson that the cultural turn preaches. More specifically, it is to confuse two very different practices. Let me explain what I mean by returning once again to the subject of science.

As we have seen, cultural theorists have questioned the claims of philosophers of science that scientific enquiry is the only practice that can get at the truth of an object by indicating that 'objective truth' is an effect or product of scientific practice and not something that scientists 'discover'. However, revealing the sociocultural construction of scientific truth is not the same thing as suggesting that those truths are illegitimate or illicit. It is simply a way of indicating that they are not the only truths in town and that judging all other truth productions – religious, sociological, literary – in terms of the norms of scientific practice is a colossally immodest thing to do. In other words, the cultural critique of scientific truth doesn't mean that people should immediately give up doing science. What it does indicate, however, is that doing science and doing a cultural analysis of science are not the same thing.

This is what H.M. Collins (quoted in Fish, 1994: 24) is getting at when he argues that the 'objects of science are made by hiding their social origins'. Collins is discussing the relationship between scientific practice – what scientists do in their laboratories and so on – and the sociological analysis of science – the delineation of the sociocultural conditions of existence of scientific practice. His point is that in order to engage in either of these two projects one must rigorously exclude – that is, forget or ignore – the imperatives of the other. As he declares, 'science – the study of an apparently external world – is constructed by not doing the sort of thing that sociology of scientific knowledge does to science . . . for science would not make sense as an institution unless it were normally the case that acting scientifically meant acting as though the sociology of science were not true' (quoted in Fish, 1994: 24). Acting scientifically means acting on the assumption of a determinate nature waiting to be described by an author-evacuated neutral observation language; acting sociologically means acting on the assumption that nature is socially constructed by the very speech acts of which it is supposedly the cause. Everything about the two practices – their respective facts, discovery procedures, mechanisms of justification, and so on – is different, and the attempt to unite them will result only in confusion.

In other words, there is no direct route from the insight that all activities are contingent and politically constructed to a special or different way of engaging in any particular activity, no politics that derives from the truth that everything is contingent and contextual. As Stanley Fish (1994: 255) has argued,

one often hears it said that once you have become aware of the political and
constructed nature of all actions, this awareness can be put to methodological use
in the practices (history, literary criticism, law) you find yourself performing; but
. . . in so far as awareness is something that can be put into play in a situation, it
will be awareness relative to the demarcated concerns of that situation and not
some separate capacity that you carry with you from one situation to another.

If the epistemological sophistication of the cultural turn does not of itself
undermine the existence of established social identities, how do we explain
the generalized 'crisis of identity' that many observers regard as *the* crucial
feature of contemporary sociocultural change in modern Western societies
(Giddens, 1991; Mercer, 1991; Hall, 1992)? In order to begin to provide
some answers to this question, our discussion of 'culture' must switch from
an exclusively epistemological to a more substantive or sociological (though
by no means atheoretical) mode. In Chapter 3, therefore, I shall concentrate upon the substantive turn to culture within one particular domain:
the world of paid work and organizations. In particular, I shall seek to
indicate the ways in which contemporary attempts to manage 'organizational culture' have major implications for the sorts of work-based
identities that are able to flourish within an enterprise.

# 3
# Governing Organizational Life

In his 1938 lecture on 'A category of the human mind: the notion of person, the notion of "self"', Marcel Mauss (1979) articulated what was to become one of the most scandalous axioms of the social sciences: the idea that the 'person' or the 'self' is a culturally and historically malleable category. Since then, anthropological evidence and historical research have indicated that the modern, Western 'idea' of the person as a largely coherent, rational, conscious and self-directed being is 'a metaphysical fiction' (Beechey and Donald, 1986: x; see also Hirst and Woolley, 1982). As Mauss (1979: 90) argued, 'Who knows if this "category", which all of us here today believe to be well founded, will always be recognized as such? It was formed only for us, among us.'

This argument regarding the contextual nature of identities can be applied without hesitation to the arena of work and employment. As Claude Lefort (1986: 142) has suggested, for example, the category of 'worker' does not connote some form of suprahistorical essence or 'spirit' – as the notion of alienation appears to indicate – since it is, as Marx himself indicated, a 'product of *history*'. It only comes into being under certain historical and cultural conditions. Similarly, notions such as 'job satisfaction' and 'motivation' are not phenomena that exist in some timeless, universal realm waiting to be discovered by, and deployed within, managerial discourse. Both the basic concepts and the practices that bestow upon them a material reality are products of changes in the imagination and organization of work.

As we saw in Chapter 2, given that any identity is basically relational in terms of its conditions of existence, any change in the latter is bound to affect the former. For example, if an employee's relations with his or her employing organization are discursively reconceptualized, then rather than having the same identity – the 'employee' – in a new situation, a new identity is established. However, as indicated in Chapter 1, for some Marxists the 'worker' is conceived as a transcendental *a priori* category representing the essence of every direct producer, 'whose historically differentiated forms in relation to the conditions of production would merely constitute empirical variations' (Laclau, 1990: 25). Hyman (1987: 40), for example, argues that 'shifting fashions in labour management' are purely and simply the outcome of a primal antagonism between labour and capital. In this vision, the identity of both labour and capital is invariably represented as stable and unchanging, while lived history is reduced to a series of 'empirical variations' on a constant theme. Labour and capital are conceived of as having an 'essential', 'real' identity that precedes or evades their dominant discursive articulation in any historical or cultural context. Needless to say, knowledge of this 'real' identity is only available to those armed with the appropriate 'gaze'.

For proponents of this sort of position, at the heart of modern work organization there lies an 'objectively' conflictual relationship. As Baldamus (1961: 105), for example, has put it, 'as wages are costs to the firm, and the deprivation inherent in effort means cost to the employee, the interests of management and wage-earner are diametrically opposed.' At one pole there stand the 'workers'. With nothing to sell but their labour power, their 'interests' can easily be delineated. Failing the complete transformation of already existing social relations, workers' 'objective' interests lie in increasing wages, reducing working hours, minimizing 'effort', and imposing various constraints upon 'exploitation' by fighting for better conditions of employment and firmer legislative constraints upon the activities and ambitions of employers (Rose, 1990). At the opposite extreme are the employers and their 'servants of power', management and the experts of symbolic mediation – occupational psychologists and the like – who service them. Their 'objective' interests are linked to the perpetual expansion of profit through increasing productivity, deskilling work, keeping wages low, weakening the collective power of workers, and reducing their capacity to disrupt the process of accumulation, while simultaneously casting a cloak of 'ideological legitimacy' over the essentially exploitative nature of the employment relation (Braverman, 1974).

From this perspective it is obvious that nothing short of a wholesale transformation of society will eradicate the alienation residing at the heart of modern work. In this model, as indicated in Chapter 1, work entails the subordination of subjectivity. For Hyman (1987) and others, any programmes and practices that attempt to reorganize business enterprises and the subjective experience of work without tackling the fundamental antagonism between capital and labour must be little more than 'shifting fashions', because they are obviously on a hiding to nothing. How subjects are positioned by, and use, these programmes and practices is of no concern because the latter are perceived to have no effect in overcoming the 'objective' relations of alienation and exploitation.

However, for proponents of these 'shifting fashions', the worker's subjective experience of work *is* of central importance. The advocates of various discourses and practices of work reform – the Human Relations school, the Quality of Working Life movement etc. – claim to be able to restructure the employment relation so as to make work more subjectively meaningful for those performing it, while simultaneously increasing profitability. These different discourses of work represent the subjectivity of the worker not only as an object to be developed rather than repressed, but also as a crucial determinant of organizational success. Through the medium of a variety of different programmes and human 'technologies' –

the use of human scientific knowledge to specify ways of doing things in a reproducible way – they have attempted to indicate that productive work can satisfy the worker, that the activity of working can provide empowering and fulfilling personal and social relations for those performing it, and that work is a route to self-fulfilment (Rose, 1990; Hollway, 1991). As Rose (1990: 56) has argued,

> Employers and managers equipped with these new visions of work have thus claimed that there is no conflict between the pursuits of productivity, efficiency, and competitiveness on the one hand and the humanization of work on the other. On the contrary, the path to business success lies in engaging the employee with the goals of the company at the level of his or her subjectivity, aligning the wishes, needs, and aspirations of each individual who works for the organization with the successful pursuit of its objectives. Through striving to fulfil their own needs and wishes at work, each employee will thus work for the advance of the enterprise; the more the individual fulfils him or herself, the greater the benefit to the company.

While it is undoubtedly true that these discourses and practices of work reform have played, and continue to play, an active part in reproducing hierarchies of power and reward at work, or that they have been consciously deployed at various times to attenuate the power of trade unions and their prerogatives for the representation of collective interests and the defence of collective 'rights', it is equally important to note that they are not simply 'ideological' distortions; in other words, that their claims to 'knowledge' are not 'false', nor do they serve a specific social function and answer to certain pre-formed economic needs. Certainly these discourses of work reform arise in specific political contexts, and have political consequences, but they are not merely functional responses to, or legitimations of, already existing economic interests or needs. Rather than simply reflecting a pre-given social world, they themselves actively 'make up' a reality, and create new ways for people to be at work. As Miller and O'Leary (1989) have argued, the 'nature' or 'essence' of the internal world of the business enterprise is a function of changes in practices of governing economic life, rather than the converse.

'Managerial thought' and other discourses of work reform play an active role in the formation of new images and mechanisms, which bring the government of the enterprise into alignment with political rationalities, cultural values and social expectations (Rose, 1989). In the process, people come to identify themselves and conceive of their interests in terms of these new words and images and formulate their objectives in relation to them. Changes in the ways of conceptualizing, documenting and acting upon the internal world of the business organization actively transform the meaning and reality of work. As Rose (1990: 60) has suggested, these new ways of relating the attributes and feelings of individual employees to the objectives of the organization for which they work are central elements in the 'fabrication of new languages and techniques to bind the worker into the productive life of society'.

### Governing the work-based subject

If management discourses play an active role in attempts to 'govern' economic life through creating new ways for people to be at work, what exactly is the status of the term 'government' in this context? Quite obviously 'government' is not equivalent to 'the government' or 'the state', and yet, as Rose's comments suggest, various discourses of work reform appear to be intimately linked to the political culture of the time. It is a shared 'governmental rationality' (Foucault, 1991) which provides this link.

According to Foucault (1980: 221), 'government' is a form of power referring to the 'conduct of conduct': 'to govern, in this sense, is to structure the possible field of actions of others'; that is to say, government is a form of activity aiming to shape, guide or affect the conduct of some person or persons. Government as an activity can concern the relation between self and self, private interpersonal relations involving some form of control or guidance, relations within social institutions and committees and, finally, relations concerned with the exercise of political sovereignty.

For Foucault, government is a discursive activity. All forms of government rely upon a particular mode of representation: the development of a language for delineating and depicting a certain domain that claims both to capture the nature of the 'reality' represented, and, literally, to 're-present' it in a form suitable for deliberation, argumentation, scheming and intervention. Thus it is possible to see that the government of an economy, or of an organization, only becomes feasible through discursive practices that render the 'Real' comprehensible as a particular 'reality' with specific limits and distinct characteristics whose components are linked together in some relatively systematic fashion (Hacking, 1983).[1] Particular programmes of intervention and rectification, and specific 'technologies of government' follow on from this rendering of the 'Real' into the domain of thought as a 'reality'.

However, government isn't simply about the ordering of activities and processes, it is intimately concerned with 'subjectification': government operates through subjects. As Foucault (1980, 1982) argued, forms of power 'work' by constructing and maintaining the forms of subjectivity most appropriate to a given type of social practice/governmental rationality. Subjectivities are constituted by, and rendered instrumental to, a particular form of power through the medium of knowledges or technical *savoir faire* 'immanent to that form of power' (Minson, 1985: 44–5). Thus power works in and through subjectivity. Different governmental rationalities – attempts to invent and exercise different types of rule – are closely linked to conceptions and attributes of those to be governed. In other words, particular rationalities of government involve the construction of specific ways for people to be. In Ian Hacking's (1986: 234) phrase, they actively 'make up' people.

As 'government' is a 'conduct of conduct', it presupposes rather than annuls the capacity of individuals as agents. As Foucault (1982: 221) suggests,

> when one defines the exercise of power as a mode of action upon the actions of others, when one characterizes these actions by the government of men by other men – in the broadest sense of the term – one includes an important element: freedom. Power is exercised only over free subjects, and only insofar as they are free. By this we mean individual or collective subjects who are faced with a field of possibilities in which several ways of behaving, several reactions and diverse comportments may be realized. Where the determining factors saturate the whole there is no relationship of power.

The relation between government and governed therefore depends upon an 'unstable conjuncture' – it is 'agonistic' – because this relation passes through the manner in which governed individuals are willing to exist as particular subjects. As Gordon (1991: 48) has suggested, 'to the extent that the governed are engaged, in their individuality, by the propositions and provisions of government, government makes its own rationality intimately their affair.' In this sense, government is a very personal matter; it is bound up with 'ethics'. For Foucault (1984: 352) 'ethics' has a very particular meaning: 'the kind of relationship you ought to have with yourself, *rapport a soi* . . . which determines how the individual is supposed to constitute himself as a moral subject of his own actions'. Ethics are thus conceived as the means by which individuals come to understand and act upon themselves in relation to the true and the false, the permitted and the forbidden, the desirable and the undesirable (Rose, 1989).

As indicated above, the government of economic life in the twentieth century has entailed a range of attempts to shape and regulate the relations that individuals have with society's productive apparatus. From 'scientific management' through 'human relations' up to and including the contemporary programmes of 'excellence', the activities of individuals as workers have become 'an object of knowledge and the target of expertise, and a complex web of relays has been formed through which the economic endeavours of politicians and businessmen have been translated into the personal capacities and aspirations of subjects' (Miller and Rose, 1990: 19). In other words, the identity of the 'worker' has been differentially constituted in the changing practices of governing economic life. 'Workers' and 'managers' have been 'made up' in different ways – discursively re-imagined and reconceptualized – at different times through their positioning in a variety of discourses of work reform.

For the remainder of this chapter I will concentrate on the ways in which people are presently 'made up' at work by exploring the contemporary management discourse of 'excellence' and its relationship to the political rationality of 'enterprise'. In particular, I will indicate how the expertise of 'excellence' provides the means whereby the politico-ethical objectives of neo-liberal government in the UK (or Thatcherism as it has popularly been known), the economic objectives of contemporary business and the self-actualizing and self-regulating capacities of human subjects are linked together into a functioning network.

## Enterprise culture and the discourse of excellence

From the outset, the Thatcherite project not only involved an economic revival but also a moral crusade. As Margaret Thatcher herself argued, as early as 1975, 'serious as the economic challenge is, the political and moral challenge is just as grave, and perhaps more so, because economic problems never start with economics' (quoted in Hall, 1988: 85). It was the difficult, often faltering, attempt to weave these economic and moral strands together that produced the 'enterprise culture' as the symbol and goal of Thatcherism.

Although the concept of an enterprise culture was not at all well defined in policy terms when the Conservatives first won power in 1979, it has since become extremely important in 'justifying many of the policies the government has adopted, and in characterising the long term objectives of its programme and the kind of society it wants to see emerge' (Gamble, 1988: 137). Basically, the government argued that the permissive and anti-enterprise culture that had been fostered by social democratic institutions since 1945 had become one of the most serious obstacles to reversing decline. The economic and moral regeneration of Britain therefore necessitated exerting pressure on every institution to make it supportive of enterprise.

In Britain, attempts to construct a culture of enterprise have proceeded through the progressive enlargement of the territory of the market – the realm of private enterprise and economic rationality – by a series of redefinitions of its object. Thus, the task of creating an enterprise culture has involved the reconstruction of a wide range of institutions and activities along the lines of the commercial business organization, with attention focused, in particular, on its orientation towards 'the sovereign consumer'. At the same time, however, the market has also come to define the sort of relation an individual should have with him or herself, and the 'habits of action' he or she should acquire and exhibit. Enterprise refers here to the 'kind of action or project' that exhibits 'enterprising' qualities or characteristics on the part of individuals or groups. In this latter sense an enterprise culture is one in which certain enterprising qualities – such as self-reliance, personal responsibility, boldness and a willingness to take risks in the pursuit of goals – are regarded as human virtues and promoted as such. As Keat (1990: 3–4) has indicated, in the contemporary discourse of enterprise, these two strands – the 'institutional' and the 'ethical' – are intricately interwoven:

> on the one hand, the conduct of commercial enterprises is presented as a (indeed the) primary field of activity in which enterprising qualities are displayed. And given that these qualities are themselves regarded as intrinsically desirable . . .

this serves to valorize engagement in such activities and hence, more generally, the workings of a free market economy. On the other hand, however, it is also claimed that in order to maximise the benefits of this economic system, commercial enterprises must themselves be encouraged to be enterprising, i.e. to act in ways that fully express these qualities. In other words, it seems to be acknowledged that 'enterprises are not fully enterprising', and enterprising qualities are thus given an instrumental value in relation to the optimal performance of a market economy.

According to Colin Gordon (1991: 43), enterprise has become an approach capable, in principle, 'of addressing the totality of human behaviour, and thus, of envisaging a coherent, purely economic method of programming the totality of governmental action'. In other words, enterprise can be understood to constitute a particular form of 'governmental rationality' (Foucault, 1991). As such, it is not simply reducible to the politico-ethical project of Thatcherism. Rather than having its original essence in, and uniquely belonging to, the policies of successive Conservative administrations, the rationality of enterprise permeates a plethora of discourses, programmes and technologies developed outside the field of formal or 'official' government. For example, one area in which the vocabulary of enterprise has played a central structuring role is in management discourse.

According to Wood (1989: 387), one of the most distinctive features of 'new wave management' is the shift it attempts to initiate from 'reactive to proactive postures', from 'bureaucratic' to 'entrepreneurial styles of management' and, possibly most importantly, the new forms of work-based identity it tries to forge among all members of an organization. For Wood, the appeal of the new management discourse of excellence has as much, if not more, to do with the *cultural* reconstruction of work-based identities as with the 'values of the technologies or organizational forms they propose'.

As Wood's comments indicate, one of the key elements in the contemporary discourse of work reform is the attention devoted to questions of 'culture' and 'identity'. A cursory inspection of any number of recent management texts reveals the primacy accorded to 'culture change programmes' as panaceas for all manner of organizational ills (Ouchi, 1981; Peters and Waterman, 1982; Peters, 1987; Kanter, 1990).[2] In this literature, culture is paramount because it is seen to structure the way people think, make decisions and act in organizations. Culture is represented as an answer to the problems thrown up by the increasingly dislocated ground upon which globalized capitalism operates. As Laclau (1990: 56), for example, has argued, the less organizations are able to rely upon a framework of stable social and political relations, the more they are forced to engage in a project of 'hegemonic construction'. In other words, the effects of dislocation require constant 'creativity', and the continuous construction of collective operational space that rests less on inherited objective forms (bureaucracy) and more on *cultural* reconstruction. Thus 'new wave management' is concerned with changing people's values, norms and attitudes so that they make the 'right' and necessary contribution to the success of the organization for which they work. To this end, excellence encourages managers to view the most effective and excellent organizations as those with 'strong cultures' – patterns of meaning which enable all members of an organization to *identify* with the goals and objectives of the company for which they work.

According to Deleuze (1992: 3), among others, the corporation only becomes 'cultural' – develops a 'soul' – once 'the market' has achieved a position of pre-eminence. The discourse of excellence is therefore both symptom and effect of the increasing de-differentiation of economy and culture. As Jameson (1990: 29) has argued, the colonization of culture by the market does not imply the disappearance or extinction of the cultural; rather, it suggests a situation in which 'the corporate is now at one with culture'.

In effect, the 'institutional' and 'ethical' imperatives propounded by the advocates of excellence are very similar to those proclaimed within the neo-liberal project of enterprise culture: economic and moral revival through a programme of 'cultural change'. Like contemporary neo-liberal political rationalities, the 'search for excellence' requires a veritable 'cultural revolution', one in which organizations and their members learn to 'thrive on chaos' (in the decentred, global, free-market economy) and to renew continually their enterprising spirit. Thus, the vocabulary of enterprise is a central structuring element in both of these projects. However, as indicated above, excellence is not reducible to 'Thatcherism at work'. Although the discourse of enterprise, and contemporary attempts to create an enterprise culture in the UK are virtually synonymous with the politico-ethical project of Thatcherism, they are not reducible to this phenomenon. Rather, enterprise as a 'governmental rationality' has entered people's daily lives in a number of ways not directly related to the policy initiatives of successive Conservative administrations (Robins, 1991). At the same time, this also suggests that the removal of Margaret Thatcher from office in no way heralded the end of the project of enterprise. Indeed, as Hall (1991: 10) has recently argued, the 'entrepreneurial revolution' to which Thatcherism contributed with such passionate brutality 'is still working its way through the system'.

Although the *cultural reconstruction of identity* is central to the excellence project, contemporary management discourse has been largely ignored within cultural analysis. Morris (1988: 22–3) has recently provided a convincing explanation for this neglect. According to her, there is a marked tendency within cultural studies to assume that somehow the economic sphere has already been accounted for. Within this tradition, a potentially de-alienated sphere of consumption is often counterposed to an alienated, deskilled and already determined world of paid employment. So, while cultural analysis has paid considerable attention to the 'pleasures' and 'play' of identities within contemporary cultures of consumption, it has tended to relegate the world of work and employment 'to the realm of the *déjà vu*'.

Meanwhile, within the sociology of work and employment, for example, where 'economic life' is the central focus, the excellence phenomenon has been accorded some considerable, though narrowly focused, attention. But while its theoretical underpinnings have been criticized, its empirical incidence debated, and its internal contradictions exposed (Storey, 1989), there has been little notice paid to the subjectivizing aspects of the excellence project, and their relationship to the politico-ethical objectives of neo-liberal government in the UK. However, as I argued above, questions of discourse, subjectivity and identity have a key role to play in understanding the excellence phenomenon and its links with the governmental rationality of enterprise.

## Work-based identity and management discourse

A concern with the production of particular work-based identities is not unique to contemporary management discourse. Throughout this century multifarious schemes have been advocated by a plethora of schools of thought which attempt, both consciously and unconsciously, to eradicate conflict and contestability from organizational life through integrating the work-based human subject and the organization. This objective can be seen to underlie such seemingly diverse approaches as the Mayoite Human Relations school (Roethlisberger and Dickson, 1939; Mayo, 1949), the 'Organizational Psycho-Technologists' (Argyris, 1957; McGregor, 1960; Herzberg, 1968) and the Quality of Working Life movement (Davies and Cherns, 1975), for example. Each of these projects assumed that it was possible (and indeed necessary) to reconcile the needs and desires of management and workers through the deployment of their own particular 'expertise'. In effect, whether articulated in terms of a 'need' for 'belonging' (Mayo et al.), or as a desire for 'self-actualization' (Argyris et al.), what unites all of these projects is a concern with the production and regulation of particular work-based subjectivities. According to Miller and Rose (1988: 172), these various schools of thought construct

> images of the enterprise, techniques of management, forms of authority, and conceptions of the social vocation of industry which can align the government of the enterprise with the prevailing cultural values, social expectations, political concerns and personal ambitions ... They have provided means for linking together changing political rationalities and objectives, the ceaseless quest of business for profitability and a basis for managerial authority, with interventions aimed at the subjectivity of the worker.

The excellence project is firmly established on this trajectory. It follows in the footsteps of its predecessors in seeking to construct a vision of the enterprise as an 'organic entity', but it does so through the articulation of a new vocabulary of the employment relationship in which the worker's relation to his or her work is re-imagined in line with prevailing ethical systems, political rationalities and, of course, the profitability imperative. Within the discourse of excellence the internal world of the enterprise is reconceptualized as one in which productivity is to be improved, production and service quality assured, flexibility enhanced, and 'innovation developed through the active engagement of the self-fulfilling impulses of all the organization's members' (Rose, 1989: 16).

Some critics of excellence within the social sciences have emphasized the similarities between contemporary management discourse and previous programmes of work reform, and, in particular, its close resemblance to the Human Relations school (Turner, 1986; Silver, 1987). However, by concentrating almost exclusively on continuity and homogeneity within management discourse, these critics tend to downgrade the new ways for people to be at work which are present within the contemporary discursive formation. Within the Human Relations tradition, for example, the worker is considered, first and foremost, as a *social* creature seeking fulfilment of his or her needs to 'belong' in the group relations of the workplace. With the contemporary 'entrepreneurial order' (Miller and O'Leary, 1989) however, the worker is represented as an *individual* in search of *meaning* in work, and wanting to achieve fulfilment through work. Excellent organizations are those that 'make meaning for people' by encouraging them to believe that they have control over their own destinies; that, no matter what position they may hold in an organization, their contribution is vital, not only to the success of the company for which they work, *but also to the enterprise of their own lives.* Peters and Waterman (1982: 81, 45), for example, approvingly quote Nietzsche's axiom that 'he who has a *why* to live for can bear most any *how*.' They argue that 'the fact . . . that we think we have a bit more discretion leads to much greater commitment' and that 'we desperately need meaning in our lives, and will sacrifice a great deal to institutions that will provide meaning for us. We simultaneously need independence, to feel as though we are in charge of our destinies, and to have the ability to stick out.' In this vision, work is a sphere within which the individual constructs and confirms his or her identity. Excellent organizations get the most out of their employees, not by manipulating group human relations to secure a sense of 'belonging', but by harnessing 'the psychological striving of individuals for autonomy and creativity and channelling them into the search of the firm for excellence and success' (Miller and Rose, 1990: 26).

In other words, excellent companies seek to cultivate 'enterprising subjects' – autonomous, self-regulating, productive individuals (Gordon, 1987; Rose, 1989, 1990). Here, enterprise refers to those plethora of 'rules for conduct' for everyday life mentioned earlier: energy, initiative, self-reliance and personal responsibility. This 'enterprising self' is a calculating self; a self that 'calculates *about* itself, and that works *upon* itself in order to better itself' (Rose, 1989: 7–8) Thus, enterprise designates a form of rule that is intrinsically 'ethical' in Foucault's sense of the term: good government is to be grounded in the ways individuals govern themselves; as well as being inherently 'economic', enterprising self-regulation accords well with Jeremy Bentham's rallying cry of 'Cheap Government!'

For Peters and Waterman (1982: 238–9), excellent organizations are those which create a 'powerful focus of identification' by activating the individual's capacities for 'self-motivation' and 'enterprise':

> there was hardly a more pervasive theme in the excellent companies than *respect for the individual*. That basic belief and assumption were omnipresent . . . what makes it live at these companies is a plethora of structural devices, systems, styles and values all re-inforcing one another so that the companies are truly unusual in their ability to achieve extraordinary results through ordinary people . . . These companies give people control over their destinies; they make meaning for people. They turn the average Joe or Jane into winners. They let, even insist that, people stick out. They accentuate the positive.

For the advocates of excellence, governing the organization in an enterprising manner requires a judicious mixture of centralized control and individual autonomy. According to Peters and Waterman (1982: 318), excellent companies must be 'simultaneously loose and tight': 'organizations that live by the loose/tight principle are on the one hand rigidly controlled, yet at the same time allow (indeed, insist on) autonomy, entrepreneurship, and innovation from the rank and file.' Thus, the excellent firm is one that engages in a *controlled de-control*, or, to deploy Foucault's (1988b) terminology, one that 'totalizes' and 'individualizes' at one and the same time.

According to its proponents, the key to 'loose/tight' is 'culture': the effective management of symbols, meanings, beliefs and values is held to transform an apparent contradiction – between increasing central control and extending individual accountability and responsibility – into 'no contradiction at all' (Peters and Waterman, 1982: 321). If an organization has an appropriate culture of excellence, if all its members adopt an enterprising relationship to self, then efficiency, economy, autonomy, quality and innovation all 'become words that belong on the same side of the coin' (Peters and Waterman, 1982: 321).

Although the recourse to culture by advocates of excellence is often criticized within the social sciences for its 'remarkable vagueness' (Howard, 1985), Peters (1987: 404), for example, is adamant that the 'corporate culture' only finds life 'in details, not broad strokes'. In other words, the culture of the business enterprise is only operationalized through particular practices and technologies – through 'specific measures' (Hunter, 1987). Rather than being some vague, incalculable 'spirit', the culture of enterprise is inscribed into a variety of mechanisms – application forms, recruitment 'auditions', communication groups and the like – through which senior managers in excellent companies seek to delineate, normalize and instrumentalize the conduct of persons in order to achieve the ends they postulate as desirable. Thus, governing the business organization in an excellent manner involves cultivating enterprising subjects through the development of a (simultaneous loose/tight) 'enabling and empowering vision' (Peters, 1987) articulated in the everyday practices of the organization.

## The enterprising subjects of excellence

According to the doyenne of contemporary management discourse, Rosabeth Moss Kanter (1990: 9–10), 'by 1983' the figure of the entrepreneur had become 'the new culture hero' of the Western world. According to Kanter, the term 'entrepreneur' no longer simply implied the founder of an independent business venture; rather, it had traversed its traditional limits and now referred to the application of 'entrepreneurial principles to the traditional corporation, creating a marriage between entrepreneurial creativity and corporate discipline, cooperation and teamwork'.[3] This 'intrapreneurial' or 'post-entrepreneurial' ('because it takes entrepreneurship a stage further') 'revolution' therefore provides the possibility for every member of an organization to express 'individual initiative' and to develop fully their 'potential' in the service of the corporation. In effect, enterprising excellence offers the individual the opportunity to feel 'in business for oneself inside the modern corporation', and therefore the all important experience of 'ownership' (Pinchot, 1985; Kanter, 1990; Sabel, 1990).

Hence, while 'enterprise' still designates an economic form, it also indicates a category of activity to be encouraged by specific programmes of intervention and rectification in economic life, and a certain way in which aspects of economic, social and cultural life should be 'problematized and programmed' (Rose, 1989: 3–4). Problems are conceptualized in terms of a 'lack of enterprise'; the solutions to which are to be found by actively fostering and utilizing the 'enterprising capacities' of individuals, 'encouraging them to conduct themselves with boldness and vigour, and to drive themselves hard to accept risks in the pursuit of goals' (Rose, 1989: 3–4). Individuals are deemed capable of identifying themselves with the goals and objectives of their employing organization to the extent that they interpret them as both dependent upon and enhancing their own skills of self-development, self-presentation, self-direction and self-management.

The enterprising vision of excellence provides a novel image of the worker and the organization, and their relationship one with the other. It posits a 'post-hierarchical', entrepreneurial future where the 'old bureaucratic' emphasis on order, uniformity and repetition is gradually replaced by an entrepreneurial emphasis on 'can do' creativity (Kanter, 1990)[4] The choice presented is stark: to survive in the dislocated, decentred, increasingly competitive and chaotic global economy 'companies must either move away from bureaucratic guarantees to post-entrepreneurial flexibility or . . . stagnate' (Kanter, 1990: 356). The message is clear: organizations must shift from 'formality' to 'flexibility' in all their activities and relations. 'Formal rules' as to how work should be done must be replaced by 'implicit expectations' as to how work should be done. This requires that all employees make the goals and objectives of their employing organization their own personal goals and objectives, thus ensuring that they will deploy their 'autonomy' and 'creativity' correctly from the organization's point of view. Hence, again, there is the insistence on the construction and promulgation of a 'strong corporate culture' which reconciles the autonomous aspirations of the self-steering individual employee with the collective entrepreneurialism of the flexible corporation. According to Peters and Waterman (1982: 72) 'virtually all the excellent companies are driven by just a few key values, and then give lots of space to employees to take initiatives in support of these values – finding their own paths, and so making the task their own.'

Thus the 'expertise' of excellence provides techniques for mapping the cultural world of the business organization in terms of its success in engaging with and building upon the motivations and aspirations of its inhabitants. Through the medium of various technologies and practices inscribed with the presuppositions of the enterprising self – techniques for reducing dependency by reorganizing management structures ('delayering'); for cutting across internal organizational boundaries (the creation of 'special project teams', for example); for encouraging internal competitiveness through small group working; and for eliciting individual accountability and personal responsibility through peer review and performance appraisal schemes etc. – the internal world of the business organization is reconceptualized as one in which customers' demands are satisfied, productivity enhanced, quality assured, innovation fostered and flexibility guaranteed through the active engagement of the self-fulfilling impulses of all the organization's members. In this way, the autonomous subjectivity of the productive individual has become a central economic resource; that is, the 'strategic human resource' (Storey, 1989).

Within the discourse of excellence, work is characterized not as a painful obligation imposed upon individuals, nor as an activity only undertaken by people for the fulfilment of instrumental needs and satisfactions. Work is itself a means for self-fulfilment, and the road to company profit is also the path to individual self-development and growth. In this way, the worker is made 'subject', in that the worker is both 'subject to someone else by control and dependence, and tied to his own identity by a conscience or self-knowledge. Both meanings suggest a form of power which subjugates and makes subject to' (Foucault, 1982: 212). In other words, a person's sense of who he or she is is constituted and confirmed through his or her positioning within particular relations of power. These relations are both 'technological' and 'economical': 'technological', in that they are exercised in and through specific 'knowledges'; 'economical' in that their effect is to create and sustain a 'self-governing' subject. According to Gordon (1991: 44), enterprise is the contemporary 'care of the self' which government commends as the corrective to collective greed.

As Foucault (1988c: 92) has argued, the exercise of power 'depends on an unstable conjuncture'. Power is always productive, not merely repressive of culture. And it is precisely the positive aspects of power/knowledge relations which makes them so plausible, so effective/seductive. Thus, the expertise of excellence can be seen to play the role of 'cypher' between people's evaluations of themselves and the 'programmatic' aspirations of economic authorities (Rose, 1990). The 'power' of this 'expertise' lies in its promise of an effectiveness lodged in objectivity, and its manifest commitment to people's sense of who they are. As Rose (1989, 1990), for example, has argued, expertise is constitutive of subjectivity. Its language permeates people's ways of thinking, its judgements enter into people's evaluations, and its norms into their calculations. At the very moment when they aspire to freedom and try to realize autonomy, people are bound not only to expert knowledge but to the project of their own identities.

Thus the establishment of connections and symmetries between the self-development of the worker and the increased competitiveness and flexibility of the corporation

> enables an alignment to take place between the technologies of work and the technologies of subjectivity. For the entrepreneurial self, work is no longer necessarily a constraint upon the freedom of the individual to fulfil his or her potential through strivings for autonomy, creativity and responsibility. Work is an essential element in the path to self-realization . . . The government of work now passes through the psychological strivings of each and every individual for self-fulfilment. (Miller and Rose, 1990: 27)

### Enterprise, excellence and the New Right

It is now possible to see how the language of enterprise does not simply attempt to fashion the way owners and managers of capital calculate and activate business strategies in the market place, it is also inscribed within contemporary management discourse where it has been formulated into a series of technologies of regulation for governing the internal life of the modern corporation in order to secure business success. This success is premised upon an engagement by the organization of the 'self-fulfilling impulses' of all its individual employees, no matter what their role within the enterprise. Excellence plays the role of 'relay' between objectives that are economically desirable and those that are personally seductive, 'teaching the arts of self-realization that will enhance employees as individuals as well as workers' (Rose, 1989: 16). The discourse of excellence brooks no opposition between the mode of self-presentation required of managers and employees, and the ethics of the personal self. Becoming a better worker is represented as the same thing as becoming a more virtuous person, a better self. In other words, within the discourse of excellence, *technologies of power* – 'which determine the conduct of individuals and submit them to certain ends or domination, an objectivizing of the subject' – and *technologies of the self* – 'which permit individuals to effect by their own means or with the help of others, a certain number of operations on their own bodies and souls, thoughts, conduct and way of being, so as to transform themselves in order to attain a certain state of happiness, purity, wisdom, perfection or immortality' – are imperceptibly merged (Foucault, 1988a: 18). The values of self-realization, of personal responsibility, of 'ownership', accountability and self-management are both personally attractive and economically desirable.

This 'autonomization' and 'responsibilization' of the self, the instilling of a reflexive self-monitoring which will afford self-knowledge and therefore, self-mastery, makes paid work (no matter how 'objectively' alienated, deskilled or degraded it may appear to social scientists) an essential element in the path to self-fulfilment and provides the *a priori* that links together work and non-work life. The 'employee', just as much as the 'sovereign consumer', is represented as an individual in search of meaning and fulfilment, one looking to 'add value' in every sphere of existence. Paid work and consumption are just different playing grounds for the same activity; that is, different terrains upon which the enterprising self seeks to master, better and fulfil itself. In the discourse of excellence the relations between production, consumption, between the 'inside' and 'outside' of the corporation, and, crucially, between work and non-work based identities, are progressively blurred (Sabel, 1990).

However, the expertise of excellence does not just act as a 'relay' between the self-steering capacities of subjects and the goals of industry, it also plays a vital 'translating role' between the government of the enterprise and the politico-ethical objectives of neo-liberal government in the UK. Through deployment of the vocabulary of enterprise, contemporary management discourse establishes 'connections and symmetries' between the concerns of owners and managers of capital to maximize the performance and pro-ductivity of their organizations, political concerns about the government of the productive, moral and cultural life of the nation, and techniques for the government of the subject. Excellence helps link these together into a 'functioning network' (Miller and Rose, 1990) 26–7).

Thus the New Right's belief that Britain's moral and economic regeneration can only come about through the destruction of the 'dependency culture' and its replacement by a culture of enterprise is mirrored almost exactly in the logic of excellence. What is seen as an increasingly competitive and chaotic global free market 'that can't be bucked' demands that the corporation – like the state – shed its 'dependency mentality' and cultivate some 'entrepreneurial spirit'. 'The traditional corporation is in such turmoil that it can no longer carry the weight of . . . society's expectations of permanence, to which a variety of welfare benefits are tied' (Kanter, 1990: 357).

According to the Confederation of British Industry (1988: 59–60), for example, the 'productivity imperative' calls for a restructured corporation with 'lower manning levels and more flexible and wider job specification'. In turn, this is deemed to require 'a necessary parallel change . . . towards greater individual responsibility on the part of all employees and, in consequence, the development of self-management at all levels'. Again the message is clear: 'the free ride is over, you're on your own.' From now on it's up to individuals to secure their own future through their own efforts. In 'post-entrepreneurial' times people's careers are more dependent on their own resources . . . This means that some people who know only bureaucratic ropes are cut adrift. It means that incomes are likely to fluctuate rather than increase in an orderly fashion every year . . . It means more risk and uncertainty . . . No longer counting on the corporation requires people to build resources in themselves, which ultimately could result in more resourceful people. (Kanter, 1990: 357–8)

The assumption is that 'post-entrepreneurial strategies are more motivating for people' because they allow everyone the opportunity to be in business for themselves 'inside . . . the large corporation'. The promise is that the corporation itself 'should reap benefits too, in increased productivity' (Kanter, 1990: 357–8).

This vision of the corporation again echoes familiar ('organic') theories of society. According to critical management theorists such as Legge (1989) and Storey and Sisson (1989), 'new wave' management discourse is really 'no more or less than a reflection of the rise of the new right – whether in the UK or the USA'. For Legge (1989: 40), excellence provides that 'different language' which 'our new enterprise culture demands . . . one that asserts management's right to manipulate *and* ability to generate and develop resources'. Indeed, as Storey and Sisson (1989: 168–72) have indicated, the powerful advocacy of the 'excellence literature' has been supported massively by the government and its agencies; for example, through the Department of Trade and Industry's (the Department of Enterprise as Lord Young referred to it) 'Enterprise Initiative'. None the less, despite this committed promulgation, Storey and Sisson (1989) continue, the facts suggest that the Excellence vision is not being adopted in most organizations. So, while they acknowledge the importance of contemporary management discourse in articulating 'a coherent and convincing *Weltanschauung*', they still posit an enormous gap between representation and reality.

Interestingly, it is a self-styled 'post-Marxist', André Gorz, who takes this view of contemporary developments to its logical conclusion. Gorz (1989: 66) argues that contemporary images of the enterprise

as a place where employees can achieve personal fulfilment is . . . an essentially ideological invention. It conceals the real transformations that have taken place, namely that enterprises are replacing labour by machines, producing more and better with a decreasing percentage of the workforce previously employed, and offering privileges to a chosen elite of workers, which are accompanied by unemployment, precarious employment, deskilling and lack of job security for the majority.

While the 'transformations' Gorz refers to are 'real' enough, they are never just given, as he seems to imply, but are always discursively constituted. Unlike many other post-Marxists (Laclau and Mouffe, 1985; Hall, 1988; Zizek, 1989), Gorz views discourse and ideology as simply a negative force, hiding or distorting a more 'truthful' reality.[5] Thus, the desire to establish a clear and transparent relationship between the socially active signifier and the real relations to which it might refer is expressed in a vocabulary of truth and falsity: ideology is a simulacrum; it disguises, travesties and blurs reality and 'real' relations.

In a very orthodox (and extremely non-post-Marxist) fashion, any acknowledgement of the discursive or ideological status of excellence can also be seen to be, at one and the same time, a condemnation. As a counterweight to the 'essentially ideological' (whatever that is), Gorz appears to invite the reader to view instead what is actually (that is, non-ideologically) happening on the ground by taking a close look at 'real' material circumstances. None the less, while it is undoubtedly true that 'material circumstances' matter profoundly, these circumstances are always 'ideologically' (that is, discursively) defined. The subjects of ideology are never unified and integral selves, however; they are 'fractured, always in process and strangely composite' (Hall, 1988: 9–10). People make identifications symbolically, through social imagery, in their imaginations. To maintain a totally pejorative attitude towards ideology, to refer to it as a con-trick, distortion, or simply as a marginal or secondary concern, leads to a certain neglect of, in Reich's words, 'what goes on in people's heads' (P. Smith, 1988).

### Enterprise and excellence: ideology/antagonism/fantasy

Questions of ideology/discourse are absolutely central to the excellence project, and cannot be regarded as secondary or dependent factors. Ideology has 'real', 'material' effects which cannot be reduced to, or simply read as, the 'reflexive' accounts of some original or determining factor. As Hall (1988: 9–10) has indicated, 'all economic and political processes have discursive or ideological "conditions of existence".'

Like the New Right project of an enterprise culture, excellence is an attempt to redefine and reconstruct the economic/cultural terrain, and to 'win' social subjects to a new conception of themselves – to turn them into 'winners', 'champions' and 'everyday heroes'. As Wood (1989) has argued, excellence is about the politics of identity; contemporary management discourse attempts to enable all sorts of people, from highest executives to lowliest shopfloor employee, to see themselves reflected in the emerging conception of the 'enterprising organization', and thus to come increasingly to identify with it. In this sense, excellence can be conceptualized not only as 'cultural technology' (Hunter, 1987), but also as 'organic ideology'; as attempting to articulate into a configuration different subjects, different identities and different aspirations.

To appeal to the 'logical contradictions' of contemporary management discourse, and to the even more basic underlying 'contradictions of capitalism' (Hyman, 1987; Legge, 1989: 43), in order to show that this project can never 'really work' is to misunderstand the ways in which discourse/ideology operates. For discourse/ideology doesn't 'work' in a logical intellectual fashion. It doesn't collapse as the result of a logical contradiction because it does not obey the logic of rational discourse (Hall, 1988; Zizek, 1989). Rather, it is closer in discursive structure to the logic of 'dream-work' than to that of analytic rationalism (Hall, 1988: 86). As Wright (1987: 8) has commented, 'management thinking is superior to merely rational science in that it brings the lifeworld along with it. It entails no break with everyday experience; there is no question of having to "save the appearances" after meaning and scientific truth have taken off into a realm of their own.'

The discourse/ideology of excellence connects across different positions and divergent terrains, between seemingly disparate, and often contradictory ideas. Just like Thatcherism, excellence is 'multifaceted' – operating on several fronts at one and the same time, linking together diverse strands into a 'functioning network' (Hall, 1988: 166; Miller and Rose, 1990). Arm in arm with the New Right, excellence has unfolded a positive conception of the enterprise culture which it would be dangerous to dismiss simply as 'hype' or a 'fad'. Through deployment of the vocabulary of enterprise, excellence appears to have established a 'translatability' between the economic objectives of employers and managers of capital, changing political rationalities, and the capacities of the self.

Exactly whose identities are being discussed here? At one level it is quite clearly the 'character' of the 'manager' (MacIntyre, 1985) at whom these 'technologies of the self' are aimed. After all, it is managerial staff, rather than lower-level employees, who have sustained the remarkable sales figures of the excellence literature and attended the screenings of Tom Peters's *A Passion for Excellence* video (a common event throughout a wide range of British companies in recent years). For the manager, there is a tangible sense in which economic success, career progress and personal development intersect in this new expertise of autonomous subjectivity: the closer to the centre of the 'organizational network' you are located, the more likely it still is that the interests of organizational development and personal development coincide. In turn, this suggests that not all employees will be subjects in the new regime of the self. Those on the 'margins', or, in this case, the 'periphery', continue to be governed in more visible, and less subtle ways; subject to 'coercion' rather than 'seduction' (Bauman, 1988; Rose, 1989). Nevertheless, excellence *is* explicitly aimed at everyone. No matter what role they perform within an organization, it is argued, everybody can and will benefit from cultivating some 'enterprising spirit' and aspiring to excellence. That is how they can become virtuous, resourceful and 'empowered' human beings, so the argument goes.

Excellence is very much a crusade, promulgating the faith that everyone can be 'won over'. Almost all the 'new cultural intermediaries', or 'experts', of excellence firmly reject the idea that 'culture change' at work is only enabling for a minority of the workforce. Instead, they appear to believe that the interventions they propose in the internal world of the economic enterprise will transform what was previously a minority experience into the life of the majority. This is particularly true in relation to the notion of 'self' they encourage all workers to adopt. 'Self-management' is the key here: 'how to handle yourself to your own best advantage' (Kanter, 1990). The cultural intermediaries of excellence advise all workers to 'make a project of themselves' (Bourdieu, 1984; Featherstone, 1987; Bonner and du Gay, 1992). In other words, to work on their relations with employment, and all other areas of their lives, in order to develop a lifestyle which will maximize the worth of their existence to themselves.[6]

According to some commentators (Townley, 1989, 1994), technologies of regulation based on this faith in excellence are being deployed more extensively by employers to cover a much wider range of employees. More systematic selection and appraisal technologies – personality profiling and psychometric testing, biodata, and performance-related reviews – are being targeted at sections of the workforce they had not previously covered. As Townley (1989: 93–8) has noted, 'no longer confined to managerial levels, careful selection screening, and regular formal monitoring of performance are increasingly becoming the experience of those at lower levels of the organizational hierarchy, especially blue-collar employees.' These developments are interpreted as expressing an increasing concern among employers with the behavioural and attitudinal characteristics of the employee as an *individual*. The more extensive deployment of technologies of regulation can be seen therefore as a 'strategic' response by employers to the problems of government involved in the 'move away from the direct and technical supervision of work, to the greater degree of "discretion", or "flexibility", being devolved to the individual' (Townley, 1989: 93–8).

Although enormous gaps remain between the programmatic aspirations of employers and managers, and the actual use (or 'consumption') of these technologies in the practice of everyday working life by those at whom they are aimed, this does not mean that the whole entrepreneurial edifice of excellence can be dismissed with disdain as yet another failure. Government is an inherently Sisyphean endeavour. The impossibility of government is the very motor of the 'will to govern'. What is important here is the establishing of those 'connections and symmetries' described by Miller and Rose (1990) between changing political rationalities and objectives, the profitability imperatives of contemporary business, and interventions aimed at the subjectivity of the employee.

Since work-based identity can no longer be guaranteed in any foundational sense by 'class position', or by the 'mode of production' of themselves (Hall, 1988; Laclau, 1990), the 'subjective' moment becomes central politically, culturally and ideologically. The project of reconstruction advocated by the experts of excellence is not some side-show to the main event of global economic restructuring; rather, it is an essential element in the very process of restructuring itself. As Laclau (1990: 56), for example, has argued, 'the more dislocated is the ground on which capitalism operates, the less it can rely on a stable framework of stable social and political relations' and the more central becomes the cultural moment of 'hegemonic construction'. Excellence attempts to redefine the terms in which the social relations of work and employment are imagined. For unless people identify with and become subjects of a new conception of 'work', 'business' or 'society', it is unlikely it will emerge.

According to Hall (1988: 167), New Right ideology works by addressing 'the fears, anxieties, the lost identities of a people. It invites us to think about politics in images. It is addressed to our collective fantasies, to Britain as an imagined community, to the social imaginary.' Excellence appears to operate in a similar vein, offering people the fantasy of 'entrepreneurship'. It promotes an image of 'self-determination' at work, inviting people to feel as if they are their own bosses – to experience 'ownership' – and to become 'entrepreneurs of themselves'.

In the US context, as Guest (1990: 390) has indicated, excellence has enjoyed enormous success because, like Reaganism, it managed to capture 'the essence of the American Dream'. He argues that it is precisely because excellence plays on fantasies of 'the opportunity for progress, or growth, based on individual achievement' that it has gained 'a stubborn hold on the American mind' (Guest, 1990: 391)[7] By drawing attention to the importance of 'dreams', 'images' and 'fantasy' in the operation of excellence, Guest has performed a great service. However, it is one he quickly undermines by giving way to the desire to reintroduce a reality/representation dichotomy. While he argues that excellence addresses and connects with ordinary people's aspirations and displays 'the good intention' of turning them into 'reality', he concludes that 'the evidence suggests this is no more than a fantasy, a dream' (Guest, 1990: 391). What is this evidence? Once more it is 'objective material circumstances'.

Rather than exploring the level of 'ideological fantasy' at which excellence 'structures social reality', Guest tries to establish a clear and transparent relationship between the socially active signifier and the real relations to which it might refer. Not surprisingly, it proves impossible to break out of the ideological dream by 'opening our eyes and trying to see reality as it is', by throwing away the ideological spectacles: as the subjects of such a post-ideological, objective, sober look, free of so-called ideological prejudices, as the subjects of a look which views the facts as they are, we remain throughout 'the consciousness of our ideological dream' (Zizek, 1989: 48).

What, then, does it mean to suggest that 'ideological fantasy structures reality' itself? Well, first, it suggests that a certain 'misrecognition' characterizes the human condition. In Lacanian terms, this 'misrecognition' occurs because all attempts to capture the 'Real' symbolically ultimately fail. There is always a 'left-over', a 'surplus', separating the 'Real' from its symbolization. However, for this very reason 'misrecognition' is not synonymous with the traditional concept of 'false consciousness'. Rather than viewing ideology as a 'false' or 'illusory' representation of reality, it is reality itself which should already be conceived of as 'ideological'. As Zizek (1989: 21) argues, '*ideological" is a social reality whose very existence implies the non-knowledge of its participants as to its essence.*' Ideology is a fantasy construct that serves as a support for 'reality' itself. The function of ideology 'is not to offer us a point of escape from our reality but to offer us the social reality itself as an escape from some traumatic real kernel' (Zizek, 1989: 45).

This 'traumatic real kernel' is the 'surplus', the left-over separating the 'Real' from its symbolization. To attempt to come to terms with this 'excess' requires an acknowledgement of a certain fundamental deadlock (what Laclau and Mouffe have termed 'antagonism'), 'a hard kernel resisting symbolic integration-dissolution' (Laclau and Mouffe, 1985, 1987; Zizek, 1989). In this way it is possible to see what Laclau and Mouffe (1985) are suggesting when they say that 'Society doesn't exist'. They are certainly not lending support to the Thatcherite dictum that 'there is no such thing as Society, just individuals and their families.' Rather, they are attempting to indicate that 'the social' is 'always an inconsistent field structured around a constitutive impossibility', a fundamental antagonism. 'Society never fully manages to be society because everything in it is penetrated by its limits, which prevents it constituting itself as an objective reality' (Laclau and Mouffe, 1985: 127). However, because society is always traversed by an antagonistic split which cannot be integrated into the symbolic order, 'the stake of ideological fantasy is to construct a vision of society which does exist, a society which is not split by an antagonistic division, a society in which the relation between its parts is organic, complementary' (Zizek, 1989: 126).

The discourse/ideology of excellence operates with such a 'unitary frame of reference' (Fox, 1974). The vision it projects is of a cohesive but inherently 'flexible' organization where an 'organic' complementarity is established between 'the greatest possible realization of the intrinsic abilities of individuals at work' and the 'optimum productivity and profitability of the corporation' (Kanter, 1990). In this vision, the 'no win scenario' associated with a mechanistic, bureaucratic lack of enterprise is transformed into a permanent 'win/win situation' through the active development of a flexible, creative and organic entrepreneurialism (Pinchot, 1985: 38). For excellence, as for neo-liberal political discourse, economic and moral revival involves the construction of an appropriate culture of enterprise: enterprise is their 'ideological fantasy'. Both of these evangelical projects are engaged in a struggle against lack of enterprise, which they conceptualize as a fundamental cause of social antagonism, a disease spreading through the social body destroying initiative, innovation, creativity and the like. This debilitating lack can only be overcome, and social harmony restored, it is suggested, through the promotion and development of enterprise in both its distinct senses. In other words, the symbolic enemy – bureaucracy and its associated evils – may only be defeated by summoning up and unleashing the forces of enterprise and, in particular, the remarkable powers of its 'everyday hero' – the private, possessive, competitive, enterprising individual (man).

In their respective visions, lack of enterprise appears to be a foreign body introducing corruption to into the pure, sound social fabric. However, in effect, 'lack of enterprise' is akin to a 'symptom', the point at which the immanent social antagonism erupts on to the surface of the social, the point at which, to recall Laclau and Mouffe, it becomes apparent that the organization/society 'doesn't work'. Thus, 'lack of enterprise' is basically the means, for both excellence and for neo-liberalism, of taking into account, of representing their own impossibility. It is the expression of the ultimate impossibility of their respective projects – of their 'immanent limits'. Rather than being a positive cause of social antagonism, 'lack of enterprise' is just the expression of a 'certain blockage' – of the impossibility which prevents the organization/society from achieving its full identity as a closed, homogeneous totality.

## Conclusion

As Wright (1987) has indicated, the rise of both excellence and the New Right has prompted frequent derision and disdain from various figures who view themselves as representatives of a deep and authentic humanism (the 'artist', the 'scholar' etc.). While there may be a certain (simple) consolation in equating the contemporary discourse of enterprise with the merely philistine, Wright suggests, such a response misplaces its critical energies – indicating a powerful cultural élitism, while missing the point completely. The projects of both excellence and the New Right deserve altogether more serious attention. As Gordon (1987: 300) has argued, rather than being a travesty of genuine value, the triumph of the entrepreneur is directly related to 'a profound mutation' in governmental rationality: 'Here a certain idea of the enterprise of government promotes and capitalizes on a widely disseminated conception of individuality as an enterprise, of the person as an entrepreneur of the self.'

The key features of contemporary political rationalities and technologies of government have been the connections they have tried to establish between the self-fulfilling desires of individuals and the achievement of social and economic objectives. As Rose (1989: 24) has indicated, the success of neo-liberalism in Britain (as elsewhere in the West), with its flagship image of an enterprise culture, 'operates within a much more general transformation in "mentalities of government" in which the autonomous, responsible, free, choosing self . . . has become central to the moral bases of political arguments from all parts of the political spectrum'. It is the vocabulary of enterprise which establishes an affinity between excellence and the neo-liberal government in the UK. The expertise of excellence provides the means whereby the politico-ethical objectives of neo-liberalism in the UK, the economic objectives of contemporary business, and the self-actualizing and self-regulating capacities of human subjects are linked together into a 'functioning network'. By so doing, excellence establishes 'connections and symmetries' between 'the way we are governed by others and the way we should govern ourselves' (Rose, 1989: 3).

However, as even Miller and Rose (1990: 10) admit, 'government is a congenitally failing operation'. The 'Real' always escapes attempts to govern it because there is always a 'surplus' separating the 'Real' from its symbolization. Whether expressed in terms of 'ideology' or 'cultural technology', therefore, the most that government can hope for is to manage this 'lack of fit' without ever resolving it. None the less, at one and the same time, this very 'impossibility' of government justifies and reproduces the attempt to govern.

## Notes

1 Ian Hacking (1983) delineates the triptych Real – Representation – Reality. 'Reality' is 'a lower order concept' formed through the practice of representation. The 'Real' – in the Lacanian sense – is an impossible entity to represent fully, but its effects cannot be avoided. The 'Real' is a 'hard kernel' (Zizek, 1989) resisting symbolic integration/dissolution and yet only through trying to represent it can its effects be grasped. In other words, the 'Real' is an entity which must be constructed retroactively so that the distortions of the symbolic structure can be accounted for. As Lacan (1987: 7) puts it, 'I always speak the truth, not the whole truth because there's no way to say it all. Saying the whole truth is materially impossible: words miss it. Yet it is only through this impossibility that the truth holds onto the real.'

2 There can be little doubt that the 'excellence' literature has touched a nerve. The acknowledged leader of the field, Peters and Waterman's *In Search of Excellence* (1982), remains the best-selling business book of all time, with worldwide sales of over five million by 1985.

3 According to the cultural critic Judith Williamson (1991: 28), the language of enterprise has surpassed the boundaries imposed by even this looser definition. 'What intrigued me', she writes, 'is not only that enterprise now means business, but the fact that . . . it can be seen as . . . a personal attribute in its own right. The language has colonized our interiors; if you can't speak it, you haven't got it!'

4 As William Connolly (1987: 138) has indicated, 'equality' and 'excellence' tend to be mutually exclusive categories; 'To honor equality (an admirable thing) is also to demean excellence in certain ways: to institutionalize individualism is to sacrifice the solace and benefits of community; to exercise freedom is to experience the closure which accompanies choice among incompatible and often irreconcilable projects; to secure stable identities through gender demarcation is to exclude the hermaphrodite from such an identity and to suppress that in others which does not fit neatly into its frame; to prize the rule of law is to invite the extension of litigiousness into new corners of social life; to institutionalize respect for the responsible agent is to sow institutional disrespect for those unqualified or unwilling to exercise such responsibility; to give primacy to mathematicization in the social construction of knowledge is to denigrate individuals whose thought escapes that mold and to depreciate ways of knowing which do not fit into its frame. And lest the point be misread, to reverse these priorities would be to install another set of losses and impositions.'

5 Although the concept of 'discourse' is often viewed as superseding the notion of 'ideology' (Foucault, 1980), recent reformulations of the latter term have helped to deprive it of many of its pejorative overtones – by indicating, for example, that ideologies do not have any necessary class or political affiliation (Hall, 1988; Zizek, 1989; Laclau, 1990). As a result, 'discourse' and 'ideology' have become virtually synonymous. Because of this transposition, evident, for example, in much post-Marxist theory, both terms are used in this text.

6 As Wright (1987: 8–9) has observed, 'Excellence works in the everyday world, diversifying consumer lifestyles as it goes.' It is a defining feature of members of the new

expanding 'service'/middle class, to which the cultural intermediaries of excellence belong, to seek their 'occupational and personal salvation in the imposition of new doctrines of ethical salvation' (Bourdieu, 1984: 365). In other words, by encouraging as many people as possible to share its 'investment orientation to life' at work, as well as in all other spheres of existence, this social grouping is engaged in a symbolic action which not only produces the need for its own goods and services, but also, in the long run, legitimates itself and the lifestyle(s) it puts forward as a model.

7 Silver (1987: 124–5), another commentator on the links between 'excellence' and 'neo-conservatism' in the USA, argues that the appeal of excellence is located in its cry to American employees to 'stand tall' again, rather than feeling inferior to their international competitors (particularly the Japanese), and that this rallying call 'fell on the same receptive ground as Reagan's exhortations to the American people to "feel proud to be American", and one might argue, the same receptive ground as such popular cultural phenomena as Rambo and Rocky, which are also celebrations of extraordinary effort from ordinary people'.

# 4

# The Culture of the Customer

In Chapter 3 I indicated the ways in which the managerial discourse of excellence, operating as it were 'from above', constructs new ways for people to be at work. However, I said little or nothing about what those subjected to this discourse make or do with it. This is a significant omission for, as Laclau (1990) has argued, if subjects were simply the product of structures then a total determinism would govern social relations. Similarly, for Foucault (1982: 221), 'freedom' is an essential element in the relation between government and governed. There can be no relationship of government where the 'determining factors saturate the whole'. In effect, what both Foucault and Laclau testify to is the centrality of the category of 'dislocation'. As I argued earlier, any identity is dislocated in so far as it depends on an outside which both denies that identity and provides the conditions of its possibility at the same time.

According to Hacking (1986: 234) the discursive construction of subjectivity and identity can best be understood as a process he terms 'making up people'. Although there is no general story to be told about 'making up people' – because every category, as Mauss argued, has its own history – Hacking suggests that a partial framework for thinking of such events would consist of two mutually constitutive vectors. One is the vector of 'labelling from above', 'from a community of experts who create a "reality" that some people make their own'. Different from this, but equally important, is the vector of 'the actual behaviour of those so labelled, which presses from below, creating a reality that every expert must face'. Although, at first sight, this framework may appear to be replicating traditional dualisms associated with the project of sociology – those of object/subject, society/individual, for example – this is not in fact the case. Rather than seeing these vectors as two fully constituted objectivities, they should be viewed as *mutually constitutive* – or 'dislocated'. In other words, because the vector of 'labelling from above' never manages to constitute itself fully as an objectivity, its identity is dislocated. The very identity of 'labelling from above' depends upon a 'constitutive outside' – the second vector – which both denies that identity and provides the conditions of its possibility at one and the same time. The subject of the second vector has no 'proper' place of its own. It operates within a space delineated by, but not equivalent to, the first vector. Therefore it does not manifest itself through its own autonomous representations but in relation to its ways of 'using', or *'consuming'*, representations and technologies emanating 'from above' (de Certeau, 1984).

In this chapter I argue that exploring the 'ways of operating of consumers' is crucial to an understanding of the construction of subjectivity
and identity at work for two reasons. First, contemporary theorizing about
consumption provides some important tools for understanding the active
and creative capacities of individuals and groups in their own self-
constitution (de Certeau, 1984: Willis, 1990); in other words, it furnishes us
with important concepts for theorizing Hacking's second vector in the
'making up people' process. Secondly, if the main image informing
representations of economic life in the present is that of the 'sovereign
consumer', and if the organization of work is increasingly premised upon
'staying close to the customer', then is it not also increasingly likely that an
understanding of contemporary programmes of organizational reform –
and the work-based identities they both presuppose and constitute –
necessitates an exploration of the dynamics of contemporary consumer
culture? I begin with this latter question, examining how the 'character' of
the consumer has become a crucial element in the reinvention of
organizational life.

## Consumer culture

As indicated in Chapter 3, governing economic life in an enterprising
manner is intimately bound up with the de-differentiation of economy and
culture – with a pronounced blurring between the spheres of 'production'
and 'consumption', the 'corporate' and 'culture'. As the language of the
market becomes the only valid vocabulary of moral and social calculation,
the 'privilege of the producer' is superseded by the 'sovereignty of the
consumer', with 'civic culture' gradually giving way to 'consumer culture'
as citizens are reconceptualized as 'enterprising consumers' (Bauman, 1987;
Keat, 1990).

According to Bauman (1988: 220), for example, once the market has
made people dependent upon itself for their own reproduction, they
become, first and foremost, consumers.

> Consumer culture is a culture of men and women integrated into society as,
> above all, consumers. Features of the consumer culture explicable solely in terms
> of the logic of the market, where they originate, spill over all other aspects of
> contemporary life – if there are any other aspects, unaffected by the market
> mechanism left. Thus every item of culture becomes a commodity and becomes
> subordinated to the logic of the market either through a direct, economic
> mechanism, or an indirect psychological one. All perceptions and expectations, as
> well as life-rhythm, qualities of memory, attention, motivational and topical
> relevances are moulded inside the new 'foundational' institution – that of the
> market. (Bauman, 1987: 166)

Similarly, as Rose (1990: 102) has indicated, the 'primary economic
image offered to the modern citizen is not that of the producer but of the
consumer'. As 'consumers', people are encouraged to shape their lives by
the use of their purchasing power and to make sense of their existence by

exercising their freedom to choose in a market in which 'one simultaneously purchases products and services, and assembles, manages and markets oneself.' Within the discourse of enterprise/excellence consumers are constituted as autonomous, self-regulating and self-actualizing individual actors seeking to maximize their 'quality of life' – in other words, to optimize the worth of their existence to themselves – by assembling a lifestyle, or lifestyles, through personalized acts of choice in the market place. Thus, in an enterprise culture, freedom and independence emanate not from civil rights but from individual choices exercised in the market: 'the sovereignty that matters is not that of the king or the queen, the lord or the white man, but the sovereignty of the consumer in the marketplace' (Corner and Harvey, 1991: 11).

Within the discourse of enterprise/excellence an active, 'enterprising' consumer is placed at the moral centre of the market-based universe. What counts as 'good', or 'virtuous', in this universe is judged by reference to the apparent needs, desires and projected preferences of the 'sovereign consumer'. Thus, an enterprise culture is a culture of the customer, where markets subordinate producers to the preferences of individual consumers. Success and failure in this market-based universe are supposedly determined by the relative ability of competing producers to satisfy the preferences of the enterprising consumer (Keat, 1990: 223).

In this way, the 'character' of the customer has become a central element in attempts to reconstruct a variety of institutions and practices in both the public and private sectors.[1] In the public sector, for example, the language of enterprise/excellence has provided the rationale for programmes of intervention and rectification in, among other things, the delivery of health care and the provision of local government services. As a number of commentators have argued (Edgar, 1991; Hall, 1991), from the hospital to the railway station, and from the classroom to the museum, the public sector has found itself translated. Patients, parents, pupils and passengers have all been re-imagined as 'customers'.

However, while the character of the customer has played a vital role in the reconstruction of a wide range of public institutions and activities along market lines, it is also linked to a transformation in programmes and technologies for regulating the internal world of the private business enterprise. In other words, although the free market system provides the inherently virtuous model through which all forms of social relation should be structured, in order to guarantee that the optimum benefits accrue from the workings of this intrinsically virtuous system, it is the moral obligation of each and every commercial organization, and every member of such an organization, to become obsessed with 'staying close to the customer' (Peters and Waterman, 1982). To conform to 'the requirements of the customer' is to envisage a new type of rule and to imagine new ways for people to conduct themselves *within* the private business enterprise, as well as outside. In effect, the character of the sovereign consumer provides a novel image for the productive subject. 'The best companies have now realised that effective customer care is a crucial part of commercial success. The key is for managers to treat staff as they would hope staff would treat customers' (Clutterbuck and Crainer, 1988: 264). In truly excellent, enterprising companies, Peters and Waterman (1982: 321–3) argue, the 'external' focus on the customer is matched by an 'internal' focus on 'empowering' workers.

> cost and efficiency, over the long run, follow on from the emphasis on quality, service, innovativeness, result-sharing, participation, excitement and an external problem-solving focus that is tailored to the customer . . . Quite simply these companies are simultaneously externally focused – externally in that they are driven by the desire to provide service, quality and innovative problem-solving in support of their customers, internally in that quality control, for example, is put on the back of the individual line-worker, not primarily in the lap of the quality control department. Service standards are likewise largely self-monitored . . . This constitutes the crucial internal focus: the focus on people . . . By offering meaning as well as money they give their employees a mission as well as a sense of feeling great. Every man becomes a pioneer, an experimenter, a leader. The institution provides the guiding belief and creates a sense of excitement, a sense of being part of the best.

In reconstructing the commercial organization around the character of the sovereign consumer, the work-based subject is also reconceptualized: the employee is re-imagined as an individual actor in search of meaning, responsibility, a sense of personal achievement and a maximized quality of life. Work is now construed as an activity through which people produce and discover a sense of personal identity. In effect, workers are encouraged to view work as *consumers*: work becomes an arena in which people exhibit an 'enterprising' or 'consuming' relationship to self, where they 'make a project of themselves, and where they develop a style of living that will maximize the worth of their existence to themselves'. In other words, 'work' as an activity is re-imagined through the language of consumer culture.

One of the ways in which commercial organizations have sought to become more customer-orientated is through the technologies and practices of Total Quality Management (TQM). As Hill (1991: 399–40), for example, has indicated, the foremost principle of TQM is that 'quality is defined as conformance to the requirements of the customer'. However, the term 'customer' does not simply refer to relations between an 'inside' (the company) and an 'outside' (individual consumers); rather relationships between employees and departments within the firm are also construed in terms of the customer model: employees become each other's customers.

> *There are internal as well as external customers* . . . An organizational unit receives inputs from the previous process and transforms these to produce outputs for the next . . . As a 'customer', a unit should expect conformance to its own requirements, while as a supplier it has an obligation to conform to the requirements of others. (Hill, 1991: 400)

Although this focus on 'consumer sovereignty' is a pronounced feature of discourses of work reform within both the public and private sectors, and of restructuring programmes within manufacturing as well as service industries, it is particularly pronounced in those organizations where the quality of interactive service delivery 'has become an important source of value' (Fuller and Smith, 1991: 2; see also Hochschild, 1983; Noyelle, 1987). As 'quality of service' becomes seen as 'a prime determinant of service firms' competitive success or failure' (Fuller and Smith, 1991: 2), the links between workers and consumers have grown ever tighter. Increasingly, the character of the customer has invaded the internal world of the service organization, providing the rationale for the cultural reconstruction of work-based subjectivity and identity in services (Allen and du Gay, 1994).

As Hochschild (1983: 105–6), for example, has indicated, providing 'quality service' requires that workers identify with customers as individuals with the same wants, needs and desires as themselves. Through the use of human technologies of interpersonal management, workers are encouraged to put themselves in their customers' shoes, and thus to offer them the sort of service they themselves would ideally like to receive. As part of this process of imaginative identification, workers are often taught to view the arena in which they work as their own 'home' into which customers come as 'guests'. Thus, quality service requires workers instrumentally to assemble, manage and market aspects of their experience and identity as consumers. In the process, employees will become not only better workers, but also better selves.

Through the image of the 'sovereign consumer', the relations between production and consumption, between the 'inside' and 'outside' of the corporation, and most importantly perhaps between work-based and consumption-based identities, are progressively blurred (Sabel, 1990; du Gay and Salaman, 1992). The culture of the customer brooks no opposition between the mode of self-presentation required of people as consumers, and that required by managers and employees. The relationship to self that the employee is expected to develop builds upon and extends the identity he or she is deemed to have as a consumer: both are represented as autonomous, calculating individuals in search of meaning and fulfilment, looking to 'add value' to themselves in every sphere of existence, whether at work or at play.

As several commentators have suggested (Bauman, 1987: 167–8; Deleuze, 1992), the development of contemporary consumer culture involves a substantive change in the mode of domination central to social integration. The new mode of domination distinguishes itself by the substitution of 'seduction' for 'repression',[2] public relations for policing, advertising for authority, and needs-creation for norm-imposition. What is deemed to tie individuals to the social formation is their activity as *consumers*. 'Individuals do not need, therefore, to be repressed in their natural drives and tendency to subordinate their behaviour to the pleasure principle: they do not need to be invigilated and policed' (Bauman, 1987: 168).

Because the function of surveillance in consumer culture is now placed in the hands of the market, social surveillance gives way to 'auto-surveillance'

(Deleuze, 1992). As indicated in Chapter 3, the new image of the productive subject contained within the discourse of excellence is first and
foremost a self-regulating individual actor. Rather than relying on the
disciplinary gaze of the 'supervisor' (what Peters, 1987: 363 terms an 'out of
date cop'), attempts to govern economic life now aspire to instil and utilize
the self-directing, self-actualizing propensities and desires of subjects. In
other words, if the subject of contemporary consumer culture is defined as a
self-regulating, individual actor seeking to maximize the worth of his or her
existence to him/herself through personalized acts of choice in a market-
based universe, then the productive subject must be seen now, first and
foremost, as a consumer.

As suggested above, the prevailing image of the worker in contemporary
discourses of economic life is of an individual in search of meaning,
responsibility and a sense of personal fulfilment. This individual is not to be
policed and invigilated by others because work is defined, not as a
constraint upon freedom, but as a realm in which people represent,
construct and confirm their identity as consumers. Work is a site and an
activity which forms an integral aspect of an individual's 'style of life' as a
consumer (Rose, 1990).

If the primary image informing representations of economic life is that of
the 'sovereign consumer', and if the organization and experience of work is
increasingly structured around 'staying close to the customer', then it is
apparent that understanding the production and regulation of work-based
subjectivity and identity necessitates an exploration of the dynamics of
contemporary consumer culture and the 'ways of operating' of consumers
(de Certeau, 1984; Featherstone, 1990; Willis, 1990). It is to this latter task
that we now turn.

## Traditional representations of consumption

For what seems like an inordinate length of time, sociologists in general,
and industrial sociologists in particular, have observed that work is not 'the
central life interest' of the majority of men and women in paid employment
in modern Western societies (Mills, 1953; Dubin, 1962; Goldthorpe et al.,
1969; Fox, 1980). However, while this observation has achieved a somewhat normative status within the social sciences, it has not led to any
significant changes in the central research interests of industrial sociologists.
On the whole, the sociology of work and employment has remained firmly
wedded to a 'productionist' orientation whereby the 'public' realm of paid
work is represented as *the* vital existential sphere in contrast to the 'private'
sphere of the domestic, of consumption and leisure. Once again, the
influence of 'alienation' can be detected in the marginalization of consumption from the research agenda.

As various commentators have argued (Goldthorpe et al., 1969;
Moorhouse, 1989; Pateman, 1989), the continued attachment of many

sociologists to an old philosophical anthropology of production leads to a devaluation in all forms of 'self-creation' that take place outside the workplace. In other words, while many sociologists point to the growing importance of consumption to people's sense of who they are, because they have incorporated a Marxist emphasis on labour as the only 'real' site of human self-constitution, they tend to view consumption simply as an arena where 'alienated' workers attain derisory compensations for their lack of self-actualization in work; an overriding concern with consumption is thereby seen to reflect the subject's fundamental 'alienation' in work.[3]

In this type of critique – articulated most famously perhaps in the work of critical theorists such as Marcuse (1964) – it is because the worker is 'not at home' in 'his' work, because 'work is a calamity', that 'he' can only find satisfaction in the sphere of non-work, in the 'false', 'passive needs of personal consumption and domestic life' (Gorz, 1965: 16–17). Furthermore, consumers are regarded as fully determined by capital. Consumer desires and needs are 'created' by producers through the medium of advertising and market research and then 'satisfied' by the goods and services provided by those same producers. There is no sign of 'dislocation' here; consumers simply follow to the letter of the law a script pre-written by capital. Their very 'needs' and 'wants' are created by the market and through the manipulation of 'public opinion' by the mass media controlled by capital. In the emergent homogeneous mass culture, therefore, all material culture is reduced to the status of 'commodity', while the people that live in and through that object-world are constituted as alienated, 'passive' consumers.

Because consumption is completely determined by production in this account, there is no room for 'human agency'. 'Structure' predominates to such an extent that the universe appears to be nothing more than a self-regulating totality (Laclau, 1990: 51–2). However, it is with just such a conception of a self-regulating totality that the logic of dislocation breaks. If the category of 'production' only has meaning in relation to the category of 'consumption', if it can only constitute itself in relation to an 'outside', then production cannot fully determine consumption in the manner suggested in the mass culture critique. Rather consumption both denies the identity of production and provides its condition of possibility at one and the same time. After all, if production saturated consumption there would be no need for the term 'manipulation' in the language of the mass culture critique (Miller, 1987: 166). As Foucault (1982) argued, 'power' can only be exercised where there is freedom; to be successful in making others act in accordance with one's own wishes one requires knowledge of their motives. The fact that producers do not completely dominate consumers but must ceaselessly attempt to exercise power over them is attested by the development of motivation research as a part of modern marketing and advertising techniques (Mort, 1989). Activity under this heading is largely directed towards delineating the dreams, desires and aspirations of consumers. In other words, the cultural intermediaries of advertising, design and market research don't attempt to manipulate 'consumers' *per se*, but rather the *symbolic meanings* which are attached to products.

In his early work, for example, Baudrillard (1988: 45) exposed the essentialist conception of human nature underlying the mass culture critique by indicating ways in which the products of human labour are not aimed at the fulfilment of 'fundamental', transparent, 'needs' which lie at the basis of the materiality of humanity, but constitute a system of signs that differentiate the population: 'if we acknowledge that a need is not a need for a particular object as much as it is a "need" for difference (the desire for social meaning), only then will we understand that satisfaction can never be *fulfilled*, and consequently that there can never be a *definition* of needs.'

Similarly, Campbell (1987: 48) argues that the mass culture critique rests upon an assumption that consumption is and must always be a rational process. Therefore, in so far as 'emotion', 'imagination' and 'desire' enter into the processes through which objects are consumed by individuals then ideological 'mystification' and 'exploitation' must be at work. By projecting a unidimensional evaluation of consumption in terms of the rational calculation of 'needs', the mass culture critique is unable to delineate the dynamic cultural logic at the heart of modern consumerism. For if 'consumerism' is founded on 'desire', as Baudrillard suggests, and 'desire' can never be realized because it fulfils no possibility and has no content, then it is impossibility which 'drives' modern consumption; consumption is dynamic because disillusionment is the necessary concomitant of the acquisition of goods longed for in fantasy.

The traditional critique cannot grasp this fundamental tension. Rather than being unproblematically focused and directed at the object and the intrinsic satisfaction it might bring, 'consumer behaviour' in fact 'responds to quite different objectives: the metaphoric or displaced expression of desire, and the production of a code of social values through the use of differentiating signs' (Baudrillard, 1988: 46).[4]

## Modes of consumption

### Consumption as social differentiation

As Baudrillard's (1988) comments indicate, commodities and services have importance as signs and symbols. In other words, they have 'identity-value' and not simply or primarily 'use-value'. The consumption of goods and services is therefore important not so much for the intrinsic satisfaction it might generate but for the way in which it functions to mark social differences and act as a communicator. Style, status and group identification are aspects of identity-value, where people choose to display commodities or engage in different spheres of consumption with a view to expressing their identity as certain sorts of persons (Warde, 1992).

The suggestion that consumption activities are linked to patterns of social differentiation is not new. In his classic study of the 'conspicuous consumption' of the 'leisure class' (1899, here 1957), Veblen indicated that the consumption of goods acted as a primary index of social status. Although Veblen was particularly interested in outlining the ways in which the *nouveaux riches* of the leisure class expressed their status through distancing themselves from the world of practical necessity and of paid employment, he also suggested that no social group was entirely exempt from the practice of 'conspicuous consumption'. 'No class of society, not even the most abjectly poor, forgoes all customary conspicuous consumption. The last items of this category of consumption are not given up except under the stress of direct necessity' (Veblen, 1957: 85). In other words, no matter how ostensibly poor they may be, the consumption practices of even the lowliest social groupings tend to have identity-value as well as simply use-value. This point is picked up on and elaborated by Bourdieu (1984) in his wide-ranging examination of the economy of cultural goods and lifestyles in French society.

Although Bourdieu (1989: 14) has argued that his analyses of consumption practices 'have nothing in common with those of Veblen', it is apparent that both authors share certain assumptions. In particular, both Veblen and Bourdieu lay great emphasis on the area of 'taste' as the key dimension controlling the significance of ordinary goods.

One of Bourdieu's main aims is to rid 'taste' of its essentialist overtones. He does this by indicating the way in which Kant's notion of the 'aesthetic' as distanced contemplation is merely one perspective, that of the dominant class. The Kantian aesthetic tends towards a rejection of representation of the signified in favour of the principles of convention, the esoteric and the formal (Miller, 1987). The overt display of wealth and consumption characteristic of Veblen's leisure class is challenged by a more subtle, detached and inconspicuous form, to be appreciated only by those sufficiently cultivated or 'civilized'.

The Kantian aesthetic (or 'high' culture) achieves its meaning by contrast to what Bourdieu terms an anti-Kantian aesthetic (or 'popular' culture) with its preference for immediate entertainment, pleasure and gut emotion. For the former, beauty is created through the mode of representation, for the latter it is inherent within the subject itself (Bourdieu, 1984: 30). These differences in taste are identified by Bourdieu as an example of 'habitus'. By 'habitus' Bourdieu is referring to the unconscious dispositions, the classificatory schemes, and taken-for-granted preferences which are evident in the individual's sense of the appropriateness and validity of his or her taste for cultural goods and practices, and which not only operate at the level of everyday knowledgeability, but are also inscribed onto the body. As 'habitus', the distinction between the Kantian and anti-Kantian aesthetic is both derived from 'material conditions', and, in turn, provides an insight into the classificatory scheme which may be applied to an infinite number of actual consumption domains (Featherstone, 1982, 1987; Bourdieu, 1984; Miller, 1987).

When mapping differences in taste, the criterion deployed by Bourdieu tends to be either occupation or educational level, but both are related to a common conception of class as 'upper', 'middle' and 'working'. Bourdieu argues that each group, class or class fraction has a different habitus and, hence, a different taste structure. In other words, different 'objective conditions' are interiorized through habitus as desire expressed in taste.

> Taste is the practical operator in the transmutation of things into distinct and distinctive signs, of continuous distributions into discontinuous oppositions; it raises the differences inscribed in the physical order of bodies to the symbolic order of significant distinctions. It transforms objectively classified practices, in which a class condition signifies itself (through taste), into classifying practices, that is, into a symbolic expression of class position, by perceiving them in their mutual relations and terms of social classificatory schemes. Taste is thus the source of the system of distinctive features which cannot fail to be perceived as a systematic expression of a particular class of conditions of existence, i.e., as a distinctive lifestyle, by anyone who possesses practical knowledge of the relationships between distinctive signs and positions in the distributions – between the universe of objective properties, which is brought to light by scientific construction, and the no less objective universe of lifestyles which exists for and through ordinary experience. (Bourdieu, 1984: 174–5)

'Habitus' thereby mediates between material conditions including, but not simply reduced to, productive relations, and the observable practices of the social group.

Having indicated the ways in which taste in cultural goods functions as a marker for social class, Bourdieu goes on to map out the social field of the different tastes in lifestyles and consumption preferences. In the case of food consumption, for example, Bourdieu (1984) indicates that the working classes are found to prefer the immediacy and security of abundance, a plentiful table proclaiming itself to those around it, strong red meat, 'unpretentious' red wine, and solid breads and cheeses. Middle-class food becomes 'cuisine'. Taste here is based on knowledge of the proper methods of preparation and presentation, as well as on the 'correct' foodstuffs to eat for a well-balanced diet. For the economically dominant fraction of the upper classes, rich sauces and desserts are preferred, supplemented by rare and luxurious items such as vintage champagne and truffles. Meanwhile, the preferred food for the display of cultural capital (the dominated fraction of the upper classes) is *nouvelle cuisine*, a *repas* in which the aesthetics of minimalism are considered infinitely more important than any regard for sustenance.

In contrast to the traditional view of a grey, conformist, mass culture in which consumers' use of goods simply reflects the purposes inscribed into them by producers, Bourdieu indicates the ways in which particular constellations of taste, consumption preferences and lifestyle practices are associated with certain social groupings. In so doing he accounts for the way in which goods not only reflect distinction, but are also an instrument of it.

For Bourdieu (1989), the 'structural despair' of the mass culture critique is founded upon a 'strong objectivism' which effectively eliminates the knowledgeable consumer from social analysis. In opposition to this 'strong objectivism', Bourdieu (1989: 15) attempts to indicate the ways in which 'objective' and 'subjective' moments stand in 'dialectical relation':

> I could sum up in one phrase the gist of the analysis I am putting forward today: on the one hand, the objective structures that the sociologist constructs, in the objectivist moment, by setting aside the subjective representations of the agents, form the basis of those representations and constitute the structural constraints that bear upon the interactions; but, on the other hand, these representations must be taken into consideration particularly if one wants to account for the daily struggles, individual and collective, which purport to transform or to preserve these structures. This means that the two moments, the objectivist and the subjectivist, stand in dialectical relationship.

Although Bourdieu's work on consumption expressly attempts to navigate this dialectic, in many ways it simply ends up perpetuating a form of the mass culture critique. In particular, the attempt to map consumption practices through the use of a highly structured questionnaire leads to an extremely static picture of consumer behaviour. Although inventive and productive, Bourdieu's questionnaire can only provide quiescent responses, rather than insights into everyday practices, and, through processing, creates a normative characterization of the diverse social fractions involved, which are represented as exemplars of a larger, statistically based model of class. The dynamic interaction of 'agency' and 'structure' that Bourdieu sets out to capture is nowhere to be seen and, as a result, the consumer as an active, knowledgeable, social subject seems unduly constrained once again.

According to de Certeau (1984), for example, Bourdieu loses sight of the practices he seeks to delineate in the drive for a consistent congruence through habitus engendered by class interests and constrained possibilities. Against his best intentions, de Certeau (1984: 166) suggests, Bourdieu still assumes that consumption 'necessarily means "becoming similar to" what one absorbs, and not "making something similar" to what one is, making it one's own, appropriating, or reappropriating it'. By reducing the analysis of specific material domains to their place in social differentiation and domination, Bourdieu is unable to express what people actually make or do with the objects they consume, or to articulate what practices of consumption mean to those engaged in them.

Because Bourdieu's analysis is largely based upon the mapping of differences between goods on to differences between social groups, and because the latter are treated as prior social divisions unaltered by this process of signification, people become unilaterally trapped in positions from which they are unable to extricate themselves. In his discussion of working-class consumer behaviour, for example, people are reduced to a relationship of immediacy from which they cannot escape (Bourdieu, 1984: 386). As a result, Bourdieu ends up reiterating the oppressive hypothesis of the mass culture critique:

It is not only in music or sport that ordinary people are reduced to the role of the 'fan', the militant 'supporter' locked in a passionate, even chauvinistic, but passive and spurious participation which is merely an illusory compensation for dispossession by experts. What the relation to 'mass' (and, *a fortiori*, 'élite') cultural products reproduces, reactivates and reinforces is not the monotony of the production line or office but the social relation which underlies working class experience of the world, whereby his labour and the product of his labour, *opus proprium*, present themselves to the worker as *opus alienum*, 'alienated' labour.[5]

Although Bourdieu indicates the importance of consumption to the production and reproduction of social differentiation, he is unable to explain the ways in which consumer practices may cross-cut given social divisions, and tends to ignore all the other identity projects in the development and performance of which goods and services are employed. In the end, whether expressed through images of an overarching class interest or subsuming discourse, Bourdieu eliminates the possibility of dominated groups acting as arbiters of cultural form.

## Appropriation, recontextualization, resistance

Rather than viewing consumer behaviour as a simple expression of the will of capital, or of already existing, and seemingly immutable, social divisions, consumption, as de Certeau (1984) suggests, can be conceived of as a productive activity – a *poiesis* – which does not leave the subject, object or 'system' untouched. The dominant meanings inscribed into goods and texts in the act of their initial 'production' are not automatically and unproblematically folded into the psychic life of those at whom they are aimed. 'Meaning' is also produced by consumers in the use they make of those goods and texts in the practice of their everyday lives. So while the 'elements' used may be determined in the sphere of production, *how* these are used – to what ends and with what effects – cannot be so easily pre-established. As suggested earlier, for example, despite the enormous efforts made through advertising, design and the media to create markets for given products, profits are always dependent upon the ability of marketing staff to interpret the changes in the way in which products are used in current social relations.

One of the first attempts to articulate this gap between the lived practices of consumption of 'subordinate groups', and the plans and programmes of powerful institutions can be found in the work of what has come to be known as 'subcultural analysis' (Willis, 1978; Hebdige, 1979). Focusing on the 'subcultural worlds' of mainly white, male, working-class youth, these studies emphasized the ways in which subcultural groupings use commodities as signifiers in an active process of constructing 'oppositional' identities. Through their symbolic work of 'consuming' material culture, these groups translate commodified objects from an 'alienable' to an 'inalienable' condition; that is, from being an apparent symbol of estrangement and price value to being an artefact with particular inseparable connotations. Practices of consumption are therefore key elements in the production of an inalienable world in which objects are firmly integrated into the development of particular social relations and group identity. Thus, these studies insisted that consumption is not a passive process, but an active one involving the signifying practice which puts to use the polysemic quality of commodities as signs.[6]

More recently, the implications of this subcultural analysis have been developed into a more thoroughgoing view of contemporary consumer culture as a self-conscious critique of traditional representations of 'mass consumption'. The stress on consumer 'creativity' and polysemy has been allied to concepts derived from textual analysis to highlight the 'popular pleasures' of, and 'play' of identities within, contemporary cultures of consumption. Increasingly, consumers are represented as 'cultural experts' or *bricoleurs*, assembling their own distinctive combinations of style – lifestyles – from a wealth of available signifiers (Chambers, 1986; Fiske, 1989; Mort, 1989).

Both subcultural analysis and the more recent 'pleasures of consumption' thesis have involved not inconsiderable gains over both the 'structural pessimism' of the mass culture critique and over those theories that conceptualize consumption simply in terms of social differentiation. They have done this through, for example, insisting on seeing social subjects as active agents in the process of their own self-constitution and in indicating how *bricolage* cuts across given social divisions to produce hybrid identities. However, and unsurprisingly, both these explorations of consumption also bear interpretive costs. In particular, as a number of critics have argued (Williamson, 1986; Morris, 1988; Clarke, 1991), from the quite plausible (if increasingly banal) premise that consumption practices cannot be derived from or reduced to a mirror of production – that consumers make meanings in reception and do not simply 'receive' and 'ingest' sent messages – many studies appear to end up disconnecting consumption entirely from the forces and relations of production.[7]

Having rescued consumption from the pessimism of the mass culture critique, certain forms of cultural analysis end up inverting the errors of earlier accounts. Instead of representing consumer behaviour through an exclusively productionist frame, these accounts project a vision of consumption practices as inherently democratic and implicitly 'subversive'. As Williamson (1986: 14–15) has argued, the blatant populism of the 'pleasures of consumption' thesis leads to the virtual abandonment of any form of critical distance: all consumer behaviour becomes imbued with a romantic glow of creativity leaving no room for questions of textual quality and the 'privileged creativity necessary for the production of cultural texts and artefacts' (Willis, 1990: 153).[8]

In effect, through attempting to indicate that the cultural forms and meanings of consumption are not reducible to class and the economic – 'that consumerism doesn't simply mirror production' (Nava, 1987: 209) – cultural analysis ends up treating consumption 'as a quasi-autonomous reality diverging from another "reality" called "production" – which after Marxism, we are supposed to know quite enough about for the time being' (Morris, 1988: 21). However, if, for example, the 'economic' itself is not reducible to 'class and the economic' as traditionally conceived; if 'economic activity' is itself 'cultural', as suggested in Chapters 2 and 3, then such a division between production and consumption cannot be maintained. Rather, the relationship between production and consumption is one of dislocation. In other words, instead of representing production and consumption as two fully constituted objectivities, they should be conceptualized in terms of mutual constitution, or as Laclau (1990: 24) puts it, as 'relational semi-identities' involved in 'unstable relations of imbrication'.[9]

In some forms of contemporary cultural analysis 'imbrication' loses out to binary opposition as a de-alienated sphere of consumption is counter-posed to an alienated, deskilled and already determined world of paid employment. While exploding the myth of the 'passive consumer', cultural analysis institutes in its place the myth of the totally determined, deskilled worker. A routinized, impoverished world of paid work becomes the 'other' against which the 'pleasures of consumption thesis' constitutes its identity (du Gay and Negus, 1994).

*Production, consumption, everyday life*

Funnily enough, in their different ways, the work of both Goldthorpe et al. (1969) and that of Roy (1973) attests to the overlapping relations of production and consumption. For Goldthorpe et al. (1969) the affluent worker's relationship to work is primarily explicable in terms of 'his' identity as a consumer, whereas for Roy (1973) the symbolic construction of work-based identity involves the deployment and utilization of many of the forms, interests and communications of 'leisure'. As the work of these authors indicates, it is impossible to maintain a simple division between production and consumption, and between work and non-work identity, since these two areas of activity continually overlap.

According to de Certeau (1984), it is the 'practices of everyday life' which disrupt both the pessimistic logic of the mass culture critique and the binary oppositions of the 'pleasures of consumption' thesis, and link together work and leisure. These practices, de Certeau (1984: 21) suggests, 'imply a *logic of the operation of actions relative to types of situations*. This logic, which turns on *circumstances*, has as its precondition . . . the non-autonomy of its field of action.' Thus, these practices present themselves essentially as 'arts of making' (*arts de faire*), that is, as 'combinatory or utilizing modes of consumption' (de Certeau, 1984: xv).

This 'art of making' can be conceptualized as an active process, but also as a hidden one because it is scattered over areas defined and occupied by systems of production, and because the steadily increasing expansion of these systems no longer leaves the subjects of these practices – consumers or users – any place in which they can indicate what they make or do with the products and representations of these systems.

> To a rationalised, clamorous, and spectacular production corresponds another production, called 'consumption'. The latter is devious, it is dispersed, but it insinuates itself everywhere, silently and almost invisibly, because it does not manifest itself through its own products, but rather through ways of using the products imposed by a dominant order. (de Certeau, 1984: xii–xiii)

In this way, the polarity between production and consumption is dissolved. Practices of consumption have no proper place of their own. Rather they operate within a space delineated by, but not equivalent to, systems of production. Therefore the subject of consumption does not manifest itself through its own 'autonomous' representations, but in relation to ways of using representations and products 'from above'. In other words, the relationship between production and consumption is one of dislocation.

Procedures of consumption do not simply map onto the spaces delineated by systems of production; rather they trace 'indeterminate' trajectories that appear meaningless 'since they do not cohere with the constructed, written and prefabricated space through which they move' (de Certeau, 1984: 34).

> Although they are composed with the vocabularies of established languages (those of television, newspapers, supermarkets, or museum sequences) and although they remain subordinated to the prescribed syntactical forms (temporal modes of schedules, paradigmatic orders of spaces, etc.), the trajectories trace out the ruses of other interests and desires that are neither determined nor captured by the systems in which they develop. (de Certeau, 1984: xviii)

As indicated above, this art of consumption does not leave the subject, object or system untouched. Although consumers are caught within the grid of production, they are not reduced to it. In this sense, as de Certeau argues, 'assimilation' doesn't necessarily mean becoming similar to what absorbs, but rather suggests a situation in which one makes something similar to what one is, establishing it as one's own through appropriating or reappropriating it.[10]

In exploring the relationship between production and consumption, de Certeau's operative distinctions are between 'strategy' and 'tactics', 'place' and 'space'. Systems of production, he argues, operate with a 'strategic' logic. Here 'strategy' refers to

> the calculus of force-relationships that becomes possible when a subject of will and power (a proprietor, an enterprise, a city, a scientific institution) can be isolated from an 'environment'. A strategy assumes a place that can be circumscribed as *'proper'* (*propre*) and thus serves as the basis for generating relations with an exterior distinct from it (competitors, adversaries, 'clienteles', 'targets', or 'objects' of research). Political, economic, and scientific rationality has been constructed on this strategic model. (de Certeau, 1984: xix)

'Strategy' proceeds as if it has its own 'God's eye view' from which it can reflect on the everyday. It involves a victory of *place* over time, and a mastery of places through sight. In this sense, the exercise of strategic power is a *panoptic practice*.[11] As de Certeau conceives of it, 'strategy' shares certain similarities with Hacking's (1986) vector of 'labelling from above'. Through the interplay of power and knowledge, 'strategy' constructs a 'proper' place – a reality – that people caught within its grid are encouraged to make their own.

The power of strategic calculation lies in its ability to divide, collate and classify. However, it is precisely through this analytic fragmentation that it loses sight of what it claims to represent. In seeking to grasp the 'Real', strategy manages instead to construct a 'reality'. This reality only comes into existence through a process of 'splitting' that generates a 'surplus' which, of necessity, must remain 'other'. For de Certeau, the everyday is the space of this 'other'. 'Strategy'

> can grasp only the material used by consumer practices – a material which is obviously that imposed on everyone by production – and not the formality proper to these practices, their surreptitious and guileful 'movement', that is, the very activity of 'making do'. The strength of these computations lies in their ability to divide, but this ana-lytical ability eliminates the possibility of representing the tactical trajectories which, according to their own criteria, select fragments taken from the vast ensembles of production in order to compose new stories with them. (de Certeau, 1984: 35)

Whereas 'strategy' can count only *what* is used, it cannot grasp the *ways of using* deployed by consumers. The latter constitute the 'left-over', or 'surplus', generated by the very success of strategic rationality, and forever beyond its gaze. As de Certeau (1984: 69–70) argues, consumer practices become invisible 'in the universe of codification and generalized transparency', because 'they have no legitimacy with respect to productivist rationality . . . what is left behind by ethnological colonization acquires the status of a private activity, is charged with symbolic investments concerning everyday activity, and functions under the sign of collective or individual particulars.' To the strategic gaze, therefore, only the effects (the quantity and locus of consumed objects) of the multiform and fragmented activity of consumers remain perceptible; their actual 'ways of operating' circulate without being seen, 'discernible only through the objects that they move about and erode'. Through their signifying practices, consumers trace what de Certeau terms *'lignes d'erre'*: wandering trajectories that form unforeseeable routes, partly unreadable paths across a 'proper' place.

In contrast to the 'strategic' rationality of systems of production, procedures of consumption are 'tactical' in character: habits of action and 'ways of operating' that cannot count on a 'proper' (a spatial or institutional localization) place, nor thus on a borderline distinguishing production as a visible totality. The space of the 'tactic' is the space of the 'other'. As such it must operate within a territory delineated 'from above'.

> a tactic is a calculated action determined by the absence of a proper locus. No delimitation of an exteriority, then, provides it with the condition necessary for autonomy . . . It does not have the means to keep to itself, at a distance, in a position of withdrawal, foresight, and self-collection . . . It does not, therefore,

have the options of planning general strategy and viewing the adversary as a whole within distinct, visible, and objectifiable space. It operates in isolated actions, blow by blow. It takes advantages of 'opportunities' and depends on them, being without any base where it could stockpile its winnings, build up its own position, and plan raids. What it wins it cannot keep. This nowhere gives a tactic mobility, to be sure, but a mobility that must accept the chance offerings of the moment. It must vigilantly make use of the cracks that particular conjunctions open in the surveillance of the proprietary powers. It poaches on them. It creates surprises in them. It can be where it is least expected. It is a guileful ruse. (de Certeau, 1984: 37)

As it does not have a proper place, a tactic depends on time. While 'strategies' depend on the erosion of time through the establishment of 'place', 'tactics' depend on the use of time, of the opportunities it presents, and 'also of the play it introduces into the foundations of power' (de Certeau, 1984: 39).

As de Certeau (1984: 40) makes clear, tactical 'procedures of consumption' trace errant trajectories that fail to conform to the logic of 'place'. In this sense, consumer practices traverse strategic distinctions between 'work' and 'non-work', for example; they insinuate themselves everywhere. In contrast to the 'pleasures of consumption' thesis, de Certeau points to the presence of 'enunciative' practices and tactical techniques of consumption *within* the 'economic' sphere. '*La perruque*', for example, is an employee's own work disguised as paid work for his or her employer. It differs from pilfering in that nothing of material value is stolen, and it cannot be categorized as absenteeism because the worker is firmly located at the 'place' of work: '*la perruque* may be as simple a matter as a secretary's writing a love letter on "company time" or as complex as a cabinet-maker's "borrowing" a lathe to make a piece of furniture for his living room.' In effect, *la perruque* is a tactic whereby workers temporarily turn company time into time of their own. According to de Certeau (1984: 29), this practice is the work-based version of a tactic known outside the workplace (i.e. in another *place*) as *bricolage*. In other words, *la perruque* does not obey the 'law of place'; rather it traverses the frontiers dividing time, place and type of action into one part assigned for 'work' and one part assigned to 'leisure'. As de Certeau (1984: 29) suggests, viewed in this way it becomes apparent that 'the dividing line no longer falls between work and leisure. These two areas of activity flow together. They repeat and reinforce each other.'

Although 'tactics' are 'an art of the weak' (though not of the 'unfree'), their very existence attests to the limits of strategic rationality and, thus, of 'labelling from above'. Lodged within de Certeau's operational schema it is possible to detect a simple (and quite psychoanalytic), but not simplistic, moral: that the dynamics of subjectification are more complicated and contingent than simply identifying with the attributes, attitudes and behaviours prescribed by technologies and practices of regulation. As de Certeau (1984: xx) suggests, tactical 'procedures of consumption' introduce a Brownian movement into systems of production. While the 'wandering trajectories' of consumers are 'scattered over areas defined and occupied by systems of "production"' they are never determined nor captured by these systems within which they move, and which they cannot keep at a distance. Rather than being either completely 'autonomous' or 'totally determined', consumer behaviour is 'nomadic'. As Grossberg (1988: 384–7) has argued

> nomadic subjects are like commuters moving between different sites of daily life, who are always mobile but for whom the particular mobilities and stabilities are never entirely directed, shaped and reshaped, by the effectivities of the practices (trajectories, apparatuses etc.) within which their agency is located.

The subject's shape and effectivity are never fully guaranteed because the subject is a 'lack in the structure' (Zizek, 1989: 175). There is the 'consumer' because 'production' can never fully constitute itself as an 'objectivity'. The relationship between systems of production and procedures of consumption is therefore one of dislocation.

## Looking ahead

In the first part of this book (Chapters 1–4) I have attempted to construct a partial framework for thinking about how people are presently 'made up' at work. In particular, I have tried to indicate the ways in which contemporary discourses of organizational reform problematize the relationship between production and consumption identities. In the second part of the book (Chapters 5–7) I move on to examine the discursive construction of work-based subjectivity and identity in one particular sector of the UK economy during the 1980s and 1990s. I have chosen to focus upon the retailing sector because it offers a particularly pertinent terrain of enquiry for charting the present dislocation of production and consumption identities. As indicated in Chapter 3, for example, it is in areas such as retailing, where the quality of interactive service delivery has become an important source of value, that the introduction of customer-focused technologies and practices of 'excellence' are most pronounced.

However, before drawing upon original research in the retail sector to explore how people are 'made up' at work, I want to provide a rationale for focusing upon retailing as a crucial site in the present dislocation of production and consumption relations. In Chapter 5, therefore, I begin by delineating and examining the cultural contours of retailing, indicating the importance of the retail sector to the mode of existence and reproduction of contemporary consumer culture. I then proceed to outline some of the major 'logistical' developments occurring within the sector and to indicate how these signify a shift to a more flexible system of accumulation within retailing. The chapter concludes by considering some of the subjectivizing aspects of contemporary programmes of organizational reform within retailing both for consumers and, increasingly, for retail employees.

# Notes

1 I use 'character' in MacIntyre's (1985: 28) sense of that term: 'A *character* is an object of regard by the members of the culture generally or by some significant segment of them. He furnishes them with a cultural and moral ideal. Hence the demand is that . . . role and personality be fused. Social type and psychological type are required to coincide. The *character* morally legitimates a mode of social existence.'

2 According to Bauman (1988: 221–2), 'seduction': 'is the paramount tool of integration (of the reproduction of domination) in a consumer society. It is made possible once the market succeeds in making consumers dependent upon itself. Market-dependency is achieved through the destruction of such skills (technical, social, psychological, existential) which do not entail the use of marketable commodities; the more complete the destruction, the more necessary become new skills which point organically to market-supplied implements . . . New technical, social, psychological and existential skills of the consumers are such as to be practicable only in conjunction with marketable commodities; rationality comes to mean the ability to make the right purchasing decisions . . . .' On the other hand, 'repression' is a form of panoptic power. 'It employs surveillance, it is aimed at regimentation of the body, and it is diffused (made invisible) in the numerous institutionalizations of knowledge-based expertise . . . It is the continuous, tangible presence of repression as a viable alternative which makes seduction unchallengeable. In addition, repression is indispensable to reach the areas seduction cannot, and is not meant to, reach: it remains the paramount tool of subordination of the considerable margin of society which cannot be absorbed by market dependency and hence, in market terms, consists of 'non-consumers' . . . Repression reforges the market unattractiveness of non-consumer existence into the unattractiveness of alternatives to market dependency.'

3 C. Wright Mills' (1953: 237) famous indictment of the superficiality of modern 'leisure' expresses the traditional representation of consumption exactly: 'Each day men sell little pieces of themselves in order to try and buy them back each night with the coin of fun.'

4 For Campbell (1987: 227), the dynamism of modern consumerism, and ultimately of the West, depends upon a tension generated between the logic of rationalization and the logic of 'desire'.

5 Ironically, as Miller (1987: 156) argues, in appearing to view the working class as some form of 'authentic' humanity, whose relationship to immediacy is both proper and desirable, Bourdieu positions himself within the same old philosophical anthropology of production upon which the mass culture critique is founded.

6 As Clarke (1991: 110–11), for example, has indicated, subcultural analysis has come in for substantial criticism on a variety of grounds. One of the most trenchant criticisms has concerned the discussion of the consumption practices of these subcultural groups in terms of 'resistance'. At one level, it is argued, subcultural analyses are unspecific about what exactly is being resisted. Secondly, there is no substantial political analysis of the content or direction of these ostensible resistances. It became apparent, for example, that white, male, working-class subcultures of resistance were frequently implicated in racist and sexist practices. As a result it was not clear why their 'resistance' should be universally celebrated, nor why such resistance should be built upon politically, as the subculturalists argued. Finally, these studies have been criticized for representing subcultures as too much the product of consumers as active, rational agents; in other words, as subjects 'to whom an excess of consciousness is attributed, thus neglecting the contradictory and overdetermined character of subjectivity' (Clarke, 1991: 111).

7 Not all work in this vein is susceptible to such criticism. In an article charting the changing 'meaning' of the Italian scooter cycle, Hebdige (1981) indicates how viewing consumption as an active process has consequences for the traditional conceptualization of 'production' as a largely autonomous and determining force in the construction of social relations. According to Hebdige (1981: 44–66), the motor scooter was originally produced and marketed as the feminine equivalent of the 'macho' motorbike. These gender terms stood for a

wide range of associated connotations of industrialization and commodification, through which the childlike scooter, with its enclosed machine parts, reproduced in its relationship to the motorbike the basic asymmetry in the status of the sexes. These images were transformed, however, in a manner not envisaged by the producers – but later utilized and actively encouraged by them – but which was established through articulation with emergent polarities within British youth cultures. The motorbike became associated with the 'Rockers' in contrast to the motor scooter's appropriation by the 'Mods' in the process of their own self-constitution; the latter representing a 'softer', more European sense of style in opposition to the Rockers' 'hard', American image. The new formation was consistent with, but determined by or reducible to, the original meanings inscribed into the motor scooter in its initial production.

Hebdige's analysis indicates the centrality of 'dislocation' in understanding the relationship between forces of production and practices of consumption. It demonstrates both industry's careful reading of the market to try to differentiate material forms on the basis of already existing social divisions, in this case gender, and also the fact that the transformations of these objects in Britain provided the foundation for the formation of new social groups to whom consumer style was so integral they could not be considered prior to these material changes through which they expressed and thereby constituted themselves. In so doing, Hebdige attributes agency to both the consumer and the producer, while still retaining a sense of the larger historical forces emanating from social and technological change. However, possibilities of appropriation and recontextualization are never uniform, but vary for any given object and subject according to context. Hebdige's article indicates, for example, that although the 'meaning' of motor scooters and motorbikes was transformed according to the conceptions of youth groups, the original distinction promoted in the initial design and marketing of the goods was that of gender. There is nothing in the later trajectory of these goods to suggest that the ability of these objects to reproduce gender asymmetry was in any way deflected by the 'recontextualization' represented by these later shifts.

8  The rise to prominence of this type of analysis – what Morley (1992) has termed the 'Don't worry, be happy' school of cultural studies – in the 1980s is obviously no accident. As both Williamson (1986) and Morris (1988) suggest, the rising trajectory of the 'pleasures thesis' reflects a shift in attitudes within the academy in the face of the apparent success of the New Right in colonizing popular pleasures.

9  Though, as Laclau (1990: 24) continues, 'this does not mean, of course, that an area of the social cannot become autonomous and establish to a greater or lesser degree, a separate identity. But this separation and autonomization, like everything else, has specific conditions of existence which establish their limits at the same time.'

10  As de Certeau (1984: xvii) makes clear, although consumption is an activity of the 'weak' – 'choices are provided but not choices over choices or over the conditions under which choices are made – the cultural agenda itself' (Willis, 1990: 132) – and although consumers are fast becoming a 'silent majority' in the productionist universe, these 'users' are not a homogeneous group. Rather, 'The procedures allowing the re-use of products are linked together in a kind of obligatory language, and their functioning is related to social situations and power relationships . . . Similar strategic deployments, when acting on different relationships of force, do not produce identical effects. Hence the necessity of differentiating both the "actions" or "engagements" (in the military sense) that the system of products effects within the consumer grid, and the various kinds of room to maneuver left for consumers by the situations in which they exercise their "art".'

11  As de Certeau suggests, the establishment of a break between a place appropriated as one's own and its 'other' is accompanied by a number of important effects. First, if the 'proper' is a victory of place over time, then it allows one a certain independence with respect to circumstances. Secondly, the mastery of places through sight makes possible a *'panoptic practice* proceeding from a place whence the eye can transform foreign forces into objects that can be observed and measured, and thus control and "include" them within its scope of vision. To be able to see (far into the distance) is also to be able to predict, to run ahead of time by reading a space' (de Certeau, 1984: 36). Lastly, in these 'strategies' a specific type of *knowledge*

can be delineated, one sustained and created by the *power* to provide oneself with one's own *place*. 'In other words, *a certain power is the precondition of this knowledge* and not merely its effect or its attribute. It makes this knowledge possible and at the same time determines its characteristics' (de Certeau, 1984: 36).

# PART II

---

## 5

# Retailing and the De-differentiation of Economy and Culture

As the 1980s drew to a close a plethora of retrospective articles and programmes appeared in the media analysing, panning and celebrating perceived key moments and transitions in collective British life during the previous decade. A common theme in both business (*The Money Programme*, 7 January 1990) and cultural (*The Late Show*, 15 September 1989) programming of this type was the representation of Britain's 'retail revolution' as one of the most significant social phenomena of the age. The ubiquitous presence of retail, it was argued, extended well beyond the simple proliferation of shops and shopping centres. Retail had, in an important sense, become the defining motif of the decade, 'an approach, an ideology almost, permeating the culture'. It had, at its core, 'a celebration of the market place, which echoed strongly with the prevailing political climate' (Gardner and Sheppard, 1989: 66). As one commentator put it, 'retailing is . . . virtually the paradigm of the "enterprise culture"' (Bamfield, 1987). It is not difficult to reason why.

From dull, distributive cypher mediating between manufacturers and the public, retail was now 'imaged' as a 'leading edge' sector of Britain's 'new service economy'.[1] Murray (1988a,b), for example, argued that developments within the retail sector were playing a crucial role in 'making Fordism flexible'; that retail was a principal initiator of the shift to a new regime of accumulation based on flexible forms of production and increasingly specialized consumption practices. 'In Britain, the groundwork for the new system was laid not in manufacturing but in retailing . . . the revolution in retailing reflects new principles of production, a new pluralism of production, and a new importance for innovation. As such it marks a shift to a post-Fordist age' (Murray, 1988b: 11).

Increased concentration and centralization within the retail industry, in conjunction with the widespread introduction of electronic data processing (EDP) technologies, has facilitated the organization of the retail/distribution system and, increasingly, the production chain as well, as a 'logistic' package, allowing coordinated flexibility in the face of market changes.

This has permitted retailers to track customers more closely than ever before and to offer a significantly expanded, but carefully integrated, range of 'mass produced individualities'. According to Murray (1988b: 11), these changes are steering 'the high street from being retailers of goods to retailers of style'. Similarly, for Lash (1988) they are indicative of the 'cultural logic' of the 'new era'. In other words, the 'new regime of accumulation' is simultaneously a 'regime of signification'. That is, 'a greater and greater proportion of all goods produced comprises cultural goods' (Lash, 1990: 39).

In effect what is being attested to here, and in programmes like *The Late Show* and *The Money Programme*, is the crucial contribution of retailing to the progressive dislocation of relations between production and consumption. For social scientists interested in the ways in which production articulates with consumption in an era of widespread and intensive change – whether conceptualized as neo-Fordist, post-Fordist, flexibly specialized or disorganized capitalist – retailing would appear to offer an extremely pertinent terrain of enquiry. None the less, the sector continues to be largely neglected by social scientists. Once again, the dominant productionist bias that has inhibited social scientific discourse – only those industries that *really make* something are important – can be detected in the marginalization of retailing from the research agenda (Allen and du Gay, 1994).

In part, this chapter is an attempt to remedy this deficiency. However, my aim is not to examine the economic importance of retailing as a 'wealth creator', nor is it to delineate the 'political economy' of retailing. Rather, I am interested in exploring the ways in which the economic *folds into* the cultural in the practice of retailing in contemporary Britain. In other words, I want to examine the constitutive role of retailing in the dislocation of production and consumption relations.

To this end, first, I will delineate the cultural contours of retailing, indicating the importance of the retail sector to the mode of existence and reproduction of contemporary consumer society in the UK. Secondly, I will outline some of the major logistical developments which have allowed retailers to stay closer to the customer than ever before and which have permitted coordinated flexibility in the face of increasingly competitive and dynamic markets. This move to a more 'flexible system of accumulation' within the retail sector can be seen to involve, at one and the same time, the progressive 'culturalization' of retailing. Lastly, I will consider the subjectivizing aspects of contemporary retail change, both for consumers and, increasingly, for retail employees. I will argue that attempts by retailers to 'make up' the consumer have consequences for the way in which the social relations of employment are imagined within the retail sector.

## The cultural contours of retailing

According to a number of commentators (Murray, 1988a,b; Gardner and Sheppard, 1989), during the past decade the retail sector has played a major role in spearheading the progressive penetration of the market into all walks of British life, encouraging and facilitating the spread of consumer culture. Indeed, some have gone as far as to suggest that retail has gradually taken on '*the* leading role in the consumer economy' (Gardner and Sheppard, 1989: 66) by making more and more people dependent upon itself for their own reproduction. In other words, retail has 'colonized the everyday' through a process of increasing 'market dependency'. According to Zygmunt Bauman, 'market dependency is guaranteed once men and women, now consumers, cannot proceed with the business of life without turning themselves to the logic of the market' (Bauman, 1988: 222).

Once this degree of dependence upon the market in general, and retail in particular, is achieved, the skill of shopping attains a new status. According to Bauman (1987), rather than being one among many skills, it becomes, for the consumer, the skill to deputize for all others. Shopping therefore becomes constitutive of subjectivity in a fundamental way. Consumers need the market as a cornerstone of their sense of certainty and self-confidence because, with shopping paramount, the 'certainty that counts most and promises to compensate for all other (absent) certainties is one related to buying choices' (Bauman, 1987: 165).

At the same time, shopping not only provides a 'life project', it also becomes 'a pleasurable leisure experience' and an inexhaustible treasury of sensual stimuli (Featherstone, 1990). One of the notable recent developments in retailing, the move to out-of-town or edge-of-town shopping complexes, has involved a major redefinition of the 'shopping experience' on the part of retailers and developers. Because 'the consumer is going to spend a relatively long time in the centre it is necessary to provide a high quality of finishing and facilities', it is argued; simultaneously making the retail centre a leisure venue will 'encourage customers to stay longer and spend more money' (*Retail Week*, 23 March 1990: 16). In these retail centres, the focus is directed less towards mass-market 'routine shopping' but rather towards a more relaxed, and market-segmented, leisure shopping experience. Thus 'food courts' have appeared, along with cinema multiplexes and children's play areas and 'fantasy lands', while ordinary elements of the shopping environment such as lifts and escalators have been customized to become part of a wider leisure spectacle. Although nothing on the same scale as the Edmonton Mall in Canada, or some of the larger US shopping complexes, has appeared yet in the UK, the leisure element at both the MetroCentre in Gateshead, and the Merry Hill development in Dudley have been integral to their success (*Retail Week*, 23 March 1990: 16). In the process of redefining the shopping experience, both emotionally and geographically, through the out-of-town leisure development, retail itself is transformed. As shopping is reconceptualized as *the* premier leisure activity in contemporary consumer society, retailing is transformed into a major cultural site.

With market-dependent consumption playing a greater constitutive role in the formation of subjectivity and identity, the reproduction of the market, and therefore of the retail sector, requires the continual creation of new ways for people to be. Hence the increasing importance of the symbolic expertise of marketing, design and advertising, underpinned by knowledges and techniques of subjectivity, to the continued growth of the retail sector. These disciplines have played a vital role in the transmutation of commodities and services into desires and fantasies and vice-versa. As suggested in Chapter 4, they are not mere cyphers, simply reflecting already existing social and attitudinal difference, but active interveners, constructing differences and distinctions. In other words, they actively 'make up' the consumer.

Their major contribution to the development of the retail sector during the past decade has been the discourse of 'lifestyling': the combination of design and visual communication with techniques of market segmentation. In contrast with what might be called 'supplier-style' retailing, in which 'the key to success . . . has been a focus on homogeneity in retailing operations', lifestyling is a policy of 'tailoring a retail offering closely to the life-styles of a specific target-market segment' (Blackwell and Wayne Talarzyk, 1983: 7–8). Basically, this means 'repositioning up-market' in order to 'add value'.

The expertise of design, marketing and image construction constitutes consumers as individual actors seeking to maximise the worth of their existence to themselves by assembling a lifestyle (or lifestyles) through personalized acts of choice in a world of goods and services. Here is one leading retail design company's portrait of the 'new consumer':

> consumers have changed in the last decade . . . consumers today . . . are discriminating individuals exercising choice in an increasingly service-based economy. They are more aware of their rights and have been encouraged to make choices and stand up for themselves . . . consumers' individual needs therefore have to be recognised, not just the needs of the consumer en masse. (Fitch – RS plc, 1989: 2)

This 'consumer' has the 'right' to freedom and variety of choice and the parallel 'obligation' to take responsibility for the choices made and to make the most of his or her own individual existence. In effect, the consumer is constituted as an autonomous, responsible, self-regulating and self-actualizing individual actor – what Nikolas Rose terms an enterprising subject; a self that 'calculates about itself and works upon itself in order to better itself' (Rose, 1990: 7).

But if this is the sovereign consumer of 'lifestyling', what happens to all those who don't fit the picture? The answer is quite simple. Those who do not enter the 'lifestyle' grid – those who fall into non-key target segments – are effectively marginalized in consumer society. In a market-dependent consumer culture, those whose consumption does not matter much for the successful reproduction of capital are virtually non-people. Indeed, the maintenance of the self-identity of the enterprising consumer requires the constitution of non-consumers both as a benchmark against which to measure relative success and as a threat to be vigilant against (Bauman, 1987).

The increasing polarization between enterprising consumers – the seduced – and the effective non-consumer – the repressed – is arguably not a product of the 'malfunctioning' of consumer culture but an essential component of its mode of existence and its reproduction (Gorz, 1989: Zizek, 1989). Consumer culture can be said to create its own repressed by representing the enterprising sovereign consumer not as an exploiter, nor as a selfish egoist, but as a pathfinder, a pattern-setter whose example should be imitated; a pioneer on the road to self-fulfilment that every civilized human should aspire to follow, and a confirmation that such aspiration is realistic (Bourdieu, 1984; Bauman, 1988; Bonner and du Gay, 1992). As Bauman has argued

> The tragedy of consumer society is that it cannot reproduce itself without reproducing inequalities on an ever rising level and without insisting that all social problems must be translated into individual needs satisfiable through the individual consumption of marketable commodities. By so doing it daily generates its own handicapped, whose needs cannot be met through the market and who therefore undermine the very condition of its reproduction. (Bauman, 1987: 187)

As a leading 'player' in consumer society, retail finds itself at the heart of this dismal paradox. On the one hand, the rise of 'retail culture' can appear to be a levelling agent, bringing the pleasures of consumption to increasing numbers of people. There can be no doubt, for example, that retail has made a major contribution to the explosion in marketed material culture available for consumption, and to widening the quantity of possible 'ways of being' for consumers. At the same time, however, changing locational and marketing policies, for example, aimed at, and constituting, the 'new consumer' – the enterprising, or consuming, self – have served effectively to marginalize many of the people who do not fit into the retailers' reality 'grid'.

**The logistics of 'retail engineering'**

The growing 'culturization' of retailing in the UK is underpinned by a profound transformation of the distribution system (Murray, 1988a,b). As suggested earlier, increased levels of concentration and centralization within the retail industry, combined with the widespread deployment of EDP technologies, have permitted the retail/distribution system, and, increasingly, the whole production chain as well, to be arranged as a 'logistic' package (*Retail Week*, 2 August 1990). According to Murray (1988a: 11), for example, because the whole chain can now be organized as a single system, retailers are able to enjoy a hitherto unavailable degree of 'co-ordinated flexibility' in the face of market changes. The development of 'retail engineering', as this systematization has come to be named, allows retailers to delineate, construct and monitor the customer more intricately than ever before, and to extend significantly the range of 'mass-produced individualities' available for consumption. In other words, the 'front-to-back' visibility accorded to retail organizations through the practice of 'retail engineering' facilitates and enhances the transformation of retailing into an arena of signification.

In the following section I will outline the major processes at work within the retail sector over roughly the past three decades that have helped to transform the whole distribution system into a 'logistic' package.

## Concentration

Retail capital is one part of a wider circuit of capital located between manufacturing capital and the final consumer. It manifests itself as a number of retail enterprises competing with one another and with other *forms* of capital (Ducatel and Blomley, 1990: 208–25). One obvious way in which retailers attempt to gain competitive advantage over other retailers and other forms of capital is through the process of concentration. Indeed, one of the main features of both the UK and US retail sectors since the end of the Second World War has been the degree of concentration that has occurred. The twin features of this process have been the growth in market share attributable to the largest retailers and the local market concentration of retail outlets which has taken place at the same time. The scale of change in UK retailing can be assessed by the evidence from the 1950 census of distribution which suggests that there were 583,000 shops in the country at that time. Since then, somewhere in the region of 250,000 retail outlets have disappeared (Sparks, 1989: 44).

This huge change in retailing size has been associated with considerable mutations in structure and organizational type. The major development has been the rapid growth of the multiples at the expense of the traditional independent retailer and the cooperative retail sector. In 1980, for example, the large retail multiples (those with 10 or more outlets) accounted for 54 per cent of all retail trade through 1,300 outlets. By 1986, the multiples were achieving a 60 per cent share through less than 900 stores (Euromonitor, 1990: 41–2).[2] Overall, the retail sector can be seen to be shrinking in terms of the number of outlets, businesses and number of employees, although not in terms of volume, while the sector as a whole has become increasingly dominated and controlled by large companies.

The large multiples gain competitive advantage over the independents mainly from economies of scale and economies of replication. As they have grown larger, the multiples have been able to gain from their size in terms of their buying power from suppliers and from administrative centralization. Thus the process of concentration also entails a parallel move towards greater centralization of control. Expansion into new areas (diversification) is also easier due to the size of the enterprise. These types of benefit have also pertained from economies of replication in which a standard, or relatively standard, retail outlet or procedure can be duplicated across a large number of sites. This brings cost savings through conformity of operation, in price systems, for example. Both of these procedures have been aided by the introduction of new technology, a point to which I will return. These sorts of advantage are available to the multiples, while independents and fragmented cooperatives are often unable to benefit in the same way.

This process of concentration has passed through several stages. First, there was the local general store; then in towns and town centres, speciality stores – butchers, greengrocers, haberdashers etc. The innovation of the department store was to locate a number of speciality stores under one roof – to concentrate these specialisms spatially. The discount store sought to undercut the department store by stocking fewer lines, offering less direct service and cutting prices to increase turnover on lower margins (Bluestone and Huff Stevenson, 1981: 25–7). The development of supermarkets and superstores was based in part on an expanded selection of speciality goods in a central location. Finally, shopping malls, hypermarkets and gallerias function in a similar way to the earlier department stores in that they concentrate speciality shops (often multiples' 'segments') in a single location (Murray, 1988a: 3).

Increased concentration has not led to any diminution of competition, however; rather, it has led to intensified competition between retailers on both quality and price (Bluestone and Huff Stevenson, 1981; Rubery et al., 1987). As Craig and Wilkinson (1985: 8) have argued, the main reason for this is that while large retail firms 'can dominate the supply-side, they are faced by a multitude of buyers whose loyalty depends on price and quality. Therefore the collusion between firms to be found in concentrated industries in manufacturing does not exist in retailing and even the largest firms compete hotly with one another.'

Given the 'inherent' uncertainties of final consumption for even large multiples, retailers have sought to extend their influence over areas more amenable to their control, in particular their relations with suppliers and the overall costs of circulation. I will deal with the former first.

### The interface between manufacturing and retail capital

The continued growth of the large-scale retailing enterprise has considerably altered the relationship between retail capital and manufacturing capital. While the relationship between the two has always contained the possibility of antagonism – manufacturers have attempted to shift the cost of stockholding and risks on to the retailer, while retailers have tried to shift the burden of cost back up the line to the supplier – the balance of relative power has now shifted firmly to the side of the retailer. Whereas in the past, manufacturers tended to control the wholesalers and retailers through forward integration and control of the product, today it is backward integration from the retailer which is changing the relationship in the supply chain.

The shift in relative power is apparent at three main levels. In terms of structural change, it can be seen in the changing relative size of manufacturers of consumer goods and retailers: rapid growth and mergers of national retail chains have resulted in the largest retailing conglomerates exceeding their suppliers in terms of size of sales, assets and stockmarket capitalization. At the same time, the growing size and dominance of the major retailers has led to a reduction in the number of possible retail outlets for consumer goods, which, in turn, has been to the disadvantage of suppliers in terms of price and conditions of sale (the growth of preferential discounts for large multiples etc.). It has been noted, for example, that if neither of the UK's top supermarket chains, Sainsbury and Tesco, takes a particular new product then the manufacturer may as well not bother marketing it (Randall, quoted in Ducatel and Blomley, 1990: 221).

Secondly, retailers have increasingly amassed control over a range of functions, including physical distribution, advertising, packaging, product design and product development. This increase in the scope of retailers' activities is most clearly indicated by the growth of retailers' 'own brand' products. According to Rubery et al. (1987: 135), the latter process has been the single most significant development in shifting the balance of supplier–retailer relations. The importance to retailers in selling under their own brand name is 'the power it gives them to influence not only the price, but also design and quality'. By securing a competitive advantage over established suppliers, the retailers can then increase the pressure by widening the basis of supply both nationally and, increasingly, internationally.

Thirdly, in terms of performance, the shift of relative power between retailers and suppliers has been reflected in the profitability growth of retailing enterprises during the past 15 years relative to that achieved by consumer-goods manufacturers in the same period (Grant, 1987: 43).

Overall, the effects of increased retailer buying power upon the manufacturers of consumer goods has been to increase price competition, to reduce profitability, to increase product differentiation (particularly through advertising and new product introductions), and to increase the pressure for cost-efficiency.[3] According to Rubery et al. (1987), the increased domination of the product market by large multiple retailers, and the increasing competition between retail enterprises, are a major cause of restructuring among consumer-goods manufacturers. Changes in product markets and the consequent need for increased responsiveness in terms of price, quality, variety and variability of batch size and goods supplied was a common experience among the consumer-goods producers studied by Rubery et al. (1987), and the single most important factor shaping their policies. Increasingly, therefore, retail capital is playing a determinate role in setting the agenda for manufacturing capital:

> large multiple retailers . . . were increasingly reducing the size of orders, requiring more frequent deliveries and placing more emphasis on quality and fashion in consumer demand. The product market changes exerted a downward pressure on

prices and hence margins and required firms to supply smaller batches, with quicker deliveries, of a greater variety of goods and more frequent product changes. (Rubery et al., 1987: 33)

## Reducing circulation costs

As circulation costs incurred in retailing do not contribute to the creation of value, retailers attempt to maximize the speed-up of all retail operations in order to increase the turnover time of capital.[4] Overall, labour is the single largest cost to retailers, rising to 50 per cent of gross margins (Segal-Horn, 1987). Given the labour-intensive nature of most retailing work, reducing labour costs is considered of paramount importance to remaining competitive. Historically, the realization of this objective has involved the introduction of more productive selling techniques such as self-service shopping, together with significant changes in workforce composition in an attempt to employ cheaper sources of labour (particularly women part-timers and young people).

Possibly *the* single most important factor in containing labour costs was the introduction of self-service shopping in the 1960s. This development had dramatic effects both on the number of sales staff required by the industry and upon the organization of the labour process, transforming the nature of much retail work from specialized, personal service into two labour-intensive, repetitive and routine, low-paid occupations: shelf-filling sales assistance and cash'n'wrap till operation. Retailers could therefore recruit labour for occupations demanding little or no specialized knowledge and easily acquired skills.[5]

At the same time, however, this development also effected a trans-formation in the relationship between customers and employees, as the former took on more of the 'work' of the latter. As the scope of customer choice and autonomy – the exercise of personal 'shopping skills' – was extended within the space of the retail establishment, that of the sales floor worker was consequently reduced: 'deskilling' for the shopworker became a form of 'enskilling' for the customer. In other words, self-service functioned as a 'technique of individuation' for consumers, constituting them as self-regulating, autonomous individual subjects exercising choice in a world of goods, and offering them more apparent involvement in, and control over, the act of purchase. Thus, retailers persuaded customers that self-service was in their own interests as individuals – offering them more involvement in and apparent control over the act of purchase – while simultaneously reaping the financial benefits of reduced labour costs and increased buying power over suppliers themselves.

This deskilling of the retail labour process facilitated, accentuated and reinforced another key development: the growth of female part-time labour (Robinson and Wallace, 1974; Robinson, 1988). Whereas in 1961, only 28 per cent of the retail workforce worked part time, by 1984 this had risen to 54 per cent, making retail the largest employer of part-time labour in the private sector. This increase in the use of part-time labour has occurred almost entirely at the expense of full-time employment – the full time equivalent (FTE) level within the industry fell by over 35 per cent during that same period – thus contributing to a reduction in retailers' wage costs and to increased flexibility.[6] Savings in the former arose from less rigid schedules of working hours, the widespread association of part-time jobs with relatively low hourly rates of pay and the general exclusion of part-time employees from eligibility for fringe benefits attached to full-time employment. At the same time, greater flexibility could be derived from the ability of retailers to match labour more readily with fluctuating daily and weekly trading levels (Robinson, 1988).

As Bamfield (1980: 36) has argued, when self-service replaced personal service as the dominant mode in the organization of shopping, it permitted impressive gains to be made in productivity through the substitution of capital for labour and the transfer of functions to the customer. However, this shift turned out to be more than just a labour-saving device. The trading practice it produced led to the collapse of resale price maintenance and to the increased concentration and increased buying power of retailers.

A second strand in the reduction of circulation costs can be seen in the changing geography of store location. Here the move is towards increased centralization of provision (as well as command), thus encouraging consumers to undertake more of the 'work' of consumption and exchange. Although this development has represented a considerable capital outlay for multiple retailers, bigger units have allowed them to address larger geographic markets as well as directly reducing circulation costs. This continuing process of centralization was facilitated in the 1980s by the rapid introduction of EDP technologies. The large multiples are now highly dependent on EDP technologies for the coordination of their geographically dispersed operations. However, because these innovations have very high initial costs and minimum efficient scale of operations, firms have therefore had to be large enough to ensure cost-effective use of the equipment.

The most visible sign of the new technology is at the checkout where Electronic Point of Sale (EPoS) tills and Electronic Funds at Point of Sale (EFTPoS) facilities are being introduced in ever-increasing numbers (*Retail Week*, 19 September 1990: 22).[7] EPoS systems provide retailers with an immediate record of each item sold at the point of sale thereby facilitating significant improvements in stock management, including faster and more accurate re-ordering and reduced stockholding. Stock can now be automatically re-ordered from company warehouses or distribution depots or directly from manufacturers. At the same time, the detailed and immediately available sales data captured enables retailers to monitor the comparative sales of different products, brands, types of customers and areas, price changes and promotions and generally to identify fast- or slow-moving product lines and to modify purchasing orders accordingly.

Increasing the quantity and quality of information about the sales performance of lines in this way (and the competitive advantage and increased relative power this can bring) has been a primary aim of EPoS implementation in the UK (S. Smith, 1988: 151–2). As a former corporate marketing director of the supermarket chain Asda has argued, 'The move towards scanning is absolutely at the core of understanding how a retailer is performing . . . The ability to collect accurate information about sales and profit by line and not only collect it but order it and use it effectively is going to be one of the ways that determines the winners and losers' (Dowling, 1987).

Similarly, EFTPoS systems reduce circulation costs through speeding up the act of sale and cutting down the amount of paperwork (and staff needed to handle it) involved in ordinary credit card and cheque transactions and in the amount of cash handled (with its attendant security costs). They also help to provide more information on individual customers thus allowing for marketing experiments and targeted promotions. EDP technologies have also helped to transform the organization of the warehouse and distribution function. Alongside the installation of EPoS systems in-store, many retailers have invested heavily in the automation and centralization of warehouse and distribution operations as a whole, contributing to the substitution of 'just-in-time' for 'just-in-case'. This process of centralization and automation has engendered large cost-savings in transportation and storage expenses, for example.

As basic data-entry and data-processing are increasingly automated in stores and warehouses, costs at head office are also reduced. According to Noyelle (1987: 37), the process of technological change in large-scale retail enterprises has resulted in much head office work becoming more analytic and investigative and less involved with basic data-entry or processing. Progressively, these changes have shifted the balance of skills towards higher-level personnel.

EDP technology also allows greater management surveillance and control of the labour process.[8] Increasingly, EPoS technology is being used for labour monitoring and scheduling and for control of pilferage, allowing for a greater degree of management control over labour utilization and cost. Given the 'stochastic' nature of customer arrivals and the different levels of demand at different times of the day, the information derived from EPoS can be deployed to ensure that staff are brought in and out of the trading week when 'customers require it', in a closer 'fit' between customer flow and staffing levels.

A recently introduced software package from the computer company ICL, for example, called 'Resource Manager' provides for just such a direct link between EPoS data and staffing levels. This package takes EPoS information at 15-minute intervals throughout the working day and matches this to a file of available staff to produce a labour schedule for the week ahead. In itself this is little different from other labour scheduling systems. However, the software can also be used as an on-line tool incorporating the latest sales data to produce budget and performance plans for local management purposes.

> If, for example, a store manager has set his staffing levels at the start of the week, but for some reason sales on fresh meat are a disaster and he is falling below target, the system alerts him to this fact and he can move staff, reduce overheads in that section and bring the department back into profit. Alternatively, if sales soar in a section he can see at a glance how much over-budget he is and increase the promotional spend, perhaps to encourage even further business. (*Retail Week*, 4 May 1990: 17)

Similarly, cost minimization in the pursuit of profitability and flexibility in retail leads to segmentation via the use of alternative labour types for 'discrete' (as opposed to 'continuous') periods. The introduction of EDP technologies in association with other innovations, such as longer trading hours and the exploitation of labour law loopholes (National Insurance legislation allows for the differential treatment of groups according to the number of hours worked), have assisted, but are not the primary cause of, the increasing utilization of labour by retailers on a less than full-time basis. The highly competitive nature of the contemporary retail trade, as well as the characteristic features of retailing activity mentioned above (erratic product demand, for example), make the trade open to a particularly marked dualism in the methods of labour utilization (Robinson and Wallace, 1974; Pond, 1977; Craig and Wilkinson, 1985; Noyelle, 1987). Increasingly, therefore, retailers are purchasing labour, much as they purchase goods from manufacturers, on a 'just-in-time' basis. Complementing these changes in the structure of employment in the retail sector were associated changes in the relations of employment. As Bluestone and Huff Stevenson (1981: 44) have argued, the search for labour flexibility in retailing has involved the dissolution of 'long-term employment relations' and the growth in its place of part-time and temporary labour contracts. The decline of the internal labour market and the growing duality of employment within the retailing industry has had a deleterious effect upon the conditions of employment of those caught in, or relegated to, the secondary segments of the retail labour market.[9] As a consequence of this shift, a large majority of those employed within retail find themselves in jobs demanding limited skills, offering few opportunities for on-the-job training, and extremely limited opportunities for upward mobility. At the same time as those in the 'core' segments of this market have tended to experience some degree of 'upskilling', those in the secondary segments have been subject to a process of 'down waging' (Noyelle, 1987).

As in other industries, the transformation of employment in retailing in the late 1960s and early 1970s led to an almost total break in the link between sales floor positions and managerial positions. This means that the burden of finding mobility opportunities now rests very much on the shoulders of secondary workers themselves, and no longer on employers. The decrease in firm-specific employment opportunities has placed more workers in competition with one another, thus making it easier for employers to keep wage rates low.

The impact of decreased employer commitment towards, and increased surveillance over, the retail sales labour force is registered in the growing staff turnover rates in the industry. In their research into the department store industry in the US, Bluestone and Huff Stevenson (1981) found that the turnover of salesfloor employees had increased steadily throughout the postwar period. Annual gross turnover rates grew from 36–41 per cent in the late 1950s, to 41–45 per cent in the mid-1960s, and to 47–51 per cent in the early 1970s. The story is similar in the UK, with average turnover rates in some businesses running at 50 per cent or more by the mid-1980s (Gardner and Sheppard, 1989).

As I have indicated, the reorganization of staffing in sales occupations since the early 1960s has been orientated towards maximizing sales output per employee while reducing labour costs. As a result of this process, most major high street multiples have tended to cluster around a Taylorian mode of organizing employment. In other words, they have tended to practise an intense division of labour, a pronounced centralization of command, surveillance and control, and have reduced significantly the degree of discretion exercised by shopfloor personnel and by store managers as well. The regulation of shopfloor workers has taken a number of forms mostly involving direct supervision, combined with bureaucratic control techniques and more 'anonymous' panoptical surveillance technologies (the labour monitoring facilities of EPoS, for example). All these techniques are indicative of what Alan Fox (1974) termed 'low-trust' employment relations.

For retailers, the development of 'retail engineering' in the pursuit of competitive advantage – through concentration, centralization and cost reduction, in conjunction with the deployment of EDP technologies – has been associated with employment policies that facilitate and enhance the 'low-trust' direction and surveillance of flexible, easily substitutable salesfloor labour. The detrimental effects that these policies have had in terms of labour turnover, commitment and motivation have not been of much concern to retail employers, on the whole. By concentrating so markedly on labour utilization rather than its effectiveness, retailers have shown little interest in whether or not the employee identified with the aims and objectives of her or his employing organization. Rather, they have been concerned with fostering a greater sense of identification and 'loyalty' between customers and their own particular retail 'offering'.

In the following section I suggest that, as the battle for market share within the retail industry is increasingly articulated as a struggle for the imagination of the consumer, so labour effectiveness is now coming to be seen as a major source of competitive advantage by a growing number of retailers. In other words, new attempts by retailers to 'make up' the consumer also have repercussions for the ways in which the work-based subject of retail is produced and regulated.

### Retail: from 'numbers' to 'souls'

Until the late 1970s and early 1980s, most multiple retailers continued to pursue merchandising policies aimed at what they perceived to be a homogeneous market. The emphasis was on building sales by continuous cost and price reductions: the 'pile it high, sell it cheap' philosophy of mass merchandising. However, as concentration within the industry increased, the scope for competition on price alone was consequently reduced. Aggressive competition on price in the late 1970s produced price wars and, in the context of high inflationary times, led to decreasing profit margins in both food and non-food trade (Bamfield, 1987; Davies and Howard, 1988). However, when inflation did begin to fall in the early 1980s and disposable income grew among those lucky enough to be in paid employment, multiple retailers were faced with another problem. The higher income groups benefiting most from the Thatcherite turn were 'trading up', making more specialized demands on retail markets. The mass merchandisers found themselves in trouble as demand swung in favour of the specialist retailer (Segal-Horn, 1987).

In order to stay competitive in this environment, retailers began to seek ways both of differentiating themselves from one another on terms other than price, and of moving up-market in order to appeal to those consumers with high levels of disposable income. The policies they pursued to this end encouraged the transformation of retail from dull, distributive cypher to culture industry and hence the progressive dislocation of production and consumption. The battle for market share was rearticulated, first and foremost, as a struggle for the imagination of the consumer. 'Getting it right' economically meant getting it right culturally – offering a carefully coordinated 'unique' image, identity and atmosphere to diligently targeted 'lifestyle' consumer groupings. From thinking of customers 'only in terms of numbers', retailers also began to calculate 'in terms of the soul' (Fitch and Woudhuysen, 1987). The successful expansion of the retail industry was to be 'customer led', achieved through interventions aimed in part at the subjectivity of the consumer. Hence the increased importance of the symbolic expertise of marketing, design and advertising, underpinned by the knowledges and techniques of subjectivity, to recent developments within the retail sector.

### *Symbolic expertise in the service of retail*

The disciplines of marketing, design and advertising have played a major role in retailers' attempts to differentiate themselves from one another and to become more customer focused. As indicated earlier, their foremost contribution to developments within the sector in the past decade has been through the discourse of 'lifestyling', the combination of design and visual communication with techniques of market segmentation.

Through an assemblage of socioeconomic classification, (geo)demographics and, perhaps most importantly, 'psychographic' attitudinal and perceptual research, marketing experts group consumers into discrete 'aspirational clusters' that go on to form the basis of retailers' target market segments, or 'niches'. As Dick Hebdige has indicated, intensive forms of contemporary lifestyle research are designed to offer a 'social map of desire'. They have been developed quite deliberately to cut across traditional socioeconomic polarities and to constitute in their place a new version/vision of 'the social': 'They depend for their success on the accurate outlining and anticipation (through observation and interviews with "target" subjects) not just of what some people think they want but of what they'd like to be' (Hebdige, 1989: 53).

A retailer's 'market position' is its response to the map of desire of its target customer segment. The production of a market position

> requires a co-ordinated 'statement' to be made by merchandise selection, trading format, customer services and customer communications. The more closely the customer can identify with the 'offer' presented, the more 'comfortable' the customer will be, and he will respond in terms of shopping frequency, size of spend per visit and the proportion of total spend allocated to the favoured store and its competitors. (Knee and Walters, 1985: 16)

If, in the lifestyling process, the expertise of marketing and market research is primarily responsible for delineating and monitoring the maps of desire of targeted consumer groups, that of design and visual communication is responsible for creating a 'total image or look' for the retailer which will articulate these desires and translate them into sales. As the directors of one of Britain's leading design companies, Fitch-RS, have written:

> Design is about capturing the consumer's imagination. Through this, the consumer's time and his disposable income is captured. Design thus deals in the issues which come closest to a human being's personal reality. Designing is about needs and desires, about social circumstances; it is about touching people in the heart as well as in their pockets . . . The challenge, then, is for retailers to *use* design not as a cosmetic, but to understand the individual within the community or the catchment area and to provide for his or her behavioural, aspirational and lifestyle needs . . . Design is a way of communicating: design is sensory – people can touch it, feel it, experience it . . . In other words, design talks to people. This is the ultimate strategic significance of design to modern retailing. (Fitch and Woudhuysen, 1987)

For Fitch and Woudhuysen (1987), retailers are in the game of theatre 'or they are nothing'. For them, design is a central component in the transformation of retail into Britain's premier 'pleasure' industry.[10] The design function is not limited to interiors, signs and store planning, however; it also plays a key role in many aspects of the supply chain, including graphics, packaging, corporate identity planning and branding. Increasingly, retail design teams are linking up with suppliers to develop ranges which meet the retailer's overall 'offering' and 'statement' (Segal-Horn, 1987; Sabel, 1990). Again, the emphasis is on presenting a 'totally consistent image' in order to win over the target consumer group.

Advertising also plays a crucial role in promoting this aim. Indeed, the changing form and content of retail advertising is indicative of the 'cultural logic' driving developments within the industry. Retailers have traditionally been significant advertisers in the market place. By 1989, for example, nine out of the top 20 advertised brands were those of retailing organizations (*Retail Week*, 13 July 1990). A report in the advertising industry trade paper *Campaign* (3 May 1991: 4) announced, 'the top spending brands in Thatcher's Britain were always the retailers.'

Whereas in the 1970s retail advertising focused almost exclusively on mass-market pricing, the 1980s saw a pronounced shift towards 'lifestyle' advertising. Associated with this change was a greater use of televisual media by retailers, 'with its impeccable "image-building" credentials', rather than a wholesale reliance on local and national black and white press advertising (*Retail Week*, 13 July 1990). According to industry commentators, retailers have become aware

> that a market position based solely on price advantage can be difficult to maintain, and will not necessarily insulate them against innovation and increased competition in the marketplace. This has led to a distinction in retail advertising between 'product/price' and 'image/added value'. Essentially this involves selling the store as well as what is in the store. (*Retail Week*, 13 July 1990)

As more retailers have moved towards the latter option they have also become increasingly interested in television, for 'the selective use of television can enhance a retailer's ability to differentiate his offering in an increasingly competitive market' (*Retail Week*, 13 July 1990).

Two well-known television campaigns from the early 1990s illustrate traditional 'pile it high, sell it cheap' mass merchandisers taking the 'image/added value' approach in order to attract more affluent customers. Woolworths regenerated its children's clothes range with the aid of a series of 'junior lifestyle' adverts focusing on the up-market Ladybird brand. Meanwhile, Tesco attempted to highlight its 'exclusivity' and its 'quality' and 'green' credentials in a series of adverts centred around Dudley Moore's Euro-odyssey in search of an elusive free-range chicken. 'Desperate to distance itself from its "pile it high, sell it cheap" past, Tesco's doubled spend to emerge as 1990's biggest spending brand' (*Campaign*, 3 May 1991: 4).

These bids by retailers to differentiate themselves from their competitors were simultaneously attempts to appeal to more affluent consumers. Indeed, while the expertise of lifestyling constructs many different customer clusters, these groupings were not accorded equal weight. During the 1980s and early 1990s, for example, it was those enjoying relatively high levels of disposable income who tended to dominate lifestyle advertising. However, the important point to remember is that lifestyling has no necessary class affiliation.

The prolonged economic recession in the UK saw 'value for money' emerge as a major terrain of competition between multiple retailers. At first sight, the emergence of a concern with price appears to suggest the return of a 'pile it high' mass-market mentality among retailers. However, the crucial point about contemporary 'value for money' strategies, particularly those developed by the multiple food retailers, is the central role they allocate to choice. In other words, 'value for money' tends to refer to a particular product range – with its own brand image – that exists alongside a wealth of alternative 'branded' versions of the same basic product. So, 'value for money' doesn't dictate the entire look of the store – as 'pile it high' does – but is simply one among a range of options that the consumer can choose to 'buy into'. Alternatives are always available. Indeed, choice is not compromised but rather expanded. In this sense, contemporary 'value for money' advertising is not a break with but a development of lifestyling. 'Value for money' is a lifestyle option – a choice – among a range of options all of which are available within the space of one store.

As indicated earlier, the expertise of marketing, design and image construction, underpinned by knowledges and techniques of subjectivity, constitute consumers as individual actors seeking to maximize the worth of their existence to themselves by assembling a lifestyle (or lifestyles) through personalized acts of choice in a world of goods and services. Each commodity is imbued with a personal meaning, 'a glow cast back upon those who purchase it, illuminating the kind of person they are, or want to become' (Rose, 1990: 19). For these 'ideal-typical' consumers, therefore, shopping is an integral component of their 'life project', of their 'investment orientation to life' (Featherstone, 1990). For them, shopping is not a troublesome chore but a pleasurable experience and pre-eminent skill.

Of central import here is the view of self attributed to these 'ideal-typical' consumers. They are represented as 'consuming' or 'enterprising' subjects who make a project of their lives: they calculate about themselves and work upon themselves in order to better themselves (Rose, 1989). They seek to 'maximise and experience the range of sensations available' and are fascinated with 'identity, presentation and appearance' (Featherstone, 1990: 91). 'Today's consumers' want 'self-expression and self-fulfilment' and 'demand greater choice and specialisation' (Walters and Knee, 1985: 11). They cry: 'Don't regiment me. Don't institutionalise me. Treat me as an individual ... Today's consumers take a more qualitative, more judgemental, more egocentric view than once they did.' 'We are more leisured, more middle class, more demanding ... and we want to keep away from, as well as up with, the Jones's, we want to be individuals' (Fitch and Woudhuysen, 1987).

As articulated by the expertise of symbolic mediation, it is this dynamic, narcissistic view of self as project, as object to be continually worked on and improved, which underpins contemporary 'change' programmes in the retail sector. Expertise translates the 'consumer's search for expression and identity' into specific retail demands: for 'greater choice', 'better quality', for a more personalized, pleasurable shopping environment and experience. In turn, these demands are transmuted into specific programmes of intervention and rectification by retailers: customer care programmes, shop refurbishments, expanded product ranges, quality initiatives and the like.

### 'Close to the customer': retail's 'constitutive outside'

If, as the experts of symbolic mediation argue, consumers will only ally themselves with retail 'offers' to the extent that they construe them as enhancing their own skills of self-realization, self-presentation and self-direction, then the success of retail enterprise depends increasingly upon its ability to stay 'close to the customer'.

However, staying close to the customer is more than a matter of logistics: 'in the battle to capture consumers' spending it is becoming increasingly vital to capture their hearts and minds as well. And the only way to achieve this task is with vastly improved customer service' (*Retail Week*, 30 November 1990). In other words, labour effectiveness, the quality of personal service provided by sales floor assistance, is an increasingly vital component of the 'value added' approach to achieving competitive advantage. According to industry consultants, however, the provision of quality service

> can only come from employees who are committed to giving it. It cannot be ordered or forced on them. There are myriad 'moments of truth' in the chain of contact between the consumer and company. Management cannot stand behind people every second of the day to check that they are making the most of these moments of truth. Service can only be rendered in an efficient, cheerful and high quality way by people who feel the customer is important and are committed to doing their best. (Martin and Nicholls, 1987: 81)

Thus, staying 'close to the customer' also means gaining 'productivity through people', 'treating the rank and file as the root source of quality and productivity gain' (Peters and Waterman, 1982: 14). In order to win the 'hearts and minds' of consumers, retailers must now also 'win over' their front-line employees. An editorial in the trade journal *Retail Week* (6 July 1990), devoted to the subject of 'service', argues that 'even the most relevant plan for improving customer service issuing forth from head office will come to nothing unless those on the shopfloor are carried along with the spirit as well as the letter of any plan.' However, for retailers, the pursuit of competitive advantage has long been associated with 'low-trust' employment relations. As indicated before, retail employers have practised an intense division of labour, a pronounced centralization of command, surveillance and control and have significantly reduced the degree of discretion exercised by shopfloor personnel. Overall, the emphasis has been on the close direction and surveillance of flexible, easily substitutable sales floor labour with little attention being paid to the detrimental effects that these policies have had in terms of labour turnover, motivation and commitment.

The paradox of 'lifestyle' marketing is that it is now this very commitment and motivation which is required from staff in order to ensure the delivery of 'quality service'. An employment policy which focuses on labour utilization to the detriment of labour effectiveness is no longer seen to be consistent with the aims and objectives of staying 'close to the customer' and eliciting 'productivity through people'. Thus retail management is faced with the classic dilemma between the need to exercise control over the workforce, while at the same time requiring its enthusiastic commitment to corporate objectives. As Hyman (1987: 41) has argued, the close direction, surveillance and discipline of labour is more likely to destroy, rather than guarantee, the mobilization of discretion and diligence among the workforce. The emerging tensions between employment relations based on 'low-trust' substitutability of labour and the importance of 'service' in a customer-led retail 'strategy' are evident in Thierry Noyelle's (1987: 47) analysis of the US retailer R.H. Macy & Co.

> The reorganization of staffing in sales after the mid-1960s was oriented towards maximizing sales output per employee while containing labor costs. But the emphasis on limited sales force attachment to the company has tended to run counter to the level of employee involvement needed to maintain high standards of work quality. Quality needs to be restored if productivity is to rise again. This parallels the company's need both for re-emphasizing service as part of its upscaling strategy and for adding qualified sales personnel because the trend toward multiplication of product classifications has rendered the sales task a more demanding one than in the past.

If the 'emotional labour' of customer service cannot be fully secured or effectively guaranteed through a system of close supervision and formal rules, then other systems which 'attempt to minimize the potential area of error in the exercise of discretion' have to be brought to bear (Hochschild, 1983; Townley, 1989). This suggests a shift in emphasis away from formal direction as to how work *must be done* to 'implicit' expectations as to how work *should be done*; in other words, towards a system of indirect normative regulation, or 'government at a distance' (Miller and Rose, 1990).

When regulation takes place through close supervision and technical rules 'it is hardly a problem should the worker possess a distinct cultural identity'. However, once regulation is through 'the worker's "normative orientations"', the necessary control in work will depend on the removal of any basic cultural differences between him and his superiors' (Wickham, quoted in Townley, 1989: 106). In other words, normative regulation rests upon an identification between the individual employee and the goals and objectives of his or her employing organization. Employees 'must become aware of their central role in adding value to products and service through quality labor and to be able automatically, as if by second nature, to balance competing demands for highly individualized quality service and bottom line financial considerations' (Fuller and Smith, 1991: 13). Here the onus on direct control is transformed into an emphasis on 'culturally' produced *self*-control. Thus, the government of the retail enterprise now comes to operate through the 'soul' of the individual employee. In other words, staying 'close to the customer' and gaining 'productivity through people' require the social relations of employment within the retail industry to be re-imagined, the internal world of the retail enterprise to be reconceptualized.

## Conclusion

Over the past decade retailing has played a major role in spearheading the progressive penetration of the market into all areas of British life, encouraging and facilitating the spread of consumer culture. In the process, the relationship between what is thought of as properly 'economic' and what is thought of as properly 'cultural' has been transformed. Today, shopping has emerged as Britain's foremost leisure pursuit, and an ever-increasing proportion of the total number of goods produced comprises cultural goods, created to be, and purchased as, indicators of the individuality of taste and sense of style of the enterprising 'sovereign' consumer.

In contemporary British retailing there is no longer any room for the base/superstructure dichotomy as traditional distinctions between production and consumption have become increasingly dislocated. Retailing is increasingly a *hybrid* activity; which is to say that what is properly 'economic' and what is properly 'cultural' about retailing are inseparable, notably because, as we have seen, contemporary economic success in retailing is premised upon the production of meaning.

In other words, as the battle for market share within retailing is increasingly articulated as a struggle for the *imagination of the consumer*, the success of the retail enterprise becomes consequent upon the ability to 'win over', or more accurately 'make up' the consumer. The development of 'retail engineering' has allowed retailers to delineate and monitor consumer desires more intricately than ever before and to expand significantly the range of 'mass-produced individualities' on offer. However, staying 'close to the customer' is not just a matter of logistical engineering – of 'physical proximity' as one commentator has put it – but also of 'emotional proximity' (*Retail Week*, 31 August 1990: 2).

In attempting to 'make up' the consumer, retailers are therefore driven to 'win over' those charged with providing on-site 'emotional proximity' (the quality 'emotional labour' of servicing work): retail employees. In a truly relational manner, interventions aimed at the subjectivity of the 'enterprising' consumer have repercussions for the ways in which the work-based subject of retail is produced and regulated. Staying 'close to the customer' isn't simply a matter of 'logistical engineering' since it also implies 'engineering the soul' of the retail employee, to ensure that he or she automatically delivers the highly individualized quality service 'demanded' by the enterprising consumer.

In Chapters 6 and 7 I explore the implications of these shifts in the government of organizational life in retailing. Drawing on original research, these chapters build a picture of the ways in which contemporary discourses of organizational reform take hold in a particular context, describe how the dreams and schemes they articulate are put into operation, indicate how these discourses construct particular identities for different categories of employee and explore the ways in which the latter negotiate these identities in their everyday working lives.

## Notes

1 Retail is now one of the largest industries in the UK. By 1984, over one-third of national output came from retail sales and throughout the 1980s turnover in retailing shares on the stockmarket was one of the highest of all groups (Segal-Horn, 1987: 13).

2 The share of multiples in the UK grocery trade, for example, rose from 42 per cent in 1970 to 70 per cent in 1985, while the independents fell from 43 per cent to 18 per cent in the same period. Moreover, by 1988 the top five food retailers alone accounted for 70 per cent of the market (Gardner and Sheppard, 1989: 26).

3 Despite vociferous protestations from manufacturers about the deleterious effects of increased retailer power on the country's manufacturing base, the government (in the form of the Monopolies and Mergers Commission and the Office of Fair Trading) recently ruled that growing retailer buying power does not pose a threat to consumer choice. Given the government's continued attachment to expanding the rights of the 'sovereign consumer', and the 'culture of the customer', this judgement should come as no surprise (Grant, 1987: 44).

4 Retailing consists of the following basic functions: stockholding; assembly and break-up of loads; transport; purchase and sale. The retailer is therefore driven towards maximizing the speed-up of these operations to the point of final consumption (as well, of course, as increasing total consumption).

5 Shopfloor workers were not the only employees affected by these wide-ranging changes. The work of store management has also been subject to rationalization. The degree of control and discretion exercised by managers over a wide range of activities and decisions at store level has been considerably reduced as the greater 'visibility' available to head office from the introduction of EDP technologies, for example, allows senior management to engage in increasingly 'systemic' surveillance of the whole retail process. Typically, establishment managers in the multiple retailers have little or no say over the number of lines carried in-store, their selection or their layout. They also have a significantly reduced input into decisions about promotions, pricing, window display, staff budgets, marketing, store design and decoration and delivery schedules. On the whole, they are left with 'controlled' responsibility for sales maximization and cost control in-store (including facilitating the continuous flow of trading information to centralized departments), as well as responsibility for various people management functions, and the general atmosphere and appearance of the store (S. Smith, 1988).

6 Despite the oft-voiced claims of the major retailers to be the key employment generators of the new service economy, there has been a long-term decline in the total retail workforce since the early 1960s. As the processes of concentration, centralization and rationalization proceeded within the industry, the numbers of people employed fell. With the large multiples controlling a bigger share of the market, a greater proportion of sales is concentrated in a smaller number of shops, employing fewer people. Between 1961 and 1986, for example, the number of people employed in retail dropped by 300,000. During the same period, however, sales per employee rose by 250 per cent, on average, from £17,800 to £44,500 (Sparks, 1987; Gardner and Sheppard, 1989: 187).

7 While investment in EPoS technology in West Germany rose by 21 per cent between 1989

and 1990, investment in the UK rose by more than 40 per cent during the same period 'from a base nearly twice that of Germany' (*Retail Week*, 19 September 1990: 22).

8 It needs to be stressed that, contrary to traditional labour process analysis (Braverman, 1974), the workforce control implications of EDP technology are not the main objectives of its introduction in the UK but rather a means, and frequently a by-product, of 'the search for flexibility and adaptability in labour costs by the matching of labour inputs to customer demand or output' (Walsh, 1988: 36). Similarly, in a study of retail work in the USA, Bluestone and Huff Stevenson (1981: 39) argued that deskilling in the trade was not a primary goal in and of itself but was a by-product of other changes, in particular, cost-cutting.

9 The pattern that emerges within the trade is of, on the one hand, a 'core' comprising a small group of mostly white men who exert a large degree of control over access to well-paid managerial and professional occupations, and, on the other, a quite finely differentiated 'secondary' group which comprises both full-time and, increasingly, part-time and temporary, unskilled, low-paid, (on the whole) non-unionized, mainly female workers (but also some groups of men, especially minorities and young men).

10 Similarly, Anita Roddick, founder of the lifestyle chain, *Bodyshop*, describes shops as theatres where the shopfloor is a stage on which both shop assistants and customers are acting, and where the look, the smell, the space and the backdrop are all important ingredients of the shopping experience. For her, shops must be cultural venues, arenas of sociality, and not just sites where money and goods change hands.

# 6

# Re-imagining Organizational Identities

In Chapter 5 I argued that the struggle for market share within contemporary British retailing is increasingly articulated as a battle for the imagination and loyalty of the enterprising consumer. In attempting to stay 'close to the customer' – to achieve an organic 'emotional' and 'physical' proximity – retailers are simultaneously making up new ways for people to be both 'inside' and 'outside' the workplace. Interventions aimed at, and constituting, the subjectivity of the enterprising consumer have repercussions for the ways in which the work-based subject of retailing is produced and regulated. In other words, in contemporary British retailing, production and consumption relations and identities are increasingly dislocated.

In the following two chapters I draw upon my own empirical research in the retail sector to explore this current dislocation and to examine how people are presently 'made up' at work. In keeping with the framework I outlined in the first part of this book, my analysis of consumption and identity at work is structured around two intersecting vectors. The first of these is the vector of 'labelling from above', while the latter is the vector of the 'actual behaviour of those so-labelled'.

In this chapter, I will be concentrating upon the first of these two vectors, by delineating and examining the programmatic aspirations of senior management in contemporary retailing and by articulating the various 'technologies of government' through which these aspirations are put into operation. I argue that the internal world of the retail enterprise is being re-imagined through the managerial discourse of 'excellence', as a place where productivity is to be enhanced, customers' needs satisfied, quality service guaranteed, flexibility enhanced and creative innovation fostered through the active engagement of the 'self-actualizing' impulses of all the organization's members. I suggest that store managers and shopfloor employees within retailing are increasingly being reconceptualized as 'enterprising' subjects: self-regulating, productive individuals whose sense of self-worth and virtue is inextricably linked to the 'excellent' performance of their work and, thus, to the success of the company employing them. In other words, I argue that the contemporary 'making up' of the work-based subject as an 'enterprising self' is both the medium and outcome of the contemporary dislocation of production and consumption relations within retailing.

## The culture of the customer in retailing

Although retailing in the USA, Britain and many parts of continental Europe is highly concentrated, being increasingly controlled and dominated by a few large companies, it is not particularly homogeneous and can be disaggregated into a number of broad varieties of business. Given the obvious positional differences in the UK, for example, between a super-market chain such as Asda, and a department store like Harrods, it may seem ridiculous to suggest that they share a similar rationality of govern-ment. Yet the language deployed by senior management in both organiz-ations to describe their aspirations, and the techniques and practices through which they intend to achieve them, are analogous. The importance attributed by both to strategic thinking, customer service, cultural change, excellence, quality and ownership indicates a similar approach to the conduct of retailing.

At Harrods, for example, a stated 'commitment to excellence' in customer service, as part of a 'wider strategic change programme', led in the late 1980s to their personnel director visiting the Disney Corporation in the USA – one of Peters and Waterman's (1982) 'excellent' companies – in order to explore the possibility of transposing certain elements of their 'service through people' theme to the Knightsbridge store.[1] On his return, senior management were informed that the 'language' of Disney was absolutely right for Harrods. 'There are big similarities between Orlando and Knightsbridge', it was argued; 'like Disney, Harrods is really theatre.' It was important, the personnel director felt, for staff to realize that they were part of an 'amazing' and 'spectacular' show, a living piece of British history, and that they were engaged in producing that show for their 'guests', the customers, every minute of every trading day. It was therefore essential for the company to recruit the right sort of staff, people who would 'internalize' the 'Harrods' culture', who could 'believe in it and become part of its history and prestige'; people that would learn to feel 'ownership'. By following the Disney corporate ethos, Harrods and its 'family' of employees would therefore become more cohesive, productive, efficient and effective. In other words, through striving for excellence in customer service, Harrods as a business, and its employees, as individuals, would become more enterprising.[2]

At Asda, on the other hand, while the emotional aspirations were (unsurprisingly) more modest, the customer orientation was equally strong.

> We are in the business of satisfying people with things that they want to buy; we are not in the business of major excitement. Yes, it's very good to get interest in the stores and we are very mindful of creating a sympathetic environment . . . Yes, they want to be stimulated and interested but it's not the same experience as shopping in the high street for fashion goods. It doesn't mean to say that we go back to pile it high, sell it cheap, it means that you have to understand the frame of mind that the consumers are in when they visit the store . . . That means that we have to have an organisation structure which enables us to understand what it is that makes consumers tick, what it is so that we can organise our business

accordingly . . . Customer service is now right up front at the store, is very important, and will be a differentiating factor increasingly. We are looking very hard at the ways in which we can be innovative in delivering better services to the customers . . . The culture of service is the interesting thing . . . not recruiting whoever you can find and then trying to craft customer sensitivity and customer care onto them through training. One of the first things of all is to screen at the recruitment stage those people who are predisposed to serve.[3]

According to a former corporate marketing director at Asda, the emphasis on customer service was a crucial constitutive element of the company's move away from a 'pile it high, sell it cheap' philosophy towards a 'regenerated personality' based on quality: 'Quality has got to be paramount. People want more than range now, they want . . . good service. Expertise and quality credentials are much more important than talking about range or price.'[4] However, in attempting to 'put together an offer to match all our customers' needs', Asda was simultaneously making new demands upon its shopfloor employees. Thus 'the culture of service' that senior management envisaged demanded a new sort of work-based subject, a person 'predisposed to serve' in a manner appropriate to the reconceptualized 'personality' of Asda: to offer a highly individualized quality service to all Asda customers thus making them feel wanted and ensuring their loyalty. The move to a 'culture of service' therefore required paying more attention to the recruitment and training of employees as *individuals* and to their effective 'enculturation' into Asda's corporate norms and values. Again, the perceived excellence of Disney as a provider of 'service through people' was also utilized as a guide to action at Asda.

Disney Corporation recruit and interview people in threes to see how they interrelate one with the other, which is quite interesting. Then they spend a minimum of six weeks being trained in the business and then if they are good enough they are promoted to work on the check-out line, which is quite an interesting comparison. They even fired a girl the previous week because she was too introverted. She wasn't dishonest or inefficient, she just didn't get the requisite eye-contacts. It wasn't just about 'have a nice day', it was actually about making customers feel wanted. You walk around the average UK store and see assistants avoiding eye contact. I don't think we will necessarily be the same as the States in years to come but most certainly making people feel wanted in the store is going to be important.[5]

That retailers as different as Harrods and Asda can be seen to share a similar language for delineating and intervening in the retail domain is indicative of the power and pervasiveness of the language in question. For both companies it is through a particular rationality of government – recognizably entrepreneurial in character – that the conduct of retailing is being re-imagined and reconstructed.

'Enterprise' can be seen to provide senior management in these organizations, and the retail sector more generally, with a language which constitutes the problems of the retail domain and of the individual retail enterprise in such a way as simultaneously to offer itself as a solution to the problems it 'uncovers' and delineates. So the imperative to 'know thy customer' and 'learn from those whom you serve' constitutes the retail organization in a particular way, suggests specific means through which these imperatives might be operationalized and consequently makes up new ways for both customers and employees to conduct themselves within the retail domain.

As argued in Chapter 5, when 'customer satisfaction' becomes the benchmark by which retail success is judged, knowledge of the customer becomes increasingly crucial to competitive advantage. In recent years, those retail organizations judged to be staying 'close to the customer', assiduously tracking the market and responding, quickly and in a highly coordinated fashion, to emerging consumer trends, are heralded as the 'retail engineers' – representatives of 'best practice' and guides to action – by 'key' retailing 'opinion makers' such as industry consultants, the financial media and, most importantly, City analysts.[6]

In other words, 'retail engineer' is a term reserved for those companies deemed to be obtaining 'face-to-back visibility' throughout the production/ distribution/retail chain (and as a result blurring the traditional distinctions between production and consumption relations). Put simply, 'retail engineers' are those companies judged to be staying 'close to the customer', running their businesses in a 'market-driven' manner and hence governing in an enterprising manner.

As shown in Chapter 5, many of the constitutive elements of enterprise as a rationality of government are also central features of retail engineering. Of crucial significance is the privileged role attributed to the consumer within these discourses. Both advocate a range of interventions – the implementation of 'strategic management', changing the 'corporate culture' and so forth – aimed at saturating the 'enterprise' with the voice of the customer. A precise fit between the goods and services provided by the company and the lifestyle of the consumer is to be sought and any space between them removed.

In the following sections I concentrate upon some of the mechanisms being deployed by retailers to ensure this fit between organization and customer. I also explore the effects that the institution of these mechanisms have upon the construction of identities at work. I begin by focusing upon the turn to 'strategy' within contemporary retailing.

### 'Doing the right things right': strategy in retailing

Developing a coherent and consistent strategy is increasingly represented as a major benchmark on the path towards becoming a retail engineer, both in terms of guaranteeing consumer satisfaction and in terms of City expectations of financial performance.[7] The assumed power of the discourse of 'strategic management' can be detected in the alacrity with which it has been taken up by retailers. Across the industry, from book-sellers to supermarket chains, high street multiples have begun to deploy the discourse of strategy in earnest (Knee and Walters, 1985; Johnson, 1987; Ogbonna and Wilkinson, 1988; Marchington and Parker, 1990).

At company *A* (a multiple mixed retailer whose core business is health and beauty), for example, the discourse of 'strategic management' began to be deployed by senior executives in the mid-1980s. At that time the company was coming in for considerable criticism from the City and the financial media with regard to a series of poor financial performances. As a director of the company expressed it

> in the mid 1980s, *A* was being criticized as a company that was pretty flat in terms of its performance. It was a mature chain and it wasn't going anywhere, and therefore the prognosis was not very good. You know, flat profits over a number of years. And that rattled us; we weren't very happy about that. We didn't consider ourselves as flat and boring but clearly the City, in particular, did: '*A* is looking lost', '*A* doesn't know where it's going', '*A* doesn't know what sort of store it is any more, *A*'s lost its way.' Those were the sorts of things being flung at us.[8]

Although senior management responded quickly to try to reverse these perceptions of the company, retrospectively – through the 'always already' strategic gaze – they considered their initial response to have been 'symptomatic rather than strategic'. Only once they 'sat down and formulated a proper business strategy deliberately written out in *customer terms*' – their Secure Shopping Strategy (SSS) – my synonym deployed to respect confidentiality – did they feel able to begin to 'turn the company round in the eyes of the City'.

Similarly, at company *B* (a young women's wear division of a major clothing-to-department-store group) the language of strategy was also a comparatively recent development. In this case, developing a strategy was a response to (and, in turn, constitutive of) projected changes in the company's target market. At the same time, the managing director of the company stressed that the strategy was developed explicitly for the attention of the Board of Directors of its parent company. 'Getting strategic' was a way of projecting an aura of being 'in control' and of being 'enterprising' to the 'big boys at HQ' who were responsible for setting many of the financial, and other, guidelines within which *B* had to operate. At the same time, developing a strategy was considered a way of 'stealing a march' on the other divisions within the group, none of whom, at that stage, had begun to develop a business strategy, and who therefore looked less than 'market driven' by comparison.[9]

For senior management in both companies *A* and *B*, the deployment of strategic discourse was designed to demonstrate to various 'significant others', as well as to themselves and their own staff, exactly how 'in command' they were. In other words, the development of a corporate strategy was intended to indicate the degree to which their management of the business was increasingly 'enterprising'.

To describe strategy in retailing simply in these terms may give the impression that 'strategy' is nothing but a 'floating signifier' with no 'real' material referent, or material effects. However, this is not the impression I wish to convey. First, as the examples cited above indicate, to consider the discourse of strategy as 'immaterial' fails to perceive the very *real* sense in which 'image' and 'identity' management are crucial components of doing business in the modern world. If you can't speak it – 'strategy', 'excellence' etc. – then other people may think you haven't got it. Secondly, and more importantly, the discourse of strategy defines its object. In other words, the activity of retail management does not exist objectively and therefore meaningfully outside its dominant discursive articulation. The deployment of strategic discourse in the retail industry redefines and reconstructs what it means to be engaged in the activity of retailing. Rather than maintaining some 'real' or original identity outside of its dominant discursive articulation, retailing assumes a *new identity* through its constitution in strategic discourse.

As Knights et al. (1991: 10) have argued, the language of strategy is one in which the

> 'external' and 'internal' environment are reconstituted as a problem for which strategy offers itself as a solution. This solution takes the form of constituting and monitoring the environment in ways that produce 'knowledge' which is then used as the basis for the organization to construct strategic plans as a framework and guide to its activities. But an effect of strategic discourse is to constitute the organization and the individual subject as self-consciously aware of the competitive struggle for power and to render them 'open' to techniques of rational control and evaluation in its pursuit.

Thus, the subject of strategy – whether organizational or individual – is very much an 'enterprising' subject: a calculating, self-reflexive, 'economic' subject; one that calculates about itself and works upon itself in order to better itself.

At company *A*, for example, the development of strategic thinking was linked to an 'avalanche of printed numbers' (Hacking, 1983). The collection, collation and utilization of increasing amounts of (and the increasing quality of) information – the production of knowledge – was seen as a crucial component of the company's success. A variety of broadly 'informational' technologies – external (lifestyling) and internal (personnel auditing) market research, EPoS, Direct Product Profitability (DPP) and Value Chain Analysis – were deployed, the 'knowledge' produced from which was used to construct the company's Secure Shopping Strategy of 'Total Customer Responsiveness'.[10] So, for example, knowledge produced in this manner was used to construct a 'brand image' or 'personality' for the company, and a series of Secure Shopping Commitments (see Box 6.1), which were to act as a framework for all its activities. According to the company's merchandising director, research had shown that *A*'s personality was best imagined

> as the proprietor of our business. Controversially, she's a woman: attractive, mature, fashion conscious, friendly and approachable in a down to earth sort of way. She knows what she likes and what her customers like, and that's the sort of

Box 6.1    Company *A*'s Secure Shopping Strategy statement of commitment

# Secure Shopping

## Our Commitment
### A Better Buy at *A* – Satisfaction Guaranteed

*WELCOME*    A assures you of a very warm welcome. Our staff want to treat you as a guest, making your visit happy, and leaving you with a wish to return.

*QUALITY*    Our buyers are experts whose job is to examine products carefully, and require from our manufacturers just what we believe you would think to be the best quality for the money. Where necessary, we rigorously apply exacting quality assurance tests to ensure that our merchandise meets the standards we set. We do not sell any merchandise that we wouldn't be happy to use ourselves.

*PRICE*    We are constantly shopping the markets of the world, and we manufacture in our own factories, to bring you the value which cannot be beaten in your locality. We continually check our competitors to ensure that, for identical products, our prices are genuinely competitive. If you disagree, you have this assurance: you need only tell us, and we'll put it right for you.

*SELECTION*    In the ranges that we sell, we are confident that you will find what you want at A. As soon as fresh, new and exciting merchandise becomes available that meets our exacting standards – and yours – you will find it in our stores.

*INFORMATION*    At A you can learn all you want to know about the product you are interested in. We have knowledgeable staff. We are making our store layouts easier to follow, our merchandise displays easier to find and our signs and packaging easier to understand. All this will help you to be assured that you know before you buy.

*GUARANTEES*    It matters to us, as much as to you, that the product you buy from us performs fully to your requirements. If you aren't satisfied, please return with your sales receipt as soon as possible. We promise that we will do all that we can to put things right.

*PEACE OF MIND*    A's *Secure Shopping* has been designed to make it easier for you to get the things you need in life. A's *Secure Shopping* has been designed to take the worry out of shopping and put the pleasure back in.

merchandise she puts into her stores. It's tasteful, but not too ephemeral or outrageous, it's as up to date as it needs to be in a world where quality and durability are becoming more important . . . But neither she nor the merchandise she chooses is ever dull. Above all, our personality understands and cares for all her customers. She's sympathetic towards them and knowledgeable when they are making a serious purchase. She's also fun, and, occasionally, daring when they want to pamper themselves. And she's full of great and unusual gift ideas . . . This personality will be behind, and influence, every aspect of our retailing activity – our merchandise, the information we provide about it, the tone of our advertising and point of sale material, the way our staff talk to and greet our customers, our store layout and environment and our after sales service . . . This is *A* as we want our customers to think of her.[11]

According to senior managers at *A*, 'everything that happens' in the company is joined by the 'nodal point' of the SSS – or company 'personality' – and explicated in its terms. So, for example, when, in 1990, the company announced that hundreds of supervisory and middle management positions in-store were to be shed, this 'de-layering' programme was articulated as a fundamental element of *A*'s long-term strategy. There was no alternative. The redundancies were represented as an essential element of getting 'closer to the customer', of governing in an enterprising way: 'these changes were made to clarify accountability, increase flexibility and reduce bureaucracy.' Significantly, the changes were initiated as an empowering exercise for those 'at the sharp end of the business' – the shopfloor employees. They were being introduced, it was argued, as part of a long-term commitment by senior management to get in touch with 'some of the most important people in our business', to facilitate communication and participation, and to give those 'on the front-line' more power and autonomy in their work. Redundancy for some ('a tiny, tiny fraction of the total workforce'), while regrettable, was an empowering exercise for the majority, allowing them to experience 'ownership' and hence freely to service their customers more efficiently and effectively.[12]

According to the personnel director, news of the redundancies was well received both externally and internally because it was recognized to be of strategic importance:

Now the City, interestingly, received it very well. They knew what we were about, why we'd done it . . . As far as 'in-house' is concerned, one has to say, genuinely, that the vast majority of people, including those who are at the moment unlikely to have a job, have said 'we understand what you are doing, we know why you've done it, and we accept it. We're not happy about it, but we understand it.'[13]

'De-layering' was therefore represented as evidence of governing in an enterprising manner. *Not* to have shed the positions in question would have signified bad governance (sending the wrong signals to the City and other significant stakeholders). Meanwhile, the (mooted) 'acceptance' of the situation by those adversely affected had two major consequences. First, it legitimated the action of senior management and bolstered their claim to be governing 'strategically'. Secondly, it served further to constitute the individual employee as an enterprising subject of strategy. 'Acceptance' indicated that the individual employee was prepared to 'do the right thing' and govern her/himself in an enterprising manner.

Similarly, at Company *B* 'the strategy', as it was known, was designed to permeate all aspects of the business, reconceptualizing the internal world of the company and its relationship with its environment. 'The strategy' was based on results obtained from 'the largest piece of market research ever instigated by a division of the overall company'. The Strategy Review

Box 6.2   Strategic objectives of company *B*

# STRATEGY PAPER

## STRATEGIC OBJECTIVE

*B*'s aim is to be the most exciting and successful young fashion retailer in the world.

Our success will be measured by our ability to profitably increase our share of the stated target market of 15–24-year-old females in the UK. Additionally, international opportunities will be sought, researched, evaluated and progressed.

Increased market share will be achieved by identifying and fulfilling the wants and satisfactions of the stated target group in terms of:

Retail environment

Product

Service

document that formed a 'guide to action' was constructed by *B*'s board of directors in conjunction with external consultants who carried out a Brand Positioning and Personality Study for the company. Research from the latter revealed that the traditional market for *B*'s product – the 15–17-year-old young woman – was shrinking, while the top end of their target market, traditionally more marginal to the business – the 18–24-year-old woman – would become increasingly more important. However, it was this latter group that had proved most negative towards the company's present 'offer'. *B*'s 'noisy, fun, party image' which once they had enjoyed, it was argued, 'is a big turn-off for them now' because 'they're more aspirational, they're more individualistic, they want a more mature quality product and retail environment. They want a different shopping experience'.[14] Therefore 'the strategy' was designed to cater more to this target group by constructing a new 'personality' – physical and emotional – for *B*. This 'personality' was initiated to reflect the 'aspirational lifestyle' of this group but without losing too much of the 15–17-year-old market. Senior management hoped that the strategy would enable *B* to become 'a conveyor belt for young women from their teens to "thirtysomething"'.[15]

The strategic objectives of the company were condensed into a simple one-page statement of intent (see Box 6.2). In order to achieve these objectives and therefore 'satisfy the demands and aspirations of the target market', senior management argued that '*B* will need to address the issues simultaneously across all areas of the business.'[16] With this in mind it was decided that each area of the business would be encouraged to 'assess who its main customers were inside the business', and to set about providing the

best service possible to those customers. In effect, everything had to be
geared towards staying 'close to the customer' – both external and internal
– and, in particular, equipping the 'front-line' with the tools with which to
service the consumer in a quality manner. In this way the organization
would become more cohesive, more flexible, more accountable and, most
importantly, more profitable. Senior management viewed the strategy as
inaugurating 'a management revolution'. 'Communication, consultation
and participation' were the new watchwords of management style. The old
(and freely admitted) reactive authoritarianism of, what management
termed, JFDI (Just Fucking Do It) was out because 'the strategy'
demanded it.

> The strategy is becoming the structure of the business, in terms of all the things
> happening in the business being linked to one or more elements of the strategy
> we're trying to achieve. The strategy provides the overall rationale for every
> process in the business, the rationale for why we're doing something that was
> perhaps less obvious and less easy to associate with in the past . . . You've got to
> change your method of operating, change your approach. You've got to be more
> consultative, you've got to be bothered to take time to consult with people in
> other functions, to talk to them. I think once you've done it a few times you
> actually learn you can get a lot out of it. But it is a matter of people changing
> their style and I think it's all part of the strategy . . . You really have to learn a
> new language. It's not easy having to consult rather than just doing it yourself
> and banging it down the line. You have to think 'I should consult X, Y and Z on
> this', even though the temptation in a quick-direction changing organization like
> this is to do it yourself, because everything affects everything else. You have a
> trend in a garment area overnight and you have to deal with it on the retail side,
> and on the merchandise side etc. etc. It affects everyone so you all have to be
> more communicative, hanging it round a longer term framework, which is the
> strategy.[17]

The instigation of a new management induction programme at *B*
provides a simple illustration of the way in which the demands of the
strategy have restructured the internal world of the company. Before the
strategy was formulated, the training department had spent 18 months
designing a new induction programme for store managers. They had done
this largely under their own steam – it was seen as their own project. With
the advent of the strategy, the whole programme was reviewed and found
wanting. It didn't 'fit' with the objectives of the strategy. Neither its mode
of construction, nor its content was judged 'strategic'. The training department set about revising the programme, this time in formal consultation
with other functions, in particular its main 'customer', retail operations.
Rather than simply providing an updated introduction to the technicalities
of retail management at *B* – cash handling, systems and administration etc.
(the central elements of their first attempt) – the new programme was
considered 'strategy led'. It focused upon the importance of managers as
'inspirational leaders' and motivators of staff – the importance of obtaining
productivity through people if the company was to achieve its strategic
objectives – and stressed the necessity of store managers feeling 'personal
responsibility' for, and 'ownership' of, 'the strategy' in their own stores.

Through 'thinking and acting strategically', the training department created an induction programme that made up new ways for store managers to be at *B*.

> We're looking for managers with the right managerial skills. The fact that they can cash-up and do the admin. is not as important as being able to manage their team. To get the best out of their team. So having the right interpersonal skills and the right attitude. It's the management skills, the people skills that are most important to us now . . . The image and attitude being passed down now is one of empowerment. Managers should feel more ownership of the business at their level, to the degree that they're more responsible for it in terms of having their own budgets and recruiting and training their own staff.[18]

Thus, the deployment of strategic discourse can be seen to have an effect on identity at work. Within company *B*, the strategy sought a new type of manager and created different ways for staff to be at work. Staying close to the customer by 'satisfying the needs and aspirations of the target group' not only 'made up the customer' as a particular type – the aspirational individual etc. – it also demanded 'productivity through people'; it emphasized the importance of generating a greater sense of identification between staff and company and of encouraging every member of the organization to feel personally accountable for its success.

> The focus is very much 'inwards' in as much as we're trying to get people to, you know, 'Ask not what your country can do for you, but what you can do for your country' and to try and defuse this 'them' and 'us' between the centre and the areas and branches and make people, not 'make people', but try and give people an understanding of how they can pick things up for themselves and run with it. Yes, the centre will be looking at moving things forward but there's a lot of things that people can do for themselves. In effect, the centre becomes a facilitator for the areas and branches to get on with the job at hand, to feel 'ownership' of those jobs themselves.[19]

For senior management at *B*, the promulgation of a 'new culture of communication and consultation' was designed to ensure that high-quality, personal service could flourish in a business where improvements in operating efficiency had mainly been achieved through a rigorous centralization of control. By attempting, effectively, to give in-store staff responsibility, senior management sought to dispense with direct control – which was no longer deemed to be economically efficient – in favour of a culturally constructed form of self-regulation – the ultimate form of 'cheap government'. Store managers at *B* were redefined as skilled motivators of their staff, and encouraged to feel more personally responsible for the financial success of their own store.

> They [the shopfloor staff] need more areas where they can feel more involvement, where it's not a matter of being told exactly what to do. It's to give them more a sense of 'this is what we need to do, this is why we're doing it, these are going to be the benefits, how do you best think you can help?' . . . And giving them pieces of information and then saying: 'these are the guidelines, this is the result we have to achieve, but I'll leave it to you to do it as you think best fits. I'll leave it to *you*.' And letting them plan their own destiny. Not so much ordering directly,

otherwise it's all directives and there's no freedom at all. What we want is channelled freedom, self-management, ownership. We've got to get people to think and to participate with the business through their own decisions rather than somebody else's decision that's just being carried forward.[20]

At company *B* the demands of customer-led strategy were represented as inaugurating a shift in control away from direct JFDI dictat to a more 'trusting' communicative and consultative form of management, where individual self-development (for both store managers and shopfloor staff) and the achievement of strategic objectives were happily married. In other words, a more direct and authoritarian form of rule was to give way to a culturally controlled form of de-control, or enterprising 'government at a distance'. For senior management at company *B* and company *A*, being 'strategic' was a crucial mechanism for becoming more 'enterprising'; this attempt to be 'strategic' involved reconciling a rigorous centralization with a maximization of individual responsibility and initiative.

## Control at a distance

Another arrow in the quiver of contemporary organizational reform aimed at saturating the retail enterprise with the voice of the customer is the idea of 'cultural change'. In Chapters 2 and 3 I argued that 'culture' has emerged as a vital tool in attempts to restructure the internal world of organizations. 'Culture' is accorded a central role in attempts to stay 'close to the customer' because it is seen to structure the way people think, feel and act in organizations. The aim is to produce the sort of meanings that will enable people to make the right and necessary contribution to the success of the organization for which they work. To this end, managers are encouraged to view the most effective or enterprising organizations as those with the right culture – that specific ensemble of norms and techniques of conduct that enable the self-actualizing capacities of individuals to become aligned with the goals and objectives of the organization for which they work. In other words, the notion of 'culture' appears to offer the prospect of 'having one's cake and eating it too' (Peters and Waterman, 1982: 318) through aligning the individual's search for personal meaning with the goals and objectives of the organization for which he or she works.

Attempts to stay 'close to the customer' in retailing are constitutively linked to obtaining 'productivity through people'. It is 'culture' that provides the link. The quest for 'quality service' in contemporary retailing, for example, is represented foremost as a battle for the imagination, not only of the consumer, but also of the retail employee. The effective management of 'meanings', 'feelings' and 'beliefs' that I have spoken about is considered to be of crucial import to the delivery of this 'quality service' (Fuller and Smith, 1991; Allen and du Gay, 1994; du Gay and Negus, 1994).

At company *A*, for example, 'service' was increasingly viewed as one of the company's 'core values'. According to the merchandising director at *A*, the company shared 'the view of many commentators that service is becoming one of the really major differentiators chosen by retailers to achieve their competitive edge'.[21] However, senior management believed that a 'service orientation' could only come from shopfloor staff who were committed to giving it. It couldn't be ordered or enforced upon them. The logistics and geography of the business alone militated against the day-to-day direct supervision of shopfloor staff.[22] Thus, 'quality service' could only be fostered in the 'soul' of the retail employee and could not be simply imposed by managerial dictat. 'You have to get into people. It's this 'true involvement'. I emphasize the 'true' . . . That's the winner. You won't win by a stick. You won't win by a carrot. You'll only win by really making your people feel "I want to do this", not "have to", not "being attracted to", but "I want to". And that's really the key.'[23]

Increasingly, then, the relations of employment at company *A* were becoming 'matters of discourse' (Laclau, 1990: 185), 'getting the message across' to everyone to speak the same language – the universal discourse of Secure Shopping – and to identify themselves with the core values of the company through internalizing the corporate culture.

> You have to win hearts and minds, and it's jargon, I know, but hearts and minds, energies of every member of our staff, every single one, from those who've been with us for a long time, the cynics, the people who are always positive, the new joins that joined as a Saturday girl last Saturday in Middle Wallop, every one of them you want to win. A massive undertaking, obviously, and maybe you'll never get there, but, in principle, you had to do it so that all 40,000 odd people in *A* would eventually be singing from the same hymn sheet, in the same key, facing the same direction, knowing where they're going and you've got that harmony that says 'we're all in this together, it's a total team effort' . . . [And] you had to indicate as a company that you really meant it this time. Many companies issue a 'customer of the year' theme, or whatever. But this [the SSS] was forever. This was fundamental. And you had to get across to all our people that this is essential, that they are essential to it, that we are determined to see it through 'cause it's in everybody's interests: customers, staff, management, company, shareholders, the City. It's about us moving forward into the '90s, and, indeed, into the 21st century.[24]

For senior management at *A*, the 'responsibilizing' of staff to deliver quality service could only be achieved through the prior 'responsibilizing' of store management. Obtaining commitment at store level was seen very much as the task of individual store managers. With this in mind, managers were redefined as the effective 'owners' of their stores by being given their own budgets and performance targets, as well as responsibility for the recruitment and training of their staff. Managers were reimagined as 'inspirational leaders' motivating the 'heroes' on the front-line to deliver what the customers demanded: quality service. And, once again, individual responsibility and accountability was represented as simultaneously profitable and empowering.

> I think the pressure on line management to manage change is greater than it's ever been. That doesn't just apply to *A*. One could say that 10–15 years ago the

amount of fat in an organization was gross. Because the pressures weren't there there was a degree of relaxation. That has all changed and now you're in an ever-changing environment and you have to be ready to change, and change effectively. And pressure comes on line management to effect that change. Now we're as good as anybody, probably better than many, in terms of our selection processes, and in our training programmes for managers, but I don't under-estimate the difficulties that we have in making sure that in a thousand different sites around the country, our managers get the right message every time and communicate the message consistently and effectively. It isn't easy, and they don't always necessarily have the quality of people in every area to deliver Secure Shopping, no matter how good a manager they are. But I don't apologise for saying that managers, store managers, have more personnel requirement and more personal accountability and responsibility than they have ever had before, and quite right. We've had to devolve. I think we almost spoon fed the personnel aspect of management 10, 15 years ago, and we paid the price in a way. As far as the sales assistant, and the back shop person, is concerned in our stores the store manager is company *A*, and everything he or she portrays is what *A* is all about, and therefore it is so important that the store manager portrays the right image and conducts him or her self correctly and communicates effectively . . . And the more information we get back about our managers from staff, the tougher we'll be in getting the right managers. For *A* to throw out a store manager was unheard of. It happens now. We have to be fair to our staff, so much depends on them.[25]

Even at company *D* (a multiple mixed retailer whose core business is clothing and food), where the existence of a strong paternalist culture is deemed to have been a major element in the company's long-term success, the relationship between the organization and its members is being radically restructured to ensure 'total customer responsiveness'. The substantial welfare benefits enjoyed by staff in the past (and often represented as the main source of the company's higher than average productivity rates and substantially lower than average staff turnover rates) have increasingly come to be represented as just so much 'mollycoddling'. As one City analyst commented with regard to *D*'s paternalist policies: 'to a certain extent *D* has always been carrying a lot of fat, and it now looks as if it's time for a diet.' The implication of this and other City predictions was to signal to senior management at the company that a new regime was called for, more in tune with the 'realities of the market'. In other words, if they were to prove they were capable of governing in an enterprising manner, senior management at *D* would have to ditch the company's welfare mentality. Gradually, such a shift has begun to take place. The traditional paternalist culture has come to be imagined as fostering a 'dependency mentality', stifling the individual initiative and enterprise necessary for staying 'close to the customer' in an increasingly competitive retail environment. In a move reminiscent of neo-liberal attacks on the welfare state a senior executive at *D* argued that

> the 'Mother and Father know best' attitudes of the company are going. They were resented by intelligent, bright people in our business because, you know, mum and day don't always know best . . . We're on shifting ground and it's not what it used to be. If I could sum it up in a couple of words it is moving away

from many aspects of paternalism towards a culture of partnership. It is putting more responsibility onto individuals, in an area like development, for example, for their own self-development, to take responsibility for doing something about developing themselves; learning more about their job, more about the business, making themselves more aware about what's going on and less about waiting to go on a course to be told. And they could do that, individually, by during the course of, let's say, the appraisal process, discussing with their line boss their own preferences for further promotion, development and growth within the business, and areas that they could mutually agree should be addressed to actually get from where they are now to where they want to be, and then taking responsibility to seek out within the company all the facilities that there are available to go and get some of that.[26]

Senior management at *D* stressed that 'paternalism and bureaucracy' engendered the impression among store managers that if you kept your nose clean and did as you were told then everything would be just fine. This had to change they argued and the emphasis began to shift towards a more proactive conceptualization of the store manager's role, and that of individual shopfloor employees too:

within a store the best management do make our staff feel as if they have real, not only accountability, but authority – because one goes with the other – over the area they're responsible for. And we are making more changes in management structures [i.e. transferring more functional responsibilities on to the store manager etc.] which will actually reflect this demand for 'delegated responsibility' and encourage it further. It is increasingly recognized and rewarded in management so that people who operate in that way are promoted. Fifteen years ago people who operated in the other way [i.e. obeying orders to the letter, taking little personal initiative] would have been promoted.[27]

As developments at company *D* once again indicate, the discourse of enterprise – the development of a corporate enterprise culture – links together customer satisfaction, individual responsibility and accountability, self-development, economy and efficiency into a chain of equivalences. By making all employees more individually responsible for the success of the business, senior management at *D* assumed that everybody – from share-holders to cash 'n' wrap sales assistant – would benefit.[28] So, for example, head office costs would fall as certain functions, such as personnel, slimmed down and became facilitators to the front-line rather than dependency-inducing 'spoon-feeders'; and individual employees would be more productive as their own self-development became increasingly aligned to the development of the company as a whole, thereby simultaneously ensuring greater customer satisfaction and lower management costs. In sum, both individual and organization would become more enterprising.

Interestingly, it is at company *C* (a multiple niche retailer operating largely through franchises) that a culture of responsibilization and enterprise is perhaps most fully developed. *C* is a very atypical retailing organization in many ways. Senior management consider the company to have a 'wilfully perverse attitude to retailing', as do various significant others – the City, the media and other multiple retailers. As one City analyst recently commented: 'not many companies wait until they are capitalized at over £500 million before establishing a top-level management board, but then company *C* has never played it by the business school book.'

The company was born of, and continues to be dominated by, and infused with, the charismatic authority of its founder and managing director, a woman – an unusual enough situation in retailing – who views the business as a spiritual and moral project rather than just another retailing venture. *C* has a very distinct aesthetic and moral vision derived largely from the counter-cultural inheritance of the late 1960s and the politics of the new social movements in particular, which is deemed to permeate everything that happens in the business. However, this (distinctly New Age) 'spiritual' agenda is married to a very pronounced will to excellence, indicating that current trends in management discourse are in no way the exclusive property of New Right ideologies, as some have suggested (Silver, 1987; Legge, 1989). Indeed, senior managers at *C* regard the responsibilizing of staff as a radical empowering manoeuvre in distinct opposition to the doctrines of Thatcherism as they understand them. According to the managing director at *C*, the young people who work for the company:

> are in search of present day heroes or heroines. For them their work is about a search for daily meaning, as well as daily bread, for recognition as well as cash, for astonishment rather than torpor. They see the State has defined power as the power inherent in things – in tax revenue, in barrels of oil, in miles of road. These young people define power as the power inherent in dreams, in songs, in reach for the human spirit. They are open to leadership that has vision. (Company *C* internal documentation)

Once again the language is that of enterprise, but the political project that it articulates is very different from that advanced by the New Right (Heelas, 1992: 158ff). However, commonalities are forged in the sense that both share a vision of *how individual human beings should be*: active not passive, self-reliant, accountable and responsible for their actions.

For *C*'s managing director, the company has had to strive for excellence in all its activities because so much rides upon its continued existence, in particular its stated mission to '*educate consumers* to take an active stance on important moral issues', its 'community' work both in the UK and in developing countries, and its attitude towards the experience of work – providing 'a motivating and empowering experience for people at work'.

Although senior managers at the company were very aware of their need to placate the City and their shareholders, the development of a business strategy, built around the need for 'a culture of accountability', was represented, first and foremost, as a necessary move to avoid the company ever being taken over by 'the men in suits'. 'The Charter', as the strategy document was known, was designed to provide a structure and culture which would diminish the company's dependence upon its two founders – in the context of the rapidly increasing scale and scope of the company's operations – in particular, its managing director, by 'giving the business to its people'.

At the heart of the Charter was the idea of 'a culture of accountability' whereby every member of the organization was encouraged to become more responsible for the continued existence of the business and therefore the spiritual project it embodied. Concomitantly, increased individual accountability and responsibility was represented as the logical continuation of the managing director's vision that 'work' should empower, motivate and energize people. It was considered a means of 'infecting people with energy, excitement and enthusiasm for their jobs and the company'. By becoming more individually responsible, accountable, active and participative, every member of C could become a better worker, a better citizen and a better self.

The Charter was formulated by senior management as a series of interrelated 'principles of success'. These included caring, challenge, success, humanity and integrity. In order to ensure that every aspect of the business conformed to these principles, various working parties, or project teams, were initiated. These groups were made up of people from all levels and areas of the business directly elected by their peers. Their remit was to investigate current practice in a number of key areas of the business, and to formulate a future best possible practice in those areas in keeping with the principles of the Charter. So, for example, working parties were introduced to look at appraisal processes, induction, fundraising, environment and recruitment. The ideas emanating from these working parties were presented to the Charter Steering Committee which was made up of senior management who commented and advised on these proposals and steered them forward. This system was viewed as an aid to the reflexivity, cohesiveness, efficiency and economy of the company's operations, and as advancing the cause of individual self-reflexivity, development, responsibility and accountability of all the organization's members.

For senior management at C, the Charter was the *culture* of the company. It articulated the core values of the organization with which everyone was expected to identify.

> The culture of the company is described best in saying that there are different principles that should flow through everything that we do, and those principles are the Charter. And the Charter says we should try and challenge ourselves continuously. So it's a culture of challenge, accountability, innovation, integrity and caring. So it's committed to care in the community and care in the workplace, and interested in challenge both in the workplace and in the community . . . In terms of the feel of the company, there's a definite sense of family. The whole idea of the Charter was to bolster that sense of family. The whole idea that it was instituted, was founded on the MD and Chairman's fear that if anything happened to them that the company wouldn't continue in the same way. The MD made this video which was how the whole idea was launched. And she said: 'In 20–30 years' time I'm not going to be here to make sure that the shops carry on the way I want them to and you're the best ones to do it, because you know exactly how they should be carried on.' It's this whole 'it's yours as much as it's ours, and you have the power to make things happen'.[29]

This move towards personal responsibility, individual accountability and 'ownership' was evident throughout the company. In training and selection, for example, shopfloor staff were encouraged to play a much greater role. If store staff exercised more personal choice in creating the shopfloor team, it was argued, and took personal responsibility for training their fellow employees, then they would be more committed to their store, be more likely to serve customers in a friendly and professional manner, become more developed as people, and less able to offer excuses for poor performance. In turn, this would lead to a reduction in operational costs – fewer head office training professionals would be required, as would fewer management staff in-store – while individual employees would become more responsible for the success of their store.

> The company is very interested in us all becoming more accountable. That's how we're going forward, and that's what we've let the City know is happening. And, one thing, for example, is recruitment and selection, where the people choose the people they're going to be working for and with. And in the shops we're also letting the employees choose their colleagues. My department now has a very limited role in recruitment. We've basically devolved all responsibility for that and given it to the staff. Not so much to the management, but to the staff. So they're trained in watching auditions and that sort of thing.[30]

In every area of the business, no matter how apparently trivial, the drive for personal accountability was set to introduce changes in conduct. There was an awareness that responsibility and self-reflexivity did have financial spin-offs, but cost-cutting was not the main generator. The relationship of the individual to him or herself and to his or her company was the key. Being personally responsible was promoted as a virtue in itself: if everyone took care of themselves everything would take a turn for the better.

> yes, financially, I cannot deny we get strict objectives all the time but that is certainly not what is emphasized. It's not what people talk about. Accountability is all we hear about. Accountability means being responsible for yourself and being responsible for your job. Stop waiting to be told to do things, take the initiative and do things for yourself. Basically, becoming more enterprising. A very mundane example, I suppose, is the chairman went down to payroll where he discovered that the payroll supervisor spent incredible amounts of time answering phone calls about how much holiday time people had left, so this infuriated him. And he came up to our Charter meeting and he said: 'This is ridiculous. People have to be responsible for their own holiday. I don't want to know that people take the holiday allocated to them. If they take too much that's their problem. They're affecting people in their department and that'll sort itself out.' So what we do now is we all have our own holiday cards and people take individual responsibility for their own holiday entitlements. That's a petty example but it's indicative of the ideas that are being fed through everywhere. It's just take responsibility for yourself and your own job and take the initiative and go forward and stop asking for permission . . . But I would say the whole idea is not just accountability, but in actually making people become more accountable they're more worthy in their own eyes as well, from their own point of view as well as from the company's point of view.[31]

There was one programme at *C* which took this obsession with personal accountability to its logical conclusion. Senior management had come up with the idea of 'giving' a number of the company's centrally owned shops to staff to run as their own businesses in partnership with *C*. After six years the store would become a franchise – which management and staff could sell – but in the period leading up to that time the store would be run as a separate business – a franchisee only in terms of stock – with the management and staff earning all the profits from trading, over and above a 12 per cent management fee payable annually to company *C*. Although details of the programme had yet to be finalized, the process of preparing the selected stores for independence was firmly under way. An Ownership Development Programme had been initiated whereby a team of advisers reporting from head office would visit the stores in question

> preparing them with a special training package on how to become 'owners' in the sense of payroll, their profit and loss sheets etc. Everything like that . . . It'll be very interesting to see if all of a sudden they're not pushing for as many staff as they normally push for. Because they'll be able to see what business is really all about. They're having their security blanket removed whilst at the same time being given a chance to make more of themselves.[32]

Once again, facing the realities of the market was represented as an opportunity to develop oneself in a virtuous manner. The 'security' of central control was viewed as an impediment to the full realization of potential, and as an expensive and immoral illusion that could no longer hold:

> we've let them [store management and staff] be in their own little dream world to a certain extent as far as how the shop works is concerned . . . I would say that really the generator of this push forward is making people aware, because we realized . . . that people are just not aware. They're managing that shop, working in that shop, they're doing it, but they're not owning that shop at all. They are only just becoming aware of wage costs and how much of a percentage they have on the floor. So it's a push forward to make them more responsible.[33]

At company *C* the culture of accountability 'integrated the notions of economic health, serving customers and making meanings down the line' (Peters and Waterman, 1982: 103). However, the powerful 'aesthetic and moral vision' propagated by senior management only found life 'in details, not broad strokes' (Peters, 1987: 404). In other words, the culture of the company only functioned through particular practices and technologies, through 'specific measures' (Hunter, 1987). The discourse of enterprise takes a technological form, permeating a variety of often simple mechanisms – appraisal systems, communications groups, recruitment 'auditions' and application forms, for example – through which senior management in retail organizations seek to 'govern' the conduct of persons in order to achieve the ends they consider desirable.

As developments at company *C* illustrate, the discourse of enterprise brooks no opposition between the mode of self-presentation required of consumers, managers and employees and the ethics of the personal self. Becoming a better worker is the same thing as becoming a better self. In other words, under the regime of enterprise, *technologies of power* 'which determine the conduct of individuals and submit them to certain ends or domination, an objectivizing of the subject' – and *technologies of the self* – 'which permit individuals to effect by their own means or with the help of others, a certain number of operations on their own bodies and souls, thoughts, conduct, and way of being, so as to transform themselves in order to attain a certain state of happiness, purity, wisdom, perfection or immortality' – are imperceptibly merged (Foucault, 1988a: 18).[34] The value of self-realization, of personal responsibility and accountability, of self-promotion, self-direction and self-management are both personally attractive and economically desirable (Miller and Rose, 1990; Hollway, 1991).

In the final section of the chapter I want to focus in more detail upon the 'micro'-mechanisms through which the customer is brought into the space of the retail organization and how this process serves to blur traditional distinctions between work and consumption-based identities. In particular, I hope to show how these mechanisms seek to align the self-regulating and self-actualizing capacities of individuals as work-based subjects with the 'strategic' objectives – as delineated by senior management and their symbolic intermediary advisers – of the companies for which they work.

### Adding value to yourself

In indicating the ways in which the success of individual retail organizations is increasingly imagined through the discourse of enterprise, I have already referred to a number of technologies or mechanisms of regulation. Broadly defined, the term 'technologies' refers to 'hybrid assemblages of knowledges, instruments, persons, systems of judgement, buildings and spaces, underpinned at the programmatic level by certain presuppositions and objectives about human beings' (Rose, forthcoming). In my discussions of technologies of regulation within the internal world of retail organizations I have most often referred to those techniques that rely upon human scientific knowledge to channel human conduct into certain reproducible patterns. In discussing developments at company *A*, for example, I indicated that a variety of new technologies was deployed to give effect to the strategic aspirations of senior management. These included techniques for promoting motivation through the construction of a regime of values within the firm, and techniques for reducing dependency by reorganizing management structures. I argued that these mechanisms were inscribed with the presuppositions of the enterprising self, striving for fulfilment and personal meaning. In other words, these technologies were infused with the values of self-realization, self-direction and self-management; they sought to act upon the personal capacities of subjects, channelling the conduct of individuals into certain patterns.

As the autonomous subjectivity of the retail employee has emerged as a vital economic resource – the 'strategic human resource' – senior managers in the industry have become increasingly dependent upon an objective knowledge, a scientific expertise and rational technology of the personal and interpersonal. As several commentators have argued (Hollway, 1984, 1991; Rose, 1990), during the past decade there has been a substantial growth in the practical involvement of psychological expertise in the everyday life of the modern business enterprise with psychologically trained experts carrying out such tasks as selection, appraisal, promotion and job evaluation either as permanent employees or as private consultants.

Although, at first sight, the image of the entrepreneur seems far removed from the world of psychotherapeutics, this opposition does not appear to hold. As Rose (1990: 14) has argued,

> therapeutics can forge alliances between the liberation of the self and the pathways to personal success, promising to break through the blockages that trap us into powerlessness and passivity and underachievement. Hence therapeutics can appeal to both sides of the employment contract: it will make us better workers, at the same time, it will make us better selves. Therapy can thus offer to free each of us from our psychic chains. We can become more enterprising, take control of our careers, transform ourselves into high fliers, achieve excellence and fulfil ourselves, not *in spite of* work, but *by means of* work.

In other words, psychotherapeutic technologies of the self are designed to cut across divisions between 'work' and 'non-work' life; between both the 'top' and 'bottom' and the 'inside' and 'outside' of the corporation. Within the discourse of enterprise there is no longer room for any contradiction or conflict between the motives and desires of the employee as an individual and the goals and objectives of the organization for which he or she works. The individual human being at work, as much as outside of it, is considered to be engaged in a project to shape his or her life as an autonomous individual driven by motives of self-fulfilment. In short, no matter what role they may perform, all people produce themselves at work.

There is a considerable amount of evidence from within the retailing industry that suggests that enterprising technologies of regulation are being deployed quite extensively by retailers, that these technologies are covering a much wider range of employees, and that in certain important respects they are blurring the distinction between what it means to be a consumer and what it means to be a retail employee.

At the British multiple mixed retailer W.H. Smith, for example, up to 300 middle managers were assigned for 'retraining' following a large-scale survey of management style in which staff were asked to comment upon their manager's performance across a wide range of competencies. During 1990 and 1991 the company surveyed 3,500 of its 16,000 staff in 'one of the first schemes in Britain allowing staff to assess managers'. Each employee was asked to complete, anonymously, a questionnaire rating his or her manager's qualities. On a scale of 1–5, the 400 managers whose performance was assessed rated an average 4.52 for being 'prepared to make decisions', but only 3.12 for being 'someone I could go to if I have personal problems'. Other low ratings included 'someone who keeps me motivated', 'someone who is prepared to change his or her view if I have something useful to add', and 'someone who creates a happy working environment'.

The company's retail and personnel training manager said that senior management had expected managers to perform better in traditional roles because the company had trained them to do so in the past: 'those are things we have concentrated on, and they are the traditional measures of a good manager, but we are now saying that a manager's job is broader than it was in the past and we are asking more of them.' As a result of the exercise, all managers deemed to require 'retraining' attended an assessment centre where they were interviewed by an occupational psychologist, informed of their individual result, and offered guidance on how to work on themselves in order to better themselves and become more motivational and inspirational managers of people.[35]

While at first sight, this exercise seems to have had little to do with 'saturating the company with the voice of the customer' (Whiteley, quoted in Miller and O'Leary, 1993: 198), nothing could be further from the truth. Attempts by retail organizations to re-imagine the role and conduct of store managers – turning them from direct controllers to empowering facilitators of staff – are constitutive elements of governing in an enterprising manner; in other words, they are essential components of creating a 'customer-driven company'. As this example highlights, market-orientated organizational reforms often serve to turn employees into each other's customers as well as encouraging them to focus upon the needs of (external) traditional customers (Hill, 1991). Retail employees, like staff in other service industries, are increasingly encouraged to take on the role of both customer and servicer in the workplace, through, for example, providing 'consumer reports' on their own managers (just as customers are encouraged to provide reports on the quality of service they receive from staff at the point of purchase), as well as providing quality service to external customers. In these ways, work and consumption relations become increasingly enmeshed (see for example, Fuller and Smith, 1991).

Similarly, at British department store chain Dickens & Jones, senior management's 'pursuit of service excellence' led to an exercise analogous to that at W.H. Smith, this time aimed primarily at shopfloor staff. The company employed the services of a private consultancy to act as anonymous 'professional' shoppers who systematically surveyed the performance of sales employees against a predetermined and weighted set of means. Although these professional shoppers remained anonymous, staff were informed of their presence and the purpose of the exercise. Over a one-month period, 184 full- and part-time staff in London were individually assessed on four separate occasions, each time by different consultant shoppers. Emphasis was placed on manner of approach, attitude/rapport, efficiency and farewell. The score was recorded then tabulated to arrive at an overall assessment. These were communicated to staff, individually, in the form of an appraisal and then used 'to reward levels of excellence and/or identify training needs'. In order to celebrate individual 'heroes', senior management at the company presented each employee attaining 80 per cent or over with a gift voucher and certificate, and then invited them to attend a champagne party in their honour.[36]

Two crucial points emerge from examining these cases. First, in both, a distinct interrelation can be delineated between enterprising 'technologies of power' – an objectivizing of the work-based subject through the use of devices of calculation: an examining, quantifying and grading of individuals – and enterprising 'technologies of the self' – practical psychotherapeutic counselling through which people can work upon themselves to better themselves, as workers and human beings. Through the deployment of such technologies senior management at these companies have shifted the form of control exercised over staff away from close, formal direction towards a more entrepreneurial, indirect form of government – or controlled de-control – which relies for its effectiveness upon the self-regulating capacities of its employees as subjects.

Secondly, in both cases the technologies deployed have had the effect of blurring distinctions between work and consumption identities. Both examples gave practical effect to the objective of 'saturating the company with the voice of the consumer'. In the first case, shopfloor employees were re-imagined as internal 'customers' providing consumer reports on their managers. In the second example, shopfloor staff were assessed and rewarded in terms of the degree to which their conduct conformed to the requirements of external customers. As these examples indicate, the delivery of quality service – to both internal and external customers – is deemed to necessitate employees becoming aware of their crucial role in 'adding value' through quality 'emotional labour', both to themselves and to the company for which they work.

According to both the managing and retail operations director at company *B*, the 'excellent customer service demanded by our customers' entailed a new approach to the recruitment, selection and training of both managers and staff. No longer content to 'recruit in haste and repent at leisure', senior management were looking for a particular 'type of personality' to service their stores. The personnel and training department at *B* was charged with developing a number of programmes to give effect to these aspirations. In conjunction with a range of other departments, as well as a private management consultancy, they worked to create a formal 'person specification' for the job of sales assistant which would act as a guide for store managers in selecting 'staff with the right image and attitude'. At the same time personnel and training staff were also considering the introduction of psychometric testing for sales assistant positions.[37] With regard to training, the emphasis shifted away from a primary concern with technical skills – till operation and dressing-room procedures – towards a more concerted focus on the development of interpersonal skills and self-learning. The behavioural and attitudinal characteristics of shopfloor employees as individuals were now seen to be of vital importance: 'we are saying that personality and the way people behave are as important to us as any other factor.'[38]

At some of the company's newer stores, staff were being trained to view customer care as a series of skills which could be learnt. Through interpersonal training in transactional analysis, for example, staff in these stores were taught how to 'effectively manage a transaction with a customer'. In transactional analysis each individual is represented as exhibiting three types of 'ego states' in social relations: those of Parent, Adult and Child. Thus any interaction between two individuals can be analysed in terms of whether it is Parent–Child, Adult–Adult, Adult–Child etc., and therefore effectively managed to obtain a favourable outcome.

> So when a customer comes in you identify whether they're Parent, Adult or Child, and you respond accordingly to get an 'uncrossed' transaction. If they come in and you want to move them out of one mode and into another, then you respond to their stimulus and then you move into Adult, or Parent, or Child and it works ... We want 'uncrossed' transactions and not 'crossed' ones because they work in a positive direction. It's all about being aware of what mode the customer is in and responding accordingly.[39]

Training in transactional analysis at company *B* was an attempt to provide staff with a new way of seeing, and intervening in, social relations. Moreover, not only was transactional analysis deployed to assist staff in managing customer interactions 'in a positive manner', it was also deemed to provide a technique for helping staff to help themselves; that is, to turn themselves into empowered human beings. According to *B*'s training manager, it was this 'self-producing' aspect of transactional analysis that was highlighted to staff:

> the first thing they realize is that transactional analysis and customer care, or 'how to handle other people', is a *skill*. It's 'my skill is being challenged here. Because I'm not stretching myself I'm not dealing with this customer the right way.' And once they realize it's a skill, and they can do something about it, they take it on board. It's very much an empowering thing that way. If they have a customer who goes away still arguing then they've failed. The challenge is to turn the customer around and that's how the whole thing is sold.[40]

The deployment of transactional analysis in customer-care training was a crucial aspect of what senior management regarded as a move towards 'enterprising up' the company and its staff, making them more 'customer driven'. Via the medium of 'soft', 'cultural' technologies such as transactional analysis, employees at company *B* were being encouraged to become aware of their central role in adding value both to themselves and to the company for which they worked by providing quality service to customers. It was through such mechanisms that the quest for 'emotional proximity' between customer and organization was operationalized and that specific ways for the shopfloor employees of company *B* to conduct themselves were delineated. In other words, these micro-technologies were deployed to align the self-actualizing capacities of retail employees as subjects with the organizational goal of staying 'close to the customer'.

Although several similar mechanisms were deployed at company *A* to ensure the delivery of their Secure Shopping Strategy, the centrepiece of the company's attempts to become more customer driven was the introduction of their Quality Team (QT) programme. In a speech to staff launching the company's strategy in-store, the managing director highlighted the introduction of QTs as the key to the future success of the business.

> There are many exciting aspects to our Secure Shopping Strategy but I highlight in particular the introduction of Quality Teams into every area and department of the company which will allow all of you to become involved in a very real and meaningful way in changing some of the things we do for the better. I strongly believe that throughout this huge company amongst our staff there is an enormous wealth of talent, experience and skills that is not being allowed to be used fully. At last we will have a means of taking full advantage of that and I hope allow everyone to feel that they are contributing to our progress in a very positive way.[41]

Quality teams were *A*'s equivalent of 'Quality circles'. However, unlike some quality circle programmes, QTs were articulated as an integral component of *A*'s 'overall business strategy'; in other words, they were represented as a mechanism intended to promote continuous business improvement. According to senior management within the company, QTs constituted the central technique through which the 'hearts and minds' of the company's workforce would be harnessed to the pursuit of 'staying close to the customer'. Quality teams were seen to be the key

> to changing round the way we think of our front-line troops. And throughout the company there is this recognition now that they have got a very major contribution to make. They know all the wrinkles. They actually know half the answers. And we're beginning to grow more and more aware that 75 per cent of our problems are management driven, it may be 90 per cent for all I know. And actually staff have 90 per cent of the answers: 'why are they doing it this way? If only they'd listen to us.' So this Quality Team approach, I believe, is the beginning of the answer because it's starting to say 'We need you. You've got talent. You know the wrinkles. Tell us and we, the managers, will listen to you' . . . so we're in a way turning our managers – and management is about controlling and suppressing isn't it? – into leaders. And leadership is about giving people countless opportunities to grow, to develop and contribute. But you don't do that overnight. That's ten years' work.[42]

Quality teams were established at each level and in each function of the business and involved all members of the company (indeed membership of a QT was mandatory, not voluntary). The 'senior' QT comprised the Board of Directors of company *A*, and the 11–12 people sitting on that forum established the overall strategic goals – the 'Whats': What We Want to Achieve. These 'Whats' were then 'cascaded' down to the next level QT chaired by the line manager from the immediate 'superior' QT. This QT then discussed the 'Hows': How they would deliver the 'Whats' that had been established by the 'superior' QT. The commitments made at this level were then cascaded down to the next 'subordinate' QT and continued in the same fashion right down to the front-line QTs in-store, which were chaired by the branch manager.

As this brief outline suggests, the QT system was very hierarchical. They were not an alternative to line management; rather, as a senior manager indicated, they 'simply involve everyone in analysing and achieving strategic objectives in a multi-level, multi-functional organization', and 'form a platform for the implementation of any major change in the future'.

In-store the Chair of the QT set the agenda indicating the 'Whats' cascading down from the immediately superior QT. The Chair's role was to guide the meeting imperceptibly and certainly not to hijack it or dominate it, ensuring that everyone got involved, that the group agreed to a series of 'Hows', and that everyone was personally committed to their implementation. In other words, the Chair had to encourage the group to gel without appearing to be in control. Guidelines on managing QTs stressed that 'self-regulation is a key to motivation' and that 'self-monitoring is a key to commitment'.

QTs were sold to staff very much as a freedom package; as an opportunity for them to become more personally involved in the running of the business, and, simultaneously, to develop themselves as individuals. Emphasis was placed on getting staff to see the 'hows' formulated by the group as the result of their own autonomous deliberation; that they 'owned' the QT process. 'Recognition and celebration of success' were also represented as vital ingredients of the QT system. '[M]ore and more now QTs are involving those front-line people in making their contribution to the delivery of Secure Shopping. And you know as well as I do that if it's your idea, you're much more committed to it than if I impose my ideas upon you. The obvious stuff, psychologically.'[43]

Through the technology of QTs, staff at *A* were encouraged to imagine that they 'owned' the business for which they worked. The psycho-therapeutic presuppositions that permeated the QT – self-monitoring as the key to commitment and so forth – structured it as a rational technology of the personal and interpersonal. Thus QTs could be seen to provide their members with an 'ethical' exercise, in Foucault's use of that term, aimed at producing a particular kind of relation to self, and, through this, the ethical demeanour and standing of a particular kind of person: the enterprising self. Here, once again, the onus on direct control was transformed into an emphasis on regulation through self-production. Via the technology of QTs, as with the other techniques outlined earlier in the chapter, the government of company *A* has come to operate through the 'soul' of its individual employees.

Technologies such as transactional analysis and quality teams are designed to incite and channel – to govern rather than simply to repress – the subjectivity of service workers. These technologies are fashioned first and foremost to assist staff in managing the service interaction; that is, to produce a pleasurable meaning for the customer and a sale for the company. At the same time, however, they are also deemed to provide service staff with the practical means of empowering themselves at work. In this way, service in occupations such as retailing can be seen to concern the simultaneous 'production of meaning' and 'production of profit'. The two goals are symbiotic. Moreover, the effective management of the service relation is deemed to provide meaning and fulfilment for the producer of the service, the retail employee, as well as the consumer of that service, the customer (Allen and du Gay, 1994: 267).

## Conclusion

In this chapter I have attempted to indicate how people are made up at work by examining the changing rationality of government that is operative within contemporary retailing. I have argued that the internal world of the retail enterprise is being re-imagined through the discourse of enterprise as one in which customers' needs and desires are to be satisfied, productivity is to be enhanced, quality service guaranteed, flexibility increased and innovation fostered through the active engagement of the self-fulfilling impulses of all the organization's members.

Through a variety of technologies and practices, the programmatic aspirations of senior management personnel have been translated into new ways for people to be at work. Within retailing organizations, store managers and shopfloor employees are increasingly represented as enterprising subjects: that is, as individuals who calculate about themselves and work upon themselves in order to better themselves; in other words, as people who live their lives as 'an enterprise of the self' (Gordon, 1987, 1991; Rose, 1990).

However, 'making up' people at work is not simply a matter of 'labelling from above'. It is equally important to examine the behaviour of those so labelled to see what they make of and do with – how they 'consume' or 'use' – the technologies to which they are subjected, and which they cannot keep at a distance. In Chapter 7, therefore, I will contrast the 'strategic' rationality, to use de Certeau's terminology, of the 'labellers', with the 'tactics' of those so labelled.

## Notes

1 Taken from an interview with the personnel director (male) of a major British department store group, December 1989. All the interviewees referred to in this chapter are white.

2 Taken from an interview with the personnel director (male) of a major British department store group, December 1989. Details of the companies involved in the research can be found in the Appendix.

3 From a talk delivered by Paul Dowling, former corporate marketing director, Asda Stores, to the Oxford Institute of Retail Management, 23 October 1987.

4 Bill McNamara, former corporate marketing director of Asda, reported in *Retail Week* 9 March 1990: 8.

5 From a talk by Paul Dowling, former corporate marketing director, Asda Stores, to the Oxford Institute of Retail Management, 23 October 1987.

6 As the personnel director of one of Britain's leading mixed retailers – and an acknowledged 'retail engineer' – informed me, although the 'customer is king, it is often the City's perception that proves to be the big test of how well you're doing.' Interview with personnel director (male), company *A*, 18 April 1990.

7 See, for example, the comments by Christopher Hopton, vice president, Bain & Co. (UK), concerning the increasing importance of strategy in retailing published in the *Retail Week* Conference Programme, March 1991: 6.

8 Interview with the personnel director (male), company *A*, April 1990.

9 Interview with the managing director (male), company *B*, July 1990.

10 According to the company's personnel director (male), for example, the level and content of training given to staff was directly related to the 'needs of the customer' as constructed by image study research. 'We do a lot of image study work. We do a lot of independent market research work to see how the customer sees *A* in all its aspects from price to quality merchandise to service, and we have to continually respond to that and that is going to influence the training we provide so we will be using our resources, training them directly in a manner that best suits what the customers want, which we determine through image study.'

11 Speech by the merchandising director (male) to all the company's store managers at the launch of the company's SSS, January 1989. The speech was videoed and relayed to all staff later in the year when the strategy was launched in-store. It is interesting to note that *A*'s competitive strategy – designed in part to indicate to an almost exclusively male City audience the 'rationality' and 'control' exhibited by the almost exclusively male senior management team at *A* – was articulated through the construction of an essentialist female 'personality' – friendly, caring, sympathetic, fashion conscious etc. – exhibiting traits supposedly considered by men to connote the irrational, the emotional and, hence, the 'uncontrolled'.

12 Interview with the personnel director (male), company *A*, April 1990.

13 Interview with the personnel director (male), company *A*, April 1990.

14 Interview with a regional controller (male), company *B*, July 1990.

15 Interview with the retail operations director (male), company *B*, July 1990.

16 Taken from the Strategy Review document, company *B*, March 1990.

17 Interview with a regional controller (male), company *B*, July 1990.

18 Interview with personnel and training executive (female), company *B*, July 1990. As the training manager at company *B* informed me, 'Before the strategy everything was done very much in isolation. Training officers would go off and do their research and write a training package. What they are now realizing is that they ought to deliver what the customer wants in their training. So it's a painful lesson they've learnt and they really learnt it through redeveloping management induction. So it's really persuading them to talk to retail operations – what do they want? Talk to the area managers – what do they say? That's what is happening now. It wasn't before. After they've done that, it's researching, checking it out, running pilots and then going live with it.'

19 Interview with a regional controller (male), company *B*, July 1990.

20 Interview with personnel and training manager (female), company *B*, September 1990.

21 Taken from the speech of the merchandising director (male) at company *A* at the launch of the company's SSS, January 1989.

22 As the personnel executive (male) of company *D* – a leading mixed multiple retailer – informed me (October 1990): the increasing size of contemporary multiple retail operations militated against the direct supervision of service delivery in-store. It was just no longer feasible physically to sustain the scope of direct labour control systems. He argued that: 'the business has grown enormously and the size factor alone actually means that you are left with no alternative in the end. You have to delegate responsibility. You cannot manage everything yourself.'

23 Interview with Secure Shopping implementation controller (male), company *A*, May 1990.

24 Interview with Secure Shopping implementation controller (male), company *A*, May 1990.

25 Interview with the personnel director (male), company *A*, April 1990. As the managing director (male) informed the company's branch managers at the launch of the SSS in 1989: 'Training is not just the function of training officers. It is the prime responsibility of every manager and every supervisor in the company. A manager is not a manager of things he is a manager of people. And better training does not require the injection of vast amounts of cash resource.'

26 Interview with the personnel executive (male), company *D*, October 1990.

27 Interview with the personnel executive (male), company *D*, October 1990.

28 For the Secure Shopping implementation controller (male) at company *A*, the benefits of adopting a customer-orientated culture of excellence were even more wide-ranging than this. He represented it as 'all part of making Britain better'.

29 Interview with the human resource manager (female), retail operations, company *C*, January 1991.

30 Interview with the human resource manager (female), retail operations, company *C*, January 1991.

31 Interview with the human resource manager (female), retail operations, company *C*, January 1991.

32 Interview with the human resource manager (female), retail operations, company *C*, January 1991.

33 Interview with the human resource manager (female), retail operations, company *C*, January 1991.

34 As noted earlier, this 'merging' means that the relationship between government and the governed passes to an increasing extent through the manner in which governed individuals are willing to exist as subjects.

35 'W.H. Smith to retrain managers in motivation', *The Financial Times*, 8 May 1991: 12. 'A good look at staffing', *Retail Week*, 19 April 1991: 18. Similar developments are afoot in a number of other multiple retailers. See, for example, ACAS Work Research Unit (1991).

36 'In pursuit of excellence', *Review: The Journal of the House of Fraser*, January/February, 1989, 11: 61.

37 As Townley (1989: 92), for example, has argued, the introduction of psychometric testing for lower-level employees is indicative of an increasing concern among employers with the behavioural and attitudinal characteristics of employees as *individuals*. Company *B* is far from being the only multiple retail chain currently considering the introduction of such technologies for the recruitment of sales staff. At multiple DIY chain B&Q, for example, following a pilot study of psychometric testing in 24 new and old stores in the late 1980s, the company decided to apply these tests to all store applicants. Further details of B&Q's integrated human resource policy can be found in ACAS Work Research Unit (1991).

38 Interview with personnel and training controller (female), company *B*, July 1990.

39 Interview with training manager (female), company *B*, September 1990.

40 According to the training manager (female) at company *B* (September 1990), the success of transactional analysis in staff training depended upon the extent to which the discourse it provided them with 'becomes part of their everyday language . . . If they don't take it on board then it won't be successful.'

41 Excerpt from a video-relayed speech by the managing director (male) to all the staff at company *A*, 1989.

42 Interview with the Secure Shopping implementation controller (male), company *A*, May 1990.

43 Interview with the Secure Shopping implementation controller (male), company *A*, May 1990.

# 7

# Consuming Organization

In Chapter 6 I attempted to show how certain categories of person are 'made up' at work in contemporary retailing by examining the new rationality of government operative within the industry. I argued that the internal world of the retail enterprise is being re-imagined through the discourse of enterprise as a place where customers' needs are to be satisfied, productivity is to be improved, quality service guaranteed, flexibility enhanced and creative innovation fostered through the active engagement of the self-fulfilling impulses of all the organization's members. I suggested that through a variety of representations, technologies and practices the programmatic aspirations of senior management personnel within the retail industry were being translated into new ways for people to be at work. Increasingly, store managers and shopfloor employees within the industry were being conceptualized as enterprising subjects: self-regulating, autonomous, productive individuals whose sense of self-worth and virtue was inextricably linked to the success of the company for which they work.

Following some suggestive remarks made by Ian Hacking (1986), this aspect of 'making up people' was described in terms of 'labelling from above': the discursive construction (by a 'community of experts') of a certain 'reality' that particular sorts of people are encouraged to make their own. However, in keeping with Hacking's schema I also argued that there was more to making up people than the vector of 'labelling from above' alone. Equally important is 'the actual behaviour' of those so-labelled, which presses from below, 'creating a reality that every expert must face'.

In this chapter I will be turning my attention to this second vector. Drawing selectively upon the work of de Certeau (1984) I focus upon the ways in which certain categories of employee within retailing organizations 'use' or 'consume' the technologies to which they are subjected and I seek to examine some of the effects that their 'tactics of consumption' have for the process of 'labelling from above.[1] In so doing, I am concerned not simply with delineating the 'active' abilities and capacities of employees as 'consumers at work' but, more importantly, with the ways in which such 'abilities' are made manifest in situations in which, first, the symbolic and material resources required for various forms of 'cultural consumption at work' are themselves unequally distributed; and, secondly, where such consumption practices are working in and through the powerful discourse of enterprise, which constructs the dominant definitions of work technologies ('hard' and 'soft') and hence their appropriate uses.

In de Certeau's (1984) terms this is the point of distinguishing between the 'strategies' of the powerful and the 'tactics' of the weak. De Certeau, it needs to be remembered, deploys the term 'strategy' in a very particular way (though his usage of the term contains strong echoes of Foucault's power/knowledge couplet) to refer to the 'calculation of power relations that become possible when a subject with will and power (a business, an army, a scientific institution) can be isolated. It postulates a *place* that can be delimited as its own and serve as a base from which relations with an exteriority . . . can be managed.' Thus, strategy involves a victory of place over time and a mastery of places through sight. In many ways, this 'strategic rationality' is equivalent to Hacking's (1986) vector of 'labelling from above'. 'Strategy' constructs, through the interplay of power and knowledge, a 'proper' place – a reality – that some people are encouraged to make their own.

In contrast to 'strategy', 'tactics' of consumption are habits of action and modes of operation that cannot count on a 'proper' (a spatial or institutional localization) place, nor thus on a borderline distinguishing the strategic as a visible totality. Thus, 'tactics' are an 'art' of the weak (though not of the unfree or totally powerless) who, given their lack of control over institutions and resources, have to operate in the margins (temporal and spatial) defined by those who are – to all intents and purposes (legally, for example) – 'in control' of such institutional resources.

### Particular biographies, specific histories

In Chapter 3, I suggested that 'government' is eternally optimistic. The 'will to govern' is characterized by a stubborn belief that the 'Real' is programmable. Hence the perceived failure of one policy, set of policies or complete 'paradigm' is always connected to attempts to devise or propose programmes that would 'work better'. As indicated in Chapter 2, the discourse of enterprise announces itself as a 'revolution' in opposition to previous failed forms of governmental endeavour. It demands a clean break with the past in order to guarantee a future that does indeed 'work better'. In so doing, it tends to forget its origins, to eradicate its initial contingency, and thus to objectify itself. In other words, in order to constitute itself as an objectivity it must break with its own conditions of emergence and instead suppose it has its own 'place' from which it can reflect upon the world and programme 'reality'. It must appear to be beyond the exigencies of the everyday, looking down from above, enjoying a 'God's eye view'.

Enterprise, like other dominant discourses, prefers a *tabula rasa* on which to write its compositions. According to the managing director of company *B*, for example, his organization was in the embryonic stages of a 'total cultural change', with 'no precedent' in the company. It was essential, he argued, that the company 'start with a clean slate . . . otherwise there's no guarantee of success.' Ideally, he would like to have seen all current sales staff removed from their positions and replaced by completely new recruits better able to fit the company's desired 'culture'. He felt that many of the people currently in post simply 'weren't up to it'; that they would not be able to deliver the 'excellent customer service' envisaged in the company's 'strategy'.[2]

In so far as the discourse of enterprise takes hold within an organization – becomes 'instituted' as it appeared to be doing in company *B* – then the system of possible alternatives to that discourse tends to vanish and the traces of its contingent conditions of possibility to fade. There was a very strong feeling expressed by most of the senior managers interviewed in company *B* that, love it or not, there really was no alternative to 'the strategy' and its programme of 'total cultural change'. Senior staff talked of *'having* to learn a new language' and of developing a new 'mind set'. For these employees, the success of the company and their own personal occupational status and future career progression were intimately interwoven. Being able to 'speak the language' of enterprise thus became an overwhelming *political* necessity for senior staff as well as an ostensibly objective prerequisite for the continued success of the business. Those senior managers who could not, or would not, learn the language were quickly identified as 'not having what it takes' and, in some cases, were duly informed that their services were no longer required.[3]

However, if the establishment of objectivity is based on exclusion, the traces of that exclusion will always somehow be present. As de Certeau (1984: 48) indicates, 'beneath what one might call the "monotheistic" privilege that panoptic apparatuses have won for themselves, a "polytheism" of scattered practices survives, dominated but not erased by the triumphal success of one of their number.' The presence of these scattered practices – de Certeau's 'tactics' – attests to the impossibility of abolishing antagonism, of creating the happy relation the organization would like to have with itself.

The power of enterprise lies in its apparent universality – in its ability to offer a standard benchmark by which all of life can be judged and, thus, a means of aligning seemingly opposed modes of existence. However, it applies this benchmark to human material which is already highly differentiated along the lines of gender, ethnicity, class and generation, for example. What cannot be determined in advance are the articulations that may result from the encounter of the discourse of enterprise with these cultural relations. In negotiating this encounter, a result may be produced which was completely unanticipated. In other words, although enterprise prefers a *tabula rasa* upon which to write its compositions, it actually seeks to produce its effects under circumstances not of its own choosing. It must make its mark through an engagement with already existing cultural relations and hence inscribe itself, for example, upon persons with *particular biographies* and upon organizations with *specific histories*. I will examine each of these in turn.

*Particular biographies*

In company *A*'s London flagship store, for example, the discursive demarcation of generational differences produced competing interpretations of the Secure Shopping Strategy (SSS) among store staff. For the store's middle-aged, male, senior sales manager (DM) the SSS was interpreted less as an empowering innovation and rather as another stage in the steady removal of skill from his job and its transference into 'the hands of the accountants at head office'. DM had joined the company over 30 years earlier 'with no formal education', when 'loyalty' and the gradual acquisition of 'shopfloor common sense' were represented as prime virtues, and had worked his way up from 'the lowest form of sales assistant' to deputy manager in one of the company's top stores. For him, the SSS signified another nail in the coffin of his dearly beloved 'art of retailing' and a further erosion in the status and skill associated with his job. Rather than interpreting the advent of the SSS as an opportunity to feel increased ownership of his store, DM viewed it as another step in a gradual process of deskilling which was destroying any opportunity for involvement and decision-making at local level.

> This year, for the first time, I am not involved in agency review. Now agency review is where we analyse how every one of my agencies [the concessions that trade in *A*'s stores] have done, whether we should give them more space or less space. And I have direct control over my department as to what is going to happen by talking it through with my manager and my area manager. We will talk it through and come to a decision. Now I am paid on, and judged by, the results I bring in so I should have 100 per cent control of what's going on downstairs, within the constraints the company puts on me. Now this year someone else from head office, who doesn't even know the store is doing my agency review for me. To me that is absolutely ludicrous. I don't care who they are, they can't come to the right conclusions until they have had an interview with me. And that is not happening. And to my mind that is demotivating. I feel as if I might as well not be here . . . They recognize I'm the expert. They turn round and tell me I'm the expert, and yet I'm not allowed to do what I want to do on my own shopfloor . . . Basically, we're not allowed to think any more. It's being controlled from head office. This is how I see the future of *A*. Everything will be controlled from head office. The direct buying will be done at head office. The directions will be coming from head office. There will be no deviating at all from head office. It doesn't matter whether you are London, Penzance or Edinburgh, it doesn't really matter providing you get a good average. Not that you're going to shine. You can't shine in that environment. All you can do is carry out the company policy. If you carry out the company policy and keep your nose clean, that's all they really want. But that's not loyalty, that's very demotivating.[4]

For DM, 'enterprise' was experienced as a debilitating constraint in opposition to a lived past within the company which, at least retroactively, appeared to him to have offered a significant sense of work-based identity. Rather than creating and sustaining a sense of individual commitment and loyalty to *A*, 'enterprise' directly assaulted an already established sense of identification with his work and with the company. The historic importance of 'shopfloor common sense', of a practical and local knowledge, had given way to the centralizing expertise of 'graduates with no experience in-store' at head office with 'their computers'.

> Because they are educated people 'paper' means a lot to them. Now for a practical person like myself, with little formal education, 'paper' means very little or nothing to me. I mean I get print-outs from the EPoS, I read them and I think, I could have told you that, I knew that, before I even read the print-out. I don't need that to tell me. I know how much I've sold of any of my goods the night I went home, not the next day when it was printed out and given to me. I make it my business to find out. If anybody's on the ball, that's what they know. EPoS is very good, it gives me lots of information and I use it. But it's not the be-all and end-all for me . . . I'm at the age – you can tell that by the way I'm talking and what I've said – where computers don't mean a lot to me. But they will mean a lot to the new people coming up. It's got to. But relying on machines to do the job for you isn't the same as shopfloor common sense.[5]

For DM the tenets of enterprise stood in opposition to everything he valued dear at *A*. However, his portrait of 'the way things were' found little resonance in the aspirations of the other departmental managers in the store – either male or female – all of whom were significantly younger than him, and most of whom were only in their early to mid-twenties. They had no experience of the idealized version of work DM elaborated, nor had they grasped it as an ideal meaning to aim for themselves. They were effectively *inside* 'enterprise' and it was all they had to work with.

> *A* has obviously changed. It used to be more paternalistic, but I never knew it then. I wasn't with *A* then so it really doesn't relate to me. So I can see what DM means when he says 'years ago they used to do this and that', but then again that's years ago and now everything is more geared specifically towards profit and things like that. And I don't think that's a bad thing. I suppose that's what counts. That's what we want.[6]

This difference in attitude rarely led to any overt antagonism between the older and younger generation but the potential for conflict was never very far from the surface. This potential was realized in spectacular fashion on one particular occasion and had a considerable if relatively short-lived effect upon the management of the store.

The completion of some building work in-store coincided with the onset of the company's Father's Day promotions programme. As usual, store layout plans arrived from head office and these included detailed instructions concerning the layout of the Father's Day promotions. As the aforementioned building work was not expected to be completed, the plans did not take account of the space the builders had been occupying in-store. As a result, a significant area of store space was left completely bare with nothing organized to occupy it. As luck would have it, the space in question fell under the jurisdiction of DM and he took visible delight in informing the store manager that he would take responsibility for filling it with his own Father's Day promotion.

For DM this unexpected development provided a perfect opportunity to show the world – not only his fellow managers and the store's customers but also head office – what the lost 'art of retailing' was all about. Indeed, such was his excitement that for a brief moment he really seemed to believe that if he put on a stunning display it could change the course of company strategy and reverse what he saw as the inexorable concentration of power in the hands of head office staff.

Using some spare stock from his own section, as well as some materials left over from previous promotions elsewhere in-store, DM created a display on a large table covered with crêpe paper and material which was then ceremoniously transported by two of his members of staff to the empty space in-store. DM was obviously very proud of his display and spent a considerable amount of time putting the finishing touches to it. However, in contrast to DM's evident enthusiasm for and pride in *his* display, which he considered exemplified an almost artisanal retail skill, the younger sales managers were both appalled and amused in equal measure. For them, the display was an ill-conceived eye-sore that clashed terribly with the otherwise consistent visual image of the store. This display would bewilder customers, they argued, and make them think they had walked into a church bazaar rather than a leading high-street retailer.

The clash between these two different understandings of how to do retailing came to a head later in the day when one of the younger sales managers, commonly regarded as one of the most ambitious and 'entre-preneurial', walked up to DM near his display and gave him a book of raffle tickets. Going slightly red around the collar, DM asked what they were for. His colleague nodded her head in the direction of the display and said 'I thought you might need them for your Oxfam raffle' and walked slowly away with a broad smile on her face. Seeing this interaction, some of the other young sales managers nearly burst into laughter. In an instant DM's face went bright red and he stormed out of the store and into the street from which he did not return for over half an hour.

For nearly two weeks after this incident DM refused to talk to the sales manager concerned and ate all his meals at a separate table in the staff canteen avoiding nearly all contact with his peers (in the process upsetting the delicate social structure of the canteen where managers always sat at one table, the concessions' staff at another, the audiovisual staff at another and so on), including the weekly store managers' meeting where oper-ational issues were normally discussed and collective management decisions reached.

For the younger sales managers, DM's ideal of the autonomous retailing of the 'artisan', as represented by his promotional display, was something they simply could not identify with. In the context of the homogeneous 'professional' visual identity they were used to in-store, it stood out as an 'amateurish' eyesore, reminding one sales manager of 'the drab old days of '60s retailing'. While in no sense buying uncritically into the discourse of enterprise, as represented by the SSS, they were more at home in its universe than they could ever be in what they saw as DM's nostalgic and increasingly irrelevant discourse of the 'art of retailing'.

This is not to say that all departmental managers appreciated the way A was changing. There was, for example, a distinct differentiation in perspective within the younger management group between those who had joined the company straight from school and who had worked their way into lower management positions, and those who had joined as graduates – both specialists and generalists. The latter tended to have more direct contact with head office in terms of induction and training, for example, and therefore saw themselves as being more 'strategic in outlook' than their store-based, non-graduate colleagues. They represented themselves as being privy to 'the big view' – as having a more 'objective' take on the company's goals and objectives – than their other colleagues who they viewed as more 'emotionally involved' with the day-to-day activities of their own particular store, and hence somewhat blinkered to the wider issues at stake in the process of organizational change.[7] In other words, the graduates saw themselves as 'cosmopolitans' in contrast to their non-graduate contemporaries whom they defined as 'locals' (Gouldner, 1957).

### Specific histories

As the above example makes clear, enterprise not only acts upon persons with particular biographies but also upon organizations with specific histories. While enterprise calls for a 'management revolution' (Peters, 1987) – a fresh start, as it were – and projects the vision of a cohesive but inherently flexible organization, work relations in companies like A and most other modern retailing corporations *already* involve the differentiation and 'fracturing' of collections of employees (managers as well as workers).

In company A, for example, managerial career progression had been intimately linked, historically, to the possession of a particular professional qualification (obtained only at degree level in universities). Because A's core business necessitated the perpetual presence of at least two professional employees in-store to deal with customers, and because the Society to which these professionals belonged had historically been able to negotiate significant remuneration for its members, A had a policy of recruiting these professionals as management trainees as well as purveyors of their own particular specialism. Thus, nearly every store manager at A, and almost every deputy manager (DM was an exception), was also a professional. As a result of this policy, professionals exercised a virtual monopoly over the senior positions within the company, whether at district, area or head office level, or in the marketing, personnel or training functions.

This structural elision of professional qualification and career progression had led to the virtual disintegration of an internal labour market for those employees who did not possess the appropriate professional training. Those who had worked their way up the ranks to the level of sales manager, and even those on the company's new non-professionalist graduate training scheme, were therefore highly unlikely to be able to further their line management careers at *A* beyond branch level.

Senior executives at *A* (themselves members of the professional élite) were very aware of the potential problems that this elemental division posed for the cultural reconstruction of *A* (and the new generalist graduate scheme was partly a response to this). However, they argued that it was not financially viable for the company to employ both a professional and a general manager in the same store. It was either one or the other. And as the former was a structural feature of the company's core business it made sense to train him or her for management as well as professional service.

None the less, despite the best efforts of senior management to play down the importance of this two-tier system, a symbolic division had emerged around this central fracturing between the 'professional mafia' and the 'rest', as the following comments from one of the company's Central London training and personnel staff indicates.

> There are two different career structures within this company. There's a structure for professionals, and there's a structure for 'others'. And in the professionals' structure people are able to get into what I see as more senior positions than people who are non-professionals. For example, I'm an assistant area training officer. My next promotion will be to area training officer. The position above that is area training and development manager and for that you have to be a professional. So there is no way I can go any further than area training officer ... My promotion prospects are limited by not being a professional and I feel that is unfair ... We have some non-professionals as store managers in Central London: in particular we have a female non-professional store manager, and I think that's terrific. I think that's a major achievement in the company. But where she goes from there, I don't know. Because she could easily manage a larger store – but will it be economically viable to do so as a non-professional because the company always needs professional cover? The other danger is that people at a supervisory level in the company see no way forward.[8]

For many sales managers, for example, the dominance of the 'professional mafia' meant that they had effectively reached the limits of their line management career at *A*. Most saw themselves as committed to a career in *A* and as enterprising managers – self-regulating, autonomous, 'go-getting', productive individuals whose sense of self-worth was intimately bound up with the successful effectuation of their work. However, career opportunities with increased personal responsibility and financial remuneration *were central tenets of their interpretation of the 'discourse of enterprise'*, and they now believed that *A* was no longer willing, or able, to offer them that. For one sales manager who had joined the company only four years earlier as a sales assistant and who had been promoted six times since then, this central fracturing was taking its toll on her sense of identification with her work and with the company. After two years in the same job, and having turned her department into the most profitable in-store within only one year of arriving, she now felt bored and in need of a fresh challenge.

I don't think I can give it 100 per cent commitment. I am committed and I am motivating myself but I can see it myself, and I'll be honest, that my standards a year ago are not my standards now. Whereas before I'd say 'I'm going to do that now', now I'll say 'It can wait till tomorrow.' If I could see a future here I'd still be going for it. I think I've got a lot to offer *A*, definitely, but they're just not going to exploit that.[9]

As Salaman (1986: 73) has argued, for example, the social patterns arising from these forms of fracturing within work organizations 'consist of social groupings of inclusion and exclusion', or to deploy Chantal Mouffe's (1991: 6) term (derived from Carl Schmitt): 'friend–enemy relations'. These groupings always involve the construction of an 'us' whose identity is only constituted in relation to a 'not us' or 'them'.

However, as the above examples indicate, such groupings do not develop solely or necessarily around the traditionally privileged site of management/ worker relations. Rather, these groupings are multiple, often seemingly contradictory to outside observers, and liable to constant realignment. As a sales assistant at company *B* suggested, 'it's not just one "us" and "them", there's loads of "us"s and "them"s in this store.'[10] These 'friend–enemy relations' cannot easily be domesticated because they derive their energy from the most diverse sources, many emanating from outside the arena of the workplace. Friend–enemy relations in contemporary retail organizations can, and often do, develop between customers and sales assistants, management and staff, local branch staff and head office staff, younger and older managers, between white and black staff, Afro-Caribbean and Asian staff, between different departments in-store, and between full- and part-time staff, with coalitions between these and other groupings frequently shifting, depending upon circumstances.

At company *A*'s flagship London store, for example, one of the largest departments was staffed almost entirely by black, predominantly African-born, women at sales assistant level (apart from one black female supervisor all the departmental management team was white). Although the personnel officer denied that 'colour' played a part in the departmental staff allocation process, it was noticeable that those departments with the lowest status ratings among staff were those with the largest number of black people working in them.[11] However, through crowding these women together in one department, a strong sense of identity had been established around ethnicity and gender, in direct opposition to the English-speaking white (though by no means exclusively male) dominance of other departments. In the canteen, for example, alongside the 'management table' and 'concessions girls' table' was what white staff termed the 'Africans' table'. According to one of the sales assistants on the department – a British-born black woman who did not see herself first and foremost in terms of 'being black', and was therefore regarded by her departmental colleagues as 'not really black' – the 'African women' tended 'to speak their own language' on the shopfloor. They did this, she suggested, so that what they considered to be 'outsiders' – that is non-black colleagues and customers, as well as management – couldn't understand what they were saying to each other and, thus, be privy to the group's dynamics in any way, shape or form. As this woman indicated, the strong collective spirit in the department, articulated around ethnicity and gender, constituted its identity in direct opposition to the individualizing discourse of enterprise projected by the company.

> Everything's black. Black men, black clothes. Everything is black oriented. Nothing – nothing but black . . . people tend to see them as a group and not as individuals at all. If one of them gets promoted it's not seen as an individual thing. They have a big celebration and see it as a black thing: one of the blacks' got promoted. It's like a rally round thing . . . Like one of the Ghanaian girls got sacked 'cause she was rude to a customer and it almost caused a riot. Things got really heavy in the department.[12]

Through an unacknowledged process of discrimination – allocating black women who were deemed 'not to communicate well' to a low-status department where personal interaction between shopfloor staff and customers was less likely to occur – 'white' management at the store inadvertently created the conditions of possibility for the emergence of a highly charged 'friend–enemy' grouping. The department developed an identity that was constituted in direct opposition to both 'being white' and 'being management'.

At company *B*'s flagship store in the West End of London similar dynamics were at work on the shopfloor. Although *B*'s sales staff acknowledged that 'the Asians tend to stick together, the blacks tend to stick together, and the whites tend to stick together', these various shopfloor groupings were united in their detestation of another cultural 'community' on the shopfloor, the agency staff (themselves highly differentiated by gender, ethnicity and so forth) who ran the various private concessions in-store. Whereas *B*'s own shopfloor staff were contractually obliged to wear (a universally detested) company uniform, concessions staff could wear their own clothes at work. This highly visible embodiment of individual choice and expression – establishing an obvious connection between work and non-work identity – was a symbol, for concessions staff, of their superiority to and difference from *B*'s own staff (*B*'s management staff were the only other employees allowed to wear clothes they had chosen themselves), and a source of great frustration and annoyance to *B*'s sales assistants.

> And then there's concessions. They tend to stick together and not get on with any other area of the shop. They sit on their own and everybody hates them. There's no integration. They themselves don't wear the uniform so they feel themselves to be that little bit better and that creates a real animosity on both sides. And that can affect the way the shop runs to a degree. Say, for example, with the concessions' dressing room. They'll never bring out our area's stuff and put it out or give it to us. They'll only bring out their own stuff. And if you take stuff over to them that isn't theirs they get all aggressive. They hate sharing a dressing room with us 'cause they think that brings them down to our level and they don't like that at all. It doesn't affect the customers, this tension, so it doesn't hurt the profits. But every now and again the changing room has to be shut because

they've allowed too many clothes to get piled up in there and that can cause aggravation for the customer . . . it's just the way it is, and you do notice it. You say 'Oh! I'm not going over to that crowd, you know what they're like'.[13]

Again, the social patterning of 'similarity versus difference' – or 'friend–enemy' – was largely inadvert – an unforeseen consequence of formal structure and process. The strategic objectives of providing a 'total' look for *B*'s sales staff through the adoption of a company uniform, as well as of highlighting the choice and range available at *B*'s stores through the deployment of concession outlets on the shopfloor, led not to the development of an organic complementarity as envisaged but to the creation of a virulent 'friend–enemy' grouping. However, while the *structure* of the grouping emerged as an unforeseen consequence of 'social engineering' by senior management at *B* and was therefore firmly 'work-based', the substance of the conflict between sales staff and concessions staff traversed the boundaries of work and non-work. For *B*'s sales staff, concessions became the enemy through being allowed to wear their own clothes at work. In other words, concessions staff were permitted to express their individuality (as 'consumers') visually *at the workplace*. In contrast, *B*'s own employees felt denied this connection between work and non-work. Instead, their individuality or desire for self-expression was denied through having to wear a uniform.

*B*'s staff brought to the workplace a romantic ethos that appeared at first sight to be perfectly attuned to the spirit of enterprise demanded by the company: the desire to make a project of themselves, to achieve self-actualization and exercise self-expression, autonomy and choice at work and, hence, to merge work and non-work identities. However, their understandings of autonomy, self-actualization and the relationship between work and consumption were very different from those promoted within the discourse of enterprise. And because they exceeded the dominant definitions, they highlighted that discursive productions continue to signify in spite of and sometimes against the intentions of their authors.

Such dissidence between the meanings inscribed in organizational changes from above and those produced by staff in their engagement with those changes was also evidenced in relation to the inauguration of a new customer care initiative at company *B* (an integral part of the company's overall strategy) entitled the 'Promise'. However, in this instance the friend–enemy grouping that emerged around this programme was potentially more serious for the company in that it took the form of a staff/customer antagonism.

A central element in *B*'s strategy was the introduction of the Promise. In line with other retailers, *B*'s senior management team was focusing increasingly upon the issue of customer service. In order to indicate to customers that *B* was a quality retailer and to promote customer loyalty, senior management introduced the company *B* Promise of 'Total Satisfaction Guaranteed'. If customers were in anyway dissatisfied with their purchases they would now be able to return them to any one of *B*'s stores, with or without a receipt, and receive an instant refund or exchange, and an apology from a company representative. *B*'s store management and staff were informed that the Promise was the company's way of differentiating their 'offer' to customers from that of their competitors, as well as a highly efficient, cost-effective mechanism for the conduct of contemporary retail business. In fact, far from losing the company money, it would generate extra sales in the long run as *B*'s reputation for quality and total satisfaction grew 'by word of mouth'. As part of introducing staff to the practice of the Promise, staff were encouraged to treat customers as if they were guests visiting their house, or as they themselves would ideally wish to be treated, and informed that under no circumstances were they to argue with customers over refunds or exchanges. Living up to the Promise, staff were informed, was the way to become a virtuous person at work.

However, for most sales staff, the Promise was seen as a guaranteed way of losing money and as pandering to the whims of customers at the expense of the company's own employees. In a curious inversion of the company's own preferred logic of identity, sales staff indicated their sense of 'ownership' of their store in their intense antipathy towards the Promise. For them, the institution of the Promise was seen as a 'criminal offence', endangering, rather than ensuring, the company's financial success. Rather than forging a new sense of subjective investment in the fortunes of the company, staff interpreted the Promise as an attack on an already established sense of relative autonomy and identification.

> Before it used to be that if they didn't have the receipt on refunds they couldn't have one. Now they get a refund or an exchange whatever! Even if there's a hole in it where the tag used to be they still get away with it, and that makes us look like fools. And if you tell your manager how ridiculous you feel they just say 'it's not your money'.[14]

For most sales assistants, the Promise was simply seen as a licence for customers to practise fraud and 'rip off' the company. More importantly, though, it symbolized for them a massive gap between the status of shop-workers and that of the customer. The Promise was viewed by sales assistants as redefining them as 'slaves' to customers' desires. Whereas the old refund policy – no receipt, no exchange or refund – had allowed sales assistants a certain imagined parity of status in their dealings with customers, they felt the Promise re-imagined sales assistants as mere cyphers in the company's will to please.

> The thing with customer service here is if customers want to change anything they're allowed to change anything, even underwear, swimwear. They're allowed to change it and I think that's one of the reasons they're losing money because they change almost everything and I don't think they should . . . Because a customer could have something she had from here which she's worn for four or five months and she'll waltz in here and she'll change it. The management say it's like our policy for customers: they want 'em to keep coming in here through us treating 'em nice. But we think it's wrong. We do it but we don't like it. I mean if we want to change anything and we don't have a receipt we won't be allowed to change it and yet a customer would, and that's all wrong, innit? We can't give

'em a credit slip any more, it's always 'give 'em the money'. Even when they suspect someone of nicking the stuff we're still encouraged to give customers their money. Sometimes they do, when they get a bit suspicious, give 'em a credit slip but nowhere as near as often as we did before this Promise happened. And I reckon since we've had this we're losing loads of money.[15]

Rather than harmonizing the relations between servicers and customers, the Promise became the site of an intense 'friend–enemy relation'. For staff, the Promise represented a loss of ownership and of self esteem for 'us', and its transference to 'them', the customers.

We're 'us' and they're 'them', yeah. What they don't seem to understand is that we're customers too. We go shopping too. It's almost like they think we're slaves. We don't leave here but go into a little corner where there's beds and we go to sleep there and get up the next morning and come out into the shop. There's no idea amongst customers that we're just at work . . . I remember one day we had to close the dressing room early because it was just stuffed full of clothes and we just had to clear up the mess and put the stuff back on the floor. And this woman comes up and says 'I want to use the dressing room.' So we explain to her and she still won't have it. So she demands to see the manager. She won't put herself in our position, she thinks she's God. So the management open it up for her and then you've got the staff unhappy saying 'Good God! What do they think we are, scum?' In a way you have to be nice. As a sales assistant you don't have the authority to tell them what to do. You have to cope with it, you've got no choice. These are the people, so we're told, who are paying our wages. There's nothing I can do about the position I'm in at the moment. And managers they answer to someone else as well. Management are accountable too, so they've got to please them too. You just have to grin and bear it.[16]

For many sales assistants the increased benefits accruing to the enterprising consumer had taken place directly at their expense. As far as they were concerned, the price of enskilling the sovereign customer was the effective erosion of any form of distinctive skill from the work they performed. This alternative sense of 'ownership' – which was only formally articulated in the context of its potential eradication – so overwhelmed the new entrepreneurial definition of 'ownership' which the Promise was deemed to express that in attempting to counter it management could often be heard telling staff not to worry about giving instant refunds because 'it's not your money'. The irony of this situation appeared somewhat lost on them.

As the examples above indicate, although the establishment of enterprise as an 'objective presence' by senior management at company *A* and company *B* involved the monotheistic privileging of this discourse, the ways in which the discourse was operationalized was far from unproblematic. While the official discourse of enterprise tries to produce particular meanings for and forms of conduct among employees in order that they will in turn produce quality service for customers and a sale for the company, it cannot completely close off the processes of the production of meaning nor totally determine how particular norms will be enacted. What cannot be guaranteed in advance are the articulations that may result from the meeting and mixing of entrepreneurial discourse with already existing cultural practices – formal and informal – and the meanings and identities they constitute.

In other words, rather than representing the institution of 'enterprise' within an organizational context as a form of 'revolution' – as prescriptive management theorists are wont to do – it is important to remember that 'newness', as Salman Rushdie (1991: 304) suggests, only enters the world in a hybrid, mongrel form, 'as *mélange*, hotchpotch, a bit of this and a bit of that'.

Avoiding the extremes of 'nothing's the same' (much prescriptive management discourse) and 'nothing's really changed' (much self-styled 'radical' criticism of management discourse), it becomes important instead to chart the processes of *cultural translation* through which organizational 'newness' is constituted. One thing seems certain, however: because 'newness' is inherently hybrid, 'organizational change' is unlikely to be a simple zero-sum game. Rather, it is likely to be a very ambivalent process.

In the following sections, I attempt to chart this ambivalence by looking in greater detail at how shifts in organizational governance differentially enable and constrain those involved in them. In particular, I examine what different categories of employee in specific retail organizations 'make' or 'do' with the technologies of organizational governance to which they are subjected.

## Tactical trajectories in retailing

As de Certeau (1984: xvii) makes clear, 'tactics' are related to 'social situations and power relationships'. For Yudice (1989: 216–17), it is apparent that these 'tactics' can be wielded not only by the lowliest of workers but rather by all employees within any organization. As he argues, it therefore becomes important to distinguish among the practitioners of tactics, otherwise the specificity of the motives for which tactics are employed will be obliterated.

### *'This is my* stock, in *my* shop'

In previous chapters I indicated that the discourse of enterprise envisages a coherent, purely economic method of programming the totality of governmental action. Attempts to create an enterprise culture within contemporary business organizations, as well as within the wider social formation, have proceeded through the progressive enlargement of the territory of the economic by a series of redefinitions of its object.

Although several critics (Armstrong, 1989; Legge, 1989) have sought to highlight an apparent contradiction at the heart of the discourse of enterprise between, on the one hand, its advocacy of an increasing role for management accounting frameworks and, on the other, the priority it accords to the self-steering and self-actualizing capacities of individuals, I suggested that enterprise brooks no opposition between the two. Rather, under the regime of enterprise, 'totalization' and 'individualization' (Foucault, 1988b) – or 'loose/tight' in Peters and Waterman's (1982) terms – proceed hand in hand, mutually reinforcing one another.

In both company *A* and company *B*, for example, store managers had experienced the effects of both an increasing centralization of control – with head office staff exerting greater influence over the selection and presentation of stock in-store – and a parallel increase in their own individual responsibility for the financial management and performance of their branches. In other words, at the same time as head office exerted greater control over individual branches, store managers were also subject to greater individual accountability through, for example, becoming designated budget-holders and by taking responsibility for the personnel and training function in-store. This autonomization and responsibilization of store management staff had rendered them more visible to the 'strategic' gaze of head office, while simultaneously encouraging them to view this 'gaze of the other' as their own – to become at one with it.

For most store managers at *A* and *B* the institution of enterprise had involved both an intensification of effort and a rationalization of resources – human as well as financial – at branch level. However, while the meanings inscribed within these developments by senior management stressed their liberating, self-fulfilling character for individual managers and excluded any reference to their possible constraining or debilitating effects, they had not been so unambiguously interpreted by those at whom they were aimed.

Rather than describing the situation as one of 'thriving on chaos', many store managers talked instead of 'just managing'.

> I can say now that there are managers in this area who will today be working 11–12 hour days. And if they were to say 'No! Sorry, I'm not doing it', they won't say it 'cause they know if they do say it their careers are finished. They know it, the area manager knows it, everybody knows it. Basically, you either cope with the pressure or you're out, and I think that's grossly unfair. And I think it's feasible that we're in a situation where people are frightened to actually make a fuss about it. So people like the area manager, who to be fair to them, can't go to their director and say 'I'm overspent on salaries' because he wants to get on as well, so he starves his area of . . . staff and that's the situation we've got into . . . I find that I personally have had enough of it.[17]

For many store managers at both *A* and *B* the demands of enterprise were experienced as all-consuming. It was not at all unusual for managers to have to come into their branches seven days a week just to cope with the operational basics. Moreover, friends and family were regularly recruited on an un-paid basis to help out with various urgent tasks they couldn't cope with on their own and couldn't afford to pay staff overtime to perform. Although most managers continued to argue that work was not their life, they were aware that company-related business was increasingly colonizing their existence.

I've had to come in here on Sundays to work, often for totally crazy reasons like putting together a new cash desk and putting it out on the floor. Things that they just won't pay to be done by Maintenance or whatever. It wasn't just me that came in it was my boyfriend who came in too. He's the one who sawed down the cash desk and made sure it was the right height and that. He goes absolutely apeshit when I ask him to come in, but you see the thing is I get so upset when it's not done, because I feel personally responsible . . . so my boyfriend came in and did the job with his brother-in-law on a Sunday, for no money. He wasn't too happy about it. He had a quiet life after it though 'cause the whole thing was getting me so tensed up. Every time my area manager came down she'd ask why there was a new cash desk out the back and why wasn't it on the floor. And I said I hadn't had time to do it. They weren't aggressively judging me on it but I kept thinking they were judging me on it so it just became something that *had* to be done. It drove me barmy, so I asked my boyfriend . . . Actually, he's been in to do loads of things for me. He's put the fitting room curtains up, he's painted departmental panels for me. He always goes loopy but I say 'Oh please! I've got to do it.'[18]

As both of the above examples indicate, store managers were structurally locked into the institution of enterprise within their companies. In order to guarantee their future they had to cope with the pressures thrust upon them in the name of the 'enterprising self'. Failure to keep up could easily result in dismissal, the blame falling squarely upon the victims themselves for not being enterprising enough – for not exhibiting the requisite virtues of individual initiative, self-reliance and so forth. Basically, the company's view was if individual managers could not cope then it was because they were not using their management skills effectively. 'The company goes on about people's time management skills. If you can't get it done within your allotted time then it's your fault because your time management skills weren't right.'[19]

However, while many store managers were prepared to admit that they were finding the pressures of increased individual accountability extremely debilitating, they did none the less testify to an intense sense of 'ownership' of their own stores. In other words, their relationship to this new rationality of government was *not* one of simply hating the changes that were taking place. It was considerably more *ambivalent* than that.

Whatever happens in the shop I take very personally. This is *my* stock in *my* shop. They do encourage you to feel a sense of ownership. They have a share scheme. You're also rewarded on your bonus systems. You're rewarded on what you do in your shop, not on what happens in your area. I mean, you do tend to think of them as your own shops.[20]

I actually feel that this is *my* shop. It's not *B*'s shop, it's *mine*. And I want it to take money, and I want it to look good. I don't know, but I think you feel personally responsible for what happens, and the way that it's run, and the way that it appears. And you feel personally injured if someone says 'Isn't this shop a mess!' You know it really gets to you. I don't know. You feel so emotionally involved with the way it's going. And I know that other people in the company, not just managers, but the buying department, the accounts department, area managers, they put in as much effort and extra time as we do as branch managers. So I think it's not just me: everyone's in the same boat sort of thing, so I don't feel bad about doing it. I don't feel like I'm being put upon because I know everyone else is being put upon too.[21]

While this sense of 'ownership' can easily appear indicative of the total assimilation of store managers to the logic of the 'strategic gaze', most managers interpreted their 'ownership' of the store rather differently. 'Ownership' meant making the store their own, *appropriating* it to their own purposes, rather than simply being transparent cyphers for the will of head office. One way in which managers represented their 'ownership' of the store was through transforming it into an extension of their own homes. Branches located in shopping centres or high streets often became sites where social relations originating outside of the workplace were reproduced. Friends 'popped in' while out shopping, and managers often invited them in to their office 'for a chat' in much the same way as they would if they were at home. In this sense the individual retail outlet tends to be much more easily appropriated for the purposes of non-work activity than most conventional office spaces ever could be. Rather than simply encouraging the progressive penetration of the market into all areas of social and cultural life, there is also a certain sense in which the structure and geography of the retail industry allows the socialization and culturalization of market relations within its own borders.[22]

At one company *B* store, the branch manager's sense of 'ownership' had led her to deliberately subvert the intent of the company's new 'self-help' training manual. *B* had recently instigated a new training programme which was designed to place the burden of in-store training upon shopfloor staff and their managers, rather than upon central resources. The idea was to jettison what senior management termed 'spoon-feeding' and to encourage individual responsibility for self-advancement. Training was to progress through three pre-determined and weighted stages, Bronze, Silver and Gold. On completion of the final module of each stage, staff were to be examined by their branch manager to ensure that they had reached the desired level of competency. If they were successful, they received a small salary increase and were then allowed to progress to the next stage.

However, as this branch manager indicated, the pressure of running a store with an inadequate staffing resource left neither sales employees nor management with time to concentrate upon the training programme. Instead of placing the burden on staff to put themselves through the training programme in their own time, as the company suggested they should, this manager simply completed all the requisite administration over a plausible, if comparatively short, period and sent it back to head office indicating that all her staff had now achieved the highest level of competence. This had the effect of creating some space for the manager with respect to head office demands, and of providing a salary increase for staff without them having to do any extra work, thus improving the morale of the shop as a whole. As this manager argued, 'head office don't have realistic expectations. I don't think you can expect an ordinary member of staff who's on a pittance and working all hours to take stuff home and work on training at home. Why should they? I wouldn't do it!'[23]

Without being able to 'keep it at a distance' this manager 'used' the company's training programme for ends rather different from those inscribed within it by its makers. In this instance, what might be described as the categorical imperative of the enterprising self – 'manage yourself to your own best advantage' – was used to open up a temporary space between the self-fulfilling impulses of the individual employee and the goals of the company, *while appearing further to align them.*

As this example indicates, 'tactics of consumption' are inherently con-textual and relational because, as de Certeau (1984: 21) argues, they have as their precondition the non-autonomy of their 'field of action'; they cannot be autonomous of official norms because *they always operate in relation to them.* In other words, there can be no 'unofficial expression' without a prior 'official' one or its possibility. As Judith Butler (1993: 15), for example, has argued, this counters 'any notion of a voluntarist subject who exists quite apart from the regulatory norms he/she opposes'. Tactics of consumption are therefore *immanent to power* and not in a relation of *external opposition* to power. According to de Certeau (1984: 37), the 'place of a tactic belongs to the other'. It has 'at its disposal no base where it can capitalize on its advantages, prepare its expansions and secure its independence with respect to circumstances' (1984: xix). As such, tactics cannot be anything but *ambivalent,* being both simultaneously enabled and constrained by circumstances.

The manager in our example knew that she could not be seen openly to resist the training programme as this would mark her out as a potential 'problem manager' and quite possibly damage her long-term career prospects with the company, something she just couldn't contemplate happening. At the same time, however, she realized that there was no realistic possibility, given the pressures on her and her staff in-store, that she could operate the training programme as head office required. Thus, in the face of multiple and conflicting demands – for her own survival and career prospects, to ensure the continued support and cooperation of her staff and hence the viability of the store and to satisfy head office's desire for quantifiable results – she took the calculated action described above.

The effects of this action highlight the *transient* and *ambivalent* nature of tactics. They were *transient* because they had no proper place of their own; they constituted a 'conjunctural operation' and hence were deployed 'on the wing' without the option of planning a general strategy. The manager in question knew that her actions were necessary simply to keep her show on the road as much as anything else. Pressures from head office were temporarily appeased but would not disappear for good as a result. She had not and could not achieve a clear 'victory' because she was not involved in a simple zero-sum game. The terrain upon which the tactics emerge and operate ensures this because, as I have indicated, it is inherently *dislocated.*

Similarly, a tactic is *ambivalent* because that which it would resist is always already part of what constitutes it. Because the place of the tactic belongs to the other (in other words to 'strategy'), the tactic can only exist *in relation* to strategy and not autonomously in *external opposition* to it. Thus the tactics deployed by this manager could not help but be ambivalent: she could not exist in external opposition to head office because head office was not simply the source of an antagonism, namely the training programme, but simultaneously the source of her own relative power and future career prospects as well. Analogously, she would not force her staff to comply with the demands of the training programme not only because she felt those demands to be unfair at a gut level but also because she could not run her store without the cooperation of staff and it was that cooperation that she felt the programme would jeopardize if it were enforced.

Although this example suggests an affinity of interests between managers and staff (an 'us') in relation to the demands of head office (a 'them') – and thus the expression of an antagonism between branch and centre – such an affinity was only temporary, the product of circumstances. Friend–enemy relations in retailing, as in other organizational contexts, are liable to constant realignment depending on circumstances.

While such friend–enemy groupings serve to exemplify a point made earlier, namely that management/worker relations should not be represented as *the* privileged site of organizational antagonisms, it would none the less be foolish to assume that relative power of different categories of employee did not differentially give them the opportunity to 'create space for themselves' at work. More often than not, for example, the ability of store managers to create space for themselves at work was dependent upon the *tactical use of their own staff*. It is to such practices that I now turn.

## Managerial tactics and power relations in-store

At company *B*, the store managers most likely to achieve swift career progression were those whose behaviour most fully (i.e. visibly) accorded with the values and meanings inscribed within the corporate culture. However, the competition for advancement within *B* was intense, and the calculated cultivation of a visible enterprising demeanour not only required managers to align themselves fully with the 'strategic gaze' but also to differentiate themselves from one another.

Some managers attempted to indicate their individual 'distinction' by deliberately understaffing their stores beyond the norms imposed by head office in order to come in under budget. This practice had the effect of signalling to area managers and to head office that the manager in question was 'one of them', a virtuous, enterprising person who could be trusted to act in *B*'s best interests. At the same time, however, it also helped to establish new norms against which the performance of other branches could then be judged. In other words, the political struggle for individual distinction among ambitious branch managers often led to the intensification of work in-store.

One highly ambitious young store manager at *B* had taken on so many extra responsibilities and understaffed her store to such an extent that she was regularly coming in to work seven days a week. Through taking on an increasing number of responsibilities with decreasing resources, this manager had gained a reputation for 'enterprise' within the company, and was firmly instituted as a potential 'high flier' (as a reward for being so 'virtuous' the company had awarded this manager one of their two coveted places on a national retail management summer school at Oxford University, a sure mark of distinction).

However, her reputation among senior management contrasted markedly with the views expressed about her by her colleagues in-store. They felt she was putting one over on head office. The impression she was creating, they argued, was of someone so devoted to the company that she had effectively given up any non-work life in order to further her career. However, while head office could measure this manager's 'enterprise' by the amount of work she had volunteered to take on and by her 'lean' staffing policy, it could not really see, they argued, how the work was getting done in-store. According to staff it was they who were lumbered with most of it while their manager took the credit. Certainly she spent lots of time 'officially' at the workplace, they agreed, but that was only part of the story. 'Officially at work' did not translate neatly into 'actually working'. This manager, they insisted, was using company time as her own time, for example, by taking extremely long lunch breaks, popping out to 'visit' other company stores and not returning before the end of the working day, by regularly inviting friends and family into the office during working hours and by constantly using the 'phone to make private calls. Meanwhile, and as a result of her actions, her subordinates had to take responsibility for the day-to-day running of the store.

> Our manager is young and ambitious and she wants to get on, and she'll probably go a long way. But she uses people. She's using me . . . because I'm running the branch for her. Where do we take the money? Here on the floor, not sitting in the office talking on the phone to friends, and taking long lunches. She's constantly in and out. I've taken a load off her back. But she's taking liberties . . . on the phone for hours talking to friends . . . Now that doesn't matter once in a while, but she's in there for an hour or more and the phone's always engaged. So if she does it everyone should be able to do it, but they can't.[24]

As this example – a distinctly managerial *'la perruque'* – indicates, managers can practise 'popular tactics' for their own ends and more profitably so because of their relative power. Indeed, the ability of store managers to create space for themselves at work is often founded upon the negation of such opportunities for those beneath them in the occupational hierarchy. Managers not only had more opportunities to practise 'tactics of consumption' at the workplace but also felt more justified in so doing because of what they saw as their greater individual responsibility for the success of the branch. Sales assistants, they argued, had an easier time of it because less was expected of them by the company. Unsurprisingly, perhaps, sales assistants didn't quite see it that way.

> The manager . . . she hates us having any of our friends coming in and won't let us receive personal calls on the phone. And if they do come in she wants us to be rude to them and say we can't talk to them. I mean, I had a friend come in who I hadn't seen for two years and I was asking how she was doing when the manager came over and in front of my friend said 'Is this your friend? Will you tell her to go?' I felt embarrassed and my friend felt embarrassed. And yet if the manager has a friend come in she'll stand there for ages chatting to them and if you say anything she says 'I work hard you know. I'm allowed five minutes off.' I mean we work hard as well but she doesn't seem to understand that . . . She pushes us to do the work while she goes up to the staff room to have a fag, or goes out shopping. Sometimes she says 'Oh, I've worked really hard, I'm going to have a couple of hours off.' Then she'll disappear to do some shopping. So it's us that's rushing around doing all the work and she turns round and says 'I've been working really hard this week', and I say 'What do you think I've been doing, sitting down all day?'[25]

In the following section I examine the tactical activities of sales assistants in retailing, indicating that their inferior access to the 'positional goods' enjoyed by management – information, financial rewards etc. – while reducing their 'room for manoeuvre' does not obliterate their opportunities to practise 'consumption' at work (de Certeau, 1984: viii). I begin by exploring the ways in which sales assistants use or consume those 'cultural technologies' through which they are being most explicitly encouraged to imagine they 'own' the business they work for.

### Sales assistants' 'tactics of consumption'

The discourse of enterprise places great emphasis upon the interpersonal skills of store management in 'winning over' employees – in generating a greater sense of identification between staff and company, and of encouraging every employee to feel personally accountable for the success of his or her branch. However, if the conduct of interpersonal relations is represented as increasingly important to the success of the retail enterprise then this presupposes, rather than annuls, the capacity of individual employees as agents. In other words, the relations between government and the governed passes through the manner in which governed individuals are willing to exist as particular subjects.

At company *A* it was through the technology of Quality Teams (QTs) that sales staff were being most explicitly encouraged to imagine that they 'owned' the business they worked for. The psychotherapeutic pre-suppositions inscribed within the QT process – self-monitoring as a key to commitment and so forth – structured it as a rational technology of the personal and interpersonal. QTs were designed to replace direct control with self-regulation. They sought to provide an ethical exercise for their members aimed at producing a particular kind of relationship to self and, through this, the ethical demeanour and standing of a particular kind of person: the enterprising self. However, delineating the structure of, and dominant meanings inscribed within, QTs says nothing about what they might mean for those at whom they are aimed. In other words, it says nothing about the ways in which this technology is 'consumed'.

The introduction of QTs in *A*'s stores was sold to staff as a 'freedom package'; as an opportunity for each individual employee within the company to become more personally involved in the running of the business and thus to develop himself or herself as an enterprising individual. QTs in-store were chaired by the branch manager. The Chair set the agenda indicating the 'Whats' (What We Want To Achieve) that had cascaded down from the immediately superior QT. The Chair's role was imperceptibly to guide the meeting and certainly not to hijack it or dominate it, ensuring that everyone got involved, that the group agreed to a series of 'Hows' and that every member of the QT was personally committed to their implementation. Emphasis was placed on getting staff to see the 'Hows' as the result of their own autonomous deliberations, thus ensuring that they felt 'ownership' of the QT. The effective 'impression management' of the QT process was thus represented as integral to its success. Any overt hint of manipulation or force was deemed to spell the kiss of death.

At one store in Central London where QTs were about to be introduced both management and staff were far from enthusiastic about its prospects. For the manager, the QT format appeared to be 'too dictatorial'.[26] Rather than mirroring the formal organizational hierarchy, he felt that the QT structure should be reversed. The 'Whats' should emanate from the bottom rather than the top, thus minimizing the possibility of employees interpreting QTs as an exercise in managerial manipulation. As things stood, he felt the QT structure would merely exacerbate his 'natural' desire to command. For staff, managerial manipulation was just the worry. They felt that QTs would mean an increased workload in an already understaffed store, and therefore anticipated the imminent arrival of QTs with trepidation, rather than with unmitigated joy.

Just before the first QT meeting was about to take place in-store, the branch manager was taken out for a drink by a facilitator – a personnel specialist assigned to initial QT meetings to help institute them and ensure their smooth running – and given a number of hints as to how to construct an appropriate atmosphere whereby everyone would feel at ease, equal in status and thus free to speak their minds. The emphasis was on creating the impression that QT meetings represented a space where normal workplace relations did not apply. So, for example, as staff assembled for the first meeting the manager made a point of signifying the egalitarian nature of the QT by going over to the staff drinks machine and switching it on to 'free vend'. However, this rather blatant gesture did nothing to alleviate the suspicions of staff; instead it served to intensify them. In a move every bit as calculated as that of their manager, staff signalled their disbelief in the apparent reversal of work relations by collectively ignoring this invitation to have a free drink, and instead walking over to the table where the meeting was to take place and sitting down in silence. Although, after a suitable time lapse, the facilitator attempted to salvage something from the manager's initial manoeuvre by offering to get people a drink, no one accepted.

Throughout the meeting staff simply responded to questions and prompts from the Chair and from the facilitator. At no point did they 'run with the meeting' themselves, as head office promotional material suggested they should/would, nor, conversely, did they explicitly attempt to railroad it. Instead, they projected an air of quiet resignation which only served further to highlight the artificiality and constructedness of the event, and thus the obvious control being exerted by the Chair and the facilitator. Behaving in this manner, staff indicated their disbelief in the QT process as a vehicle for their own 'empowerment'.

At various points in the meeting, the degree of explicit manipulation of social interaction taking place became almost too embarrassing for comfort. For example, having asked two members of staff for their opinions on how to avoid till receipts ending up on the floor of the store and having received the reply that perhaps staff could make better use of the bins under their tills, the Chair declared 'That's just what I wanted you to say.' The meaning of this comment was not lost on staff or on the facilitator who berated the manager on this interactional gaffe in her debrief of his performance after the meeting.

As the QT meeting progressed, it became increasingly apparent to staff that the Chair's main priority was to obtain three 'Hows' from them so as to ensure that, publicly (i.e. to head office) at least, the meeting could be judged a success. In other words, as long as the formal objectives cascading down from above were met then the manager/Chair could present his branch meeting as a 'success' to the Chair of the immediately superior QT meeting of which he was also a member; in effect, he would have satisfied the calculating, quantifying logic of the 'strategic gaze'.

As far as staff were concerned, however, while they had ostensibly come up with three 'Hows' of their own volition, they had made it perfectly clear in their mode of participation that they felt no personal involvement in the process by which these had been reached, nor indeed did they feel any personal responsibility for their implementation in-store. Rather, they had done just enough to avoid being sanctioned by their manager, while expressing their disbelief in the whole process at the same time. They believed they had no choice but to attend the meeting; however, they simultaneously refused to condone what it was meant to stand for.[27]

The meeting of government and governed in the domain of the QT raises some important issues about 'making up people at work'. As already indicated, the QT was represented by senior management at company *A* as a crucial mechanism through which the 'hearts and minds' of the company's workforce would be harnessed to the pursuit of staying 'close to the customer'. Emphasis was placed on the QT as a site or domain in which ordinary work relations were temporarily suspended as everyone played an equal role in 'changing some of the things we do for the better'.[28] However, it was this representation of the QT as an egalitarian space that was challenged by the consumption practices of staff who entered and conducted themselves within that space according to an entirely different frame of reference. Because the QT was an unknown – it didn't seem to have a proper place or identity – staff attempted to give it a firm identity by using it as if it were simply an extension of existing work relations. Because they did not occupy the same symbolic space as management in the normal cultural relations of the workplace, they saw no need to act any differently in the space of the QT. As Stallybrass and White (1986: 194), for example, have argued, each domain within any social ensemble is the site of production of discourse but each domain in turn can quite easily be reconstructed within the terms of other domains and according to the hierarchies and ranks governing that domain. The domain of the QT was structured according to the psychotherapeutic suppositions of enterprise and yet it was consumed by staff according to entirely different classificatory criteria. In other words, in order to domesticate this confusing space (the QT) staff classified it according to what they considered to be the most relevant symbolic categories: those derived from the cultural relations of the shopfloor. In so doing, and by sheer weight of numbers, they undermined their manager's attempts to represent the QT as an egalitarian space and forced him increasingly to conduct himself as their manager and not simply as another member of the QT.

As a result, while three 'Hows' emerged from the meeting, they did so under discursive conditions the very opposite to those envisaged by head office. In other words, they were produced in a world of managers and workers, of us and them, and not – as desired – in the organic, antagonism- and hierarchy-free world of enterprising individuality. Although the production of three 'Hows' allowed the QT technology to be reproduced, the symbolic categories through which that re-production was manifested were very different from those structuring the QT 'from above'. Through their classificatory practices, staff effectively translated the meaning and identity of the QT, while simultaneously reproducing it. In de Certeau's (1984: xiii) terms, staff appropriated the QT by using it with respect to references very different from those intended by its instigators.

Once again, however, it would be foolish to draw too many 'celebratory' conclusions concerning workforce resistance and so forth from this example. As indicated earlier, while staff translated the QT into a different discursive register, thus undermining its original intent, they also reproduced its basic conditions of existence by establishing and agreeing to implement three 'Hows'. The relationship between government and governed in the QT was not a simple zero-sum game. Staff were not acting autonomously of official norms but always in relation to them. Thus they could not escape 'enterprise' as a regulatory ideal even while their actions challenged it precisely because their actions were only called forth in relation to that ideal. As we have already seen, because 'tactics of consumption' have no place of their own – because they always take place in relation to 'labelling from above' – they cannot keep a distance from the norms of enterprise even when challenging them. So, although staff managed to translate the ideals of enterprise into the register of manager/worker difference, they did so only temporarily and ambiguously because they also reproduced the enterprising technology of the QT at the same time.

Similarly ambivalent tactics of consumption by shopfloor staff were evident in relation to the new technologies of organizational reform at company *B*. For sales assistants at company *B* one of the most detested elements of the company's strategy was the uniform they were contractually obliged to wear. Nothing highlighted the perceived status gap between *B*'s own sales staff, on the one hand, and concessions staff and customers, on the other, more than the uniform. Rather than allowing them to present 'a quality, up-market image' to customers, staff felt that the uniform robbed them of all self-respect, making them 'look like schoolchildren'. No member of staff would ever wear the uniform either to or from work but always changed into and out of it at the workplace, such was the sense of embarrassment that wearing it engendered. For staff, the uniform encapsulated the company's disrespect for them as individuals and their reduction to 'a mass of numbers'.

> They said we can wear this uniform on our way home and I said 'I wouldn't be seen dead in this, man.' I tell you one time I was late out so I thought to get home in time I better leave my uniform on instead of wearing my own clothes. And I get to the bus-stop and everyone starts laughing. One of my friends said 'What happened, man? You had a fight with your trousers?' And the man on the bus he says 'That shirt, man, it looks like someone been sick on you.' And I thought, 'Oh thanks, man.' So since then I haven't ever worn that uniform home or from home to work.[29]

Staff felt that the uniform attacked their sense of who they were and what they wanted to be seen to be; in order to be able to live with themselves in the uniform, they gradually began to accessorize it. At first this process was relatively discreet, but over time staff became more and more audacious: wearing brightly coloured Kickers and Reeboks, lots of rings, bracelets, and badges, and adding pieces of their own clothing to the basics of the uniform. They strove to make the uniform serve as an extension of their identity outside the workplace rather than allowing it to single them out as employees.

Although both store management and some head office staff had considerable sympathy with the sales assistants' complaints – they didn't think the uniform was of a high enough quality – they were not prepared to remove the uniform from service, nor to countenance any improvisation in its use by staff. The uniform, they argued, was a central element of the strategy; an integral component of the company's integrated design offering to customers. Any tampering with it was deemed harmful to the company's chosen, 'scientifically' constituted image, and was therefore unacceptable to the 'strategic gaze'.

> I don't care what they wear at 11 pm in a disco, I couldn't give a damn. But when they're at work they portray a professional image that appeals to the majority, not the minority. So they will conform. M&S (Marks & Spencer) uniform is not the most fashionable uniform in the world but it looks as smart and presentable on a 16-year-old as it does on a 59-year-old. They conform. There is a standard. You wear a court shoe. You wear stockings, or whatever. They don't rebel. In *B* there has tended to be more rebellion. The managers have got to control that, to make sure that staff and store project the right image. As I said, what they wear after work I don't really mind, but when they're at work they'll project the image we want them to project, and that's the initial bit. That's first impressions. The reason that M&S gets such high ratings on all aspects of its business is on its first impressions. You walk into the store. It's neat, it's clean, it's tidy. You see easily identifiable staff, not millions of them but you notice the uniform . . . In lots of *B*'s stores it's been the opposite . . . there is so much variety of individualism translated into the uniform that there is no longer a uniform; so many adaptations to the uniform that the image portrayed is chaotic. That first three seconds' impression is not good.[30]

As this manager's comments indicate, by adding accessories to the uniform, staff crossed a crucial boundary. Uniformity was a strategic goal; its implementation was closely monitored by both area and head offices. By adapting the uniform, staff posed a direct challenge to the 'strategic gaze', one that head office determined to meet head-on.

> Everyone just went crazy. They were rolling the trousers up, they were hanging out the shirt, wearing their own T-shirt. Then the personnel woman from head office come down and had a go at us. 'If you do not wear this shirt tucked in, trousers let loose' – 'cause everyone was wearing an elastic band wrapped round them to make them look baggy – 'they will dismiss you.' And everybody started to wear it properly. Everybody obeyed. But it's the nearest we've had to a hectic scene since I've been here.[31]

As this example serves to highlight once again, 'tactics of consumption' are inherently relational or dislocated, being both a structural inversion of and yet ambivalently dependent upon 'official norms'. Similarly, the effects of tactics are never unambiguous. Certainly, head office eventually got their way concerning the uniform and a coherent visual identity was written on the body of the staff. However, the cost of this was a generalized disillusion with the company's strategy and its discourse of empowerment, ownership and individual self-actualization. As one sales assistant put it after the clampdown by head office, 'They're talkin' about this strategy thing. They're talkin' about it for themselves . . . It means a lot to them because its *theirs*. Its not *ours*, we just work here.'[32]

While this statement is at one level extremely misleading – the strategy had everything to do with staff, they couldn't escape it – it carries an emotional punch because it highlights the inherent difficulties of 'making up people' at work. Far from operating in a neutral semantic field, entrepreneurial mechanisms of identity formation come into contact with existing classificatory practices and this can under certain circumstances lead them to become the site of an intense 'friend–enemy relation'. The introduction of a new corporate uniform in company *B* functioned in just such a way as the comments above testify. While staff could not escape the strategy, the battle over the uniform had made them certain of one thing: that to all intents and purposes the strategy was not theirs because rather than making them feel valued as individuals (as they had been told it was intended to do), it had reinforced their feelings of worthlessness – that they were simply a 'mass' of identikit drones and nothing more.

**Conclusion**

In this chapter I have attempted to extend the explanatory reach of my analysis of the contemporary dislocation of production and consumption relations within retailing by considering what different categories of employee make of and do with the technologies and representations to which they are subjected and which they cannot keep at a distance. In particular, I have explored the ways in which these different categories of employee consumed or used these technologies and representations, sometimes with respect to ends and references very different from those prescribed by the discourse of enterprise.

While I have indicated that a focus upon tactics of consumption within organizational domains attests to the limits of 'labelling from above', to the impossibility of abolishing antagonism and therefore of creating the happy relation the organization would like to have with itself, I have also stressed that this did not indicate the 'failure' – in some absolute sense – of the discourse of enterprise. Rather, I have been at pains to point to the inherently relational or dislocated nature of 'tactics of consumption at work'; to highlight both their structural inversion of and ambivalent dependence upon 'official norms' of enterprise. Because 'tactics of consumption' are *always immanent to power and not in a relation of external opposition to power*, I have argued that the effects of such tactics upon the processes of 'making up people' at work are never unambiguous.

In the final chapter of the book – which also serves as a conclusion – I examine the relationship between contemporary discourses of organizational governance and the domination of individuals as work-based subjects. In particular, I attempt to show how it might be possible to gain some critical purchase upon these discourses of organizational reform and the regime of subjectification to which they are inextricably linked.

**Notes**

1 There are signs of a re-emerging interest in the culture of paid work within certain sections of cultural studies. Both Paul Willis (1990: 14) and Angela McRobbie (1991: 15–16)

have argued that the sphere of paid work remains an extremely important source of identification: an arena in which people perform 'necessary symbolic work' and exercise 'symbolic creativity'.

2 Interview with managing director (white, male), company *B*, July 1990.

3 One area manager who had been with the company for 15 years in various capacities, and who was well known throughout *B*'s management circles as a 'non-believer' in the redemptive power of the 'strategy', was 'made an offer he couldn't refuse' shortly after being interviewed for this project. In the interview he had expressed his dislike of current developments in the company. He felt that management and staff had been 'cut to the bone', through a series of rationalizations, so that they no longer had any 'time or space' to institute the strategy. Instead, all their energies were expended on simply getting the 'day-to-day activities', of opening the store, serving customers and stocking up, done. They were in a 'permanent crisis situation' with no time to spare on anything but the very basics of the business. Overall, he felt that neither the systems were in place, nor were adequate resources available, to institute the strategy, and that, as it stood, the company *B* board had 'put the cart before the horse'. 'There's a danger that the whole thing'll fall as flat as a pancake. Those that have been in the company for a long time are thinking "we've seen this sort of thing before". In three months' time it'll have disappeared completely.' Although this was a view repeated on a number of occasions by both lower and middle management, as well as sales staff, during the course of research very few people admitted to expressing their fears publicly to senior management. Many chose to 'speak the language' of enterprise publicly for fear of otherwise not appearing to 'have what it takes'. Not long after this interview took place I learnt from a store manager at *B* that the area manager had resigned, though, as I was informed, this 'was more a case of being pushed than choosing to go' (interview with an area manager (white, male), company *B*, July 1990 and interview with a small store's manager (white, female), company *B*, July 1990).

4 Interview with deputy manager (white, male), company *A*, large store, Central London, May 1990.

5 Interview with deputy manager (white, male), company *A*, large store, Central London, May 1990.

6 Interview with sales manager (white, female), company *A*, large store, Central London, May 1990.

7 Interviews with graduate general management trainee (white, male), company *A*, large store, Central London, May 1990 and with graduate professional management trainee (black, male), company *A*, small store, Central London, June 1990.

8 Interview with area assistant training officer (white, female), company *A*, Central London, June 1990. This manager stressed that the dominance of senior positions by professionals was also, at the same time, a dominance by gender. Almost all senior executives at *A* were not only professionals but men. This degree of dominance was not mirrored at store level, however. In Central London, for example, almost 50 per cent of the store managers were women. This latter development, of quite recent origin, corresponds to the quite considerable increase in the number of women taking the professional qualification in question. However, in a now familiar pattern, the gradual increase in women among the profession has not yet produced any major disruption in gender relations within the company. Being a professional is seen to be an occupation where women can do a job while 'remaining a woman', i.e. taking care of child-rearing and attending to domestic responsibilities. In other words, the profession is well regarded as a consistent provider of well-remunerated, flexible employment opportunities. However, because *A* requires all its senior managers to be geographically mobile and to work full-time, women professionals have tended to stay at the lower levels of *A*'s management hierarchy. The dominance of white, male professionals in the higher echelons of *A*'s management hierarchy and of (mainly white) women professionals in the lower end of this hierarchy can therefore be partly explained as a consequence of the flexible employment opportunities available in the professional occupation which have enabled women, through a combination of intermittent and part-time work, to combine their domestic roles with continuing employment in the profession. Most of the female professionals I spoke to at *A*

informed me that the profession had attracted them because it appeared to be a good job for women who wanted to have children at some stage. However, that said, the increasing number of women store managers working (full-time) in London does suggest that more women will be moving into higher management positions in the future, and this is certainly widely anticipated both within the profession and within company *A* management circles.

9 Interview with sales manager (white, female), company *A*, large store, Central London, May 1990.

10 Interview with a sales assistant (white, female), company *B*, large store, Central London, August 1990.

11 As a store manager at another of *A*'s Central London stores informed me, the department to which these women had been allocated tended to be seen 'as a bit of a dustbin in terms of staff throughout the company' (interview with a store manager (white, male), company *A*, small store, Central London, June 1990).

12 Interview with a part-time sales assistant (black, female), company *A*, large store, Central London, July 1990. This black woman was the only member of the department who would agree to talk to me in an interview context. Being a white, middle-class male and wandering the shopfloor and canteen asking questions about working for *A* ensured my being labelled as the worst of all possible outsiders to the women on the department: a white management spy. Although this interviewee was able to offer interesting insights into the dynamics of the department that I would never otherwise have been privy to, she was in the strange position of being both an insider and an outsider herself. She was an insider on one level, being black, female and working closely with her colleagues on a day-to-day basis. But, partly through working only part-time and thus never sharing rest breaks with her colleagues, and partly through her antithetical attitude towards their 'black radicalism' (expressed, for example, by her having a white boyfriend, something she said her colleagues found both incredible and disgusting) which she described as 'narrow minded', on another level she was also an outsider: 'I don't think they see me as one of them 'cause if something happens they don't tell me.' It was only through wanting to express her difference from the group, to indicate her distance from their collective identity – 'let me tell you, man, you can learn nothing from your own culture . . . it's good to be different' – that she was willing to talk to me.

13 Interview with a sales assistant (white, female), company *B*, large store, Central London, July 1990.

14 Interview with a sales assistant (white, female), company *B*, Central London, September 1990.

15 Interview with a senior sales assistant (white, female), company *B*, Central London, September 1990.

16 Interview with a sales assistant (white, female), company *B*, Central London, September 1990.

17 Interview with a store manager (white, male) company *A*, small store, Central London, June 1990.

18 Interview with a store manager (white, female), company *B*, small store, Surrey, September 1990.

19 Interview with a graduate trainee manager (white, female), company *B*, small store, Hampshire, August 1990.

20 Interview with a store manager (white, female), company *B*, small store, Buckinghamshire, September 1990.

21 Interview with a store manager (white, female), company *B*, small store, Surrey, September 1990.

22 Information obtained from in-store observation and from interviews with management and staff at both company *A* and company *B*.

23 Interview with a store manager (white, female), company *B*, small store, Buckinghamshire, September 1990.

24 Interview with a supervisor (black, female), company *B*, small store, Central London, August 1990.

25 Interview with a sales assistant (white, female), company *B*, small store, Sussex, July 1990.

26 Interview with a store manager (white, male), company *A*, small store, Central London, June 1990.

27 Information obtained from observation of QT meetings and from interviews with both management and staff at a small store, company *A*, Central London, July and August 1990.

28 Quote taken from speech by the managing director (white, male) video-relayed to staff at company *A*, 1989.

29 Interview with a sales assistant (black, female), company *B*, Central London, September 1990.

30 Interview with an area manager (white, male), company *B*, July 1990.

31 Interview with a cashier assistant (black, female), company *B*, Central London, September 1990.

32 Interview with senior sales assistant (black, female), company *B*, Central London, September 1990.

# 8

# Setting Limits to Enterprise

Attempting to gain some critical purchase on the blurring of boundaries between work and consumption identities is an endeavour fraught with difficulties. Simple generalizations about the enabling/constraining effects of such shifts are apt to founder quite quickly upon the rock of difference. For, as we have seen in Chapters 6 and 7, the consequences of 'making up' people at work as enterprising subjects are multiple, uneven and often seemingly contradictory. No simple objective picture emerges that could provide an unequivocal guide to critique.

Every picture of contemporary organizational reform is perspectival rather than transcendental. Representing the death of the 'modern industrial worker' as a *universal* tragedy, for example, is simply not feasible, as feminist scholars among many others have demonstrated (Pateman, 1989). Similarly, those tempted to represent the contemporary 'enterprising up' of work organization and identity as inherently liberating and empowering are apt to avoid the questions: for whom, and at what cost? As I have attempted to indicate throughout this book, the establishment of every identity is always an ambiguous achievement, being dependent upon the simultaneous definition of difference.

The recognition of the ambivalence and contingency of identity can be a very dislocating experience. The gradual realization that what seemed certain is not so certain after all is, for those experiencing it, often very debilitating. None the less, the recognition of contingency, ambivalence and perspectivalism does not entail quietism. Accepting that a universal standpoint is not available does not mean that one must forgo the possibility of engaging in critique and evaluation. It simply entails accepting that one's point of view is simply that: a position held within a field of contestation and not a 'God's eye view' presiding over such a field.

With these provisos in mind, how should we attempt to gain some critical purchase on the contemporary dislocation of work and consumption relations? I have argued throughout this book that the discourse of enterprise through which this dislocation is effected is best understood in terms of a new rationality of government and a novel regime of subjectification. A critical analysis of this rationality of government and the regime of subjectification to which it is linked might begin by examining the ways in which it establishes new 'dividing' or 'classificatory' practices for the conduct of conduct.

## Border questions

To read the works of Peters, Kanter and other advocates of entrepreneurial organizational governance, with their continual references to and often explicit celebration of 'hybrid' organizations and the blurring of organizational boundaries, one would be forgiven for thinking that all barriers, boundaries and borders had been erased and that life was once again a plenitude. In such a world, is it any longer possible to delineate winners and losers? Indeed, isn't it more likely that the attempt to do so is pointless as something 'organic' is simply not susceptible to such demarcations and distinctions? To succumb to this logic would indeed be an abnegation of critical responsibility. For a world in which the boundaries within and among firms and between the public and private is blurring, is as Charles Sabel (1991: 46) has argued, 'not a world without boundaries. New boundaries, indeed new kinds of boundaries, are being drawn as the old fade.'

While the ethos of enterprise can be seen to blur traditional distinctions between sets of activities or spheres of action, this blurring does not signify the disappearance of boundaries *per se* but rather their re-articulation according to new principles. In other words, enterprise does not defy categorization, it simply categorizes in a different way. The ethical vocabulary of enterprise re-imagines activities and agents and their relationship to each other according to its own regulatory ideals. Thus, the entrepreneurial language of responsible self-advancement, for example, is linked to a new perception of those 'outside civility' – the excluded and marginalized who cannot or will not conduct themselves in an appropriately 'responsible' manner. Pathologies that were until recently represented and acted upon 'socially' – homelessness, unemployment and so forth – become re-individualized through their positioning within a new ethical vocabulary and hence subject to new and often more intense forms of surveillance and control. Because they are now represented as responsible individuals with a moral duty to take care of themselves, pathological subjects can blame no one but themselves for the problems they face. This individualization of the social is evidenced in the UK by the recent repositioning of the unemployed person as a 'job seeker' and the homeless person as a 'rough sleeper' (Rose, forthcoming).

It is through paying close attention to the boundary lines and distinctions that enterprise draws that we can begin to construct an approach that may lead to its de-valorization. For, in delineating what enterprise must inevitably exclude, it becomes possible to assess the costs of its establishment. Exploring the boundary lines of enterprise allows us to ask an important question: 'what does it cost existence for its truth to be produced and affirmed in this way?' (Burchell, 1993: 279). We can only begin this 'border questioning' by returning once again to the ethos of enterprise.

**The ethos of enterprise**

A key feature of enterprise as a rationality of government is the role it
allocates to the enterprise form as the privileged model for the conduct of
conduct. As Graham Burchell (1993: 275), for example, has noted, the
defining characteristic of entrepreneurial governance is the 'generalization
of an "enterprise form" to all forms of conduct – the conduct of organizations hitherto seen as being non-economic, to the conduct of government,
and to the conduct of individuals themselves'. While the concrete ways in
which this governmental rationality has been put into practice have varied
quite considerably, the forms of action they make possible for different
institutions and persons – schools, general practitioners, housing estates,
prisons and so forth – do share a general consistency and style.

As Burchell also argues (1993: 276, following Donzelot), a characteristic
feature of this style of government is the crucial role it accords to 'contract'
in redefining social relations. Thus, the changes affecting a variety of
different spheres of existence – schools, hospitals, government departments
and so on – often involve the reconstituting of institutional roles in terms
of contracts strictly defined, and even more frequently involve a contract-
like way of representing relationships between institutions, between
individuals and institutions and between individuals one with another. An
example of the former, for instance, occurs in the UK context when fund-
holding medical practices contract with hospital trusts for the provision of
health care to particular patients where previously that provision was made
directly by the National Health Service. Examples of the latter include the
relationships between central government departments in the UK and the
new executive or 'Next Steps' agencies – where no technical contract as
such exists but where the relationship between the two is governed by a
contract-like framework document which defines the functions and goals of
the agency and the procedures whereby the department will set and
monitor the performance targets for the agency (Freedland, 1994: 88).

Thus, contractualization typically consists in assigning the performance
of a function or an activity to a distinct unit of management – individual or
collective – which is regarded as being accountable for the efficient
performance of that function or conduct of that activity. By assuming active
responsibility for these activities and functions – both for carrying them out
and their outcomes – these units of management are in effect affirming a
certain kind of identity. This identity is essentially entrepreneurial in
character. In other words, the contractual relationship requires these units
of management to adopt an entrepreneurial character 'as a condition of
their effectiveness and of the effectiveness of this form of government'
(Burchell, 1993: 276). Or, to put it in the language of Tom Peters (1992:
273), 'contractualization' 'businesses' individuals and collectivities.

As Colin Gordon (1991: 42–5), for example, has argued, entrepreneurial
forms of governance, such as the use of contracts, involve the re-
imagination of the social as a form of the economic. 'This operation

works', he argues, 'by the progressive enlargement of the territory of economic theory by a series of re-definitions of its object'. 'Economics thus becomes an "approach" capable in principle of addressing the totality of human behaviour, and, consequently, of envisaging a coherent purely economic method of programming the totality of governmental action' (Gordon, 1991: 43). Enterprise can thus be seen to perform what we might term a 'levelling function' whereby formerly diverse institutions, practices, goods and so forth become subject to judgement and calculation primarily in terms of economic criteria, giving rise to the dominance of what Lyotard (1984: 46) terms the 'performativity principle'. However, it would be misguided to view this development as simply the latest and most potent manifestation of the irresistible rise of *homo economicus*.

As Gordon (1991: 43) has indicated, the subject of enterprise is both 'a reactivation and radical inversion' of traditional 'economic man'. The reactivation consists 'in positing a fundamental human faculty of choice, a principle which empowers economic calculation effectively to sweep aside the anthropological categories and frameworks of the human and social sciences'. The great innovation occurs, as I have indicated throughout this text, in the conceptualization of the economic agent as an inherently manipulable creation. Whereas *homo economicus* was originally conceived of as a subject, the well-springs of whose activity were ultimately 'untouchable by government', the subject of enterprise is imagined as an agent 'who is perpetually responsive to modifications in its environment'. As Gordon (1991: 43) points out, 'economic government here joins hands with behaviourism.' The resultant subject is in a novel sense not just an 'enterprise' but 'the entrepreneur of himself or herself'.

As we have seen, the idea of an individual life as an 'enterprise of the self' suggests that, no matter what hand circumstance may have dealt a person, he or she remains always continuously engaged (even when technically 'unemployed' or 'at leisure') in that one enterprise, and that it is 'part of the continuous business of living to make adequate provision for the preservation, reproduction and reconstruction of one's own human capital' (Gordon, 1991: 44).

Because a human being is considered to be continuously engaged in a project to shape his or her life as an autonomous, choosing individual driven by the desire to optimize the worth of his or her own existence, life for that person is represented as a single arena for the pursuit of that endeavour. In other words, because previously distinct forms of life or modes of conduct are now classified primarily, if not exclusively, as 'enterprise forms', the conceptions and practices of personhood they give rise to are remarkably consistent. Thus, as schools, government departments and so forth are re-imagined as 'enterprises' they all accord an increased priority to the 'entrepreneur' as a category of person. In this sense the character of the entrepreneur can no longer be seen as just one among a plurality of ethical personalities *but must rather be seen as assuming an ontological priority*.

As I have argued throughout this book, the conception of the individual as an 'entrepreneur of the self' is firmly established at the heart of contemporary programmes of organizational reform. In keeping with the entrepreneurial imbrication of economics and behaviourism, these programmes of reform characterize employment not as a painful obligation imposed upon individuals, nor as an activity undertaken to meet instrumental needs, but rather as a means to self-responsibility and hence self-optimization. Organizational success is therefore premised upon an engagement by the organization of the self-optimizing impulses of all its members, no matter what their formal role. This ambition is made practicable in the workplace through all those seemingly banal techniques we have come across in the course of this text: de-layering, the creation of 'special project teams', performance-related pay and so on. Performance-related pay, for example, whose deployment has increased dramatically in the past decade – most particularly in the public sector in the UK – often involves the development of a 'contract' between an individual employee and his or her line manager whereby that employee's pay or an element of his or her pay is made more dependent upon whether he or she has met, exceeded or failed to meet certain performance objectives (Milward et al., 1992: 268, 361; Marsden and Richardson, 1994).

Thus performance management and related techniques involve a characteristically contractual relationship between individual employees and the organization for which they work. This involves 'offering' individuals involvement in activities – such as managing budgets, training staff, delivering services – previously held to be the responsibility of other agents, such as supervisors, personnel departments and so forth. However, the price of this involvement is that individuals themselves must assume responsibility for carrying out these activities and for their outcomes. In keeping with the principles of enterprise, performance management and related techniques function as forms of responsibilization which are held to be both economically desirable and personally 'empowering'.

As indicated in Chapters 3 and 4, this 'autonomization' and 'responsibilization' makes paid work (no matter how objectively alienated, deskilled or degraded it may appear to social scientists) an essential element in the path to individual virtue and self-fulfilment and provides the *a priori* that links work and non-work, public and private together.

There is a real sense in the world of enterprise that 'one is always at it' because entrepreneurial discourse represents and structures life as one big 'enterprise'. As Colin Gordon (1991: 42) has indicated, enterprise as a rationality of government is involved in a diffusion of the enterprise-form throughout the social fabric 'as its generalized principle of functioning'. Whereas it once seemed easy for at least some portion of the population (mainly men, of course) to know where work stopped and leisure began, these days, as Charles Sabel (1991: 43) has argued, 'it is becoming harder to say when one is working. Activities at work become preparation for turning the family into a family enterprise that absorbs all leisure; family and leisure activities become preconditions of employability. Anticipation of these possibilities undermines the distinctions between *work, leisure,* and *family.'*

If the blurring – and effective reconfiguration – of the boundaries between work and leisure and so forth is 'empowering' for the responsi-bilized, autonomized individual, who is both its medium and outcome, then this empowerment is not without its costs. As Sabel (1991: 43) suggests, 'this enhanced autonomy is simultaneously qualified by the same situation that produced it.' As I indicated earlier, the price of being 'offered' autonomy is accepting responsibility for exercising it in particular ways and for the outcomes its exercise produces. This means that individuals are more personally exposed to the costs of engaging in any activity and more dependent on their own resources for successfully carrying it out. Once inside enterprise, therefore, one cannot hand one's autonomy back; instead one has – one is forced, in effect – to exercise it continuously in order to guarantee one's own reproduction.

This requirement that individuals become more personally exposed to the risks and costs of engaging in a particular activity is represented as a means to their empowerment because it encourages them to build resources in themselves rather than rely on others to take the risks and endure the uncertainty on their behalf. As such, entrepreneurial 'government makes its own rationality intimately their affair' (Gordon, 1991: 48). While the discourse of enterprise has come in for a vast amount of criticism, particularly from the Left (for a discussion of some of the more predictable criticisms levelled against the advocates of enterprise, see du Gay, 1991), the growing deployment of many of its key tropes by individuals and groups across the political spectrum (Osborne and Gaebler, 1992; Mulgan, 1994), and in a variety of other domains of activity, suggests that it is fast becoming something like a 'common sense' of the age.

According to some commentators (Donzelot, 1984; 1991), the emergence of enterprise as a rationality of government signifies the political exhaustion of both Left and Right rather than the dominance of the latter over the former. Indeed, Donzelot (1991: 178) views entrepreneurial technologies of individual autonomization and responsibilization as effecting potentially positive political and ethical outcomes. He regards the blurring of bound-aries between work and leisure, public and private, as in some sense a pluralizing process 'enabling the problems of the State', for example, 'to rebound back on society, so that society is implicated in the task of resolving them, where previously the state was expected to hand down an answer to society's needs'. From this perspective, entrepreneurial govern-ance involves the 'mobilization of society' through its lifting of the barriers between 'individual and society, society and state' and its subsequent hybridization 'of the public and the private, the state and the civil'.

This is an interesting analysis and one which at least has the audacity to argue from a critical perspective that entrepreneurial norms and techniques of governance should not be seen as unambiguously 'bad'. Certainly, entrepreneurial strategies aimed at reducing the scope of central government activity, for example, have forced citizens to consider fundamental questions about the scope and management of public services in which they have been able to avoid taking an interest in the past. Is this a completely bad thing? Similarly, devolved budgets and performance-related pay in industry can have the effect of encouraging workers and managers to see themselves as implicated in the life of the organization for which they work rather than as existing exterior to it. Such developments cannot be uniformly described as negative.

In making individuals more interested in their own government, enterprise can therefore be seen to open up a new domain of relations between politics and ethics. As Gordon (1991: 48), for example, has argued, 'to the extent that the governed are engaged, in their individuality, by the propositions and provisions of government . . . politics becomes, in a new sense, answerable to ethics.' By implicating individuals in a 'market game' where they assume the status of being 'entrepreneurs' of their own lives, entrepreneurial government makes its own rationality the condition of their active freedom (Burchell, 1993: 276).

With the whole ensemble of an individual's life structured as the pursuit of a range of different enterprises, such seemingly diverse forms of conduct as a person's relationship to self, their relationship to their paid work activities, to their leisure activities, their family, environment and so forth all become inscribed with the ethos of the enterprise form (Gordon, 1991: 42). The claim that enterprise is a pluralizing creed seems oddly at variance with this demand that all forms of life be re-imagined as enterprise forms. For surely the sorts of boundary crossings that enterprise seems to be engaging in – making distinct forms of life commensurable through their redefinition in economic terms – flattens difference and threatens the integrity of particular forms of life? As Stanley Fish (1994: 240), for example, has argued, if we want certain jobs to continue being done we need to maintain the vocabularies that make them possible and even conceivable. If a particular ethical vocabulary is jettisoned in favour of (or simply redefined in terms of) another, then the world that vocabulary brought into being will no longer be available to us. In the following sections I explore this issue further by enquiring into the political and ethical effects of re-imagining different forms of life as 'enterprise forms', paying particular attention to whether such a move is sufficiently pluralist (presupposing as it does a single ethical hierarchy with the 'entrepreneur' at its apex).

## Setting limits to enterprise

As I have argued throughout this book, assuming that the identity of a domain remains the same throughout all the changes it undergoes is extremely problematic. Given that any identity is basically relational to its conditions of existence, any change in the latter is bound to affect the former. If for example, the (bureaucratic) conduct of public administration is re-imagined in terms of entrepreneurial principles (as in the case of Britain and the United States in the 1990s), then rather than having the same identity – (bureaucratic) public administration – in a new situation, a new identity is established.

This has important implications for our understanding of the relationship between enterprise and difference. According to a number of commentators (Gordon, 1991; Burchell, 1993; Rose, forthcoming), the contemporary 'making up' of different locales – hospitals, public bureaus, prisons and so forth – as enterprise forms does not eliminate the particularity and specificity of those locales and lead to the creation of some 'amorphous cultural space'. It is, of course, still possible to differentiate between the experience of being taught, that of being detained in prison, being given medical treatment and so forth. In this reading, the enterprising individual is still confronted by a plurality of goods and not one singular good. Difference is not necessarily flattened out but rather re-articulated.

However, for Michael Walzer (1994: 36), while the subject of enterprise may acknowledge different sorts of goods *it always does so in the same way*: making its choices under the aegis of 'an individualized hierarchy of value'. This, he suggests, leads to a terrible one-sidedness. The idea that there is a single model of action appropriate to any number of locales is dangerous because it implies the triumph of one good over all others. In contrast to this form of 'simple equality', where the possession of one good such as 'enterprise' brings everything else in train, Walzer (1983; 1984; 1994) advocates what he terms 'complex equality', whereby different goods are distributed in accordance with different procedures, by different agents and all these differences derive from different understandings of the goods themselves. In other words, different goods constitute different distributional spheres within which specific distributive arrangements are appropriate, and justice consists in autonomous distributions, whereby the distribution of a good such as ecclesiastical office, for example, is conducted in accordance with the principles peculiar to that good and not corrupted by other goods, such as wealth, that properly belong to different spheres. For Walzer, the way to ensure pluralism, justice and equality is to practise an 'art of separation' whereby success in one distributive setting is not convertible into success in another. This account of distributive justice also has implications for our understanding of identity. For 'complex equality' presupposes and constitutes an ethical subject that is far from unified and single-minded in all its transactions; different spheres of justice give rise to different conceptions and comportments of personhood (Rorty, 1988; Walzer, 1994).

According to Amélie Rorty (1988: 7), this art of separation is most often endangered when the concerns of one particular context or life order are imported into or imposed on other, different departments of existence. Given that the entrepreneurial project is precisely concerned with diffusing the enterprise form throughout the social body, making it its 'generalized principle of functioning', we can certainly assume that enterprise may be involved in some serious 'boundary crossings'.

As I have already indicated, the defining feature of entrepreneurial government is the generalization of the enterprise form to all forms of conduct – public, private, voluntary etc. In this way, it is perfectly legitimate to suggest that a particular conception of the person as an entrepreneur, which while a 'hybrid' creation – born from the meeting of economics and behaviourism – none the less derives from and properly belongs to a particular sphere of existence (the life order of the market), is being increasingly imposed upon other departments of life (each of which has given rise to its own conceptions and practices of personhood). If this is the case, then the boundaries between distinct 'spheres' will be crossed and, I would suggest, the liberties and equalities predicated upon their 'separation' will be put into question. We can begin to judge the veracity of this argument by looking at some evidence. Let's take a topical example: the contemporary 'making up' of the public service bureaucrat as an active agent in his or her own government.

## Reinventing government

The idea that public-sector organizations need reforming has achieved a somewhat axiomatic status. To what extent and in what directions remains a matter of some considerable debate. However, one particular approach has become pre-eminent and it is this approach that underpins many of the public-sector reforms now taking place across the 'advanced' economies. This new *modus operandi* is often termed the 'New Public Management' or 'entrepreneurial governance'. According to two of its most fashionable proponents, Osborne and Gaebler (1992: 19–20), 'entrepreneurial governance' consists of ten 'essential principles' which link together to 'reinvent' the public sector.

> entrepreneurial governments promote *competition* between service providers. They *empower* citizens by pushing control out of the bureaucracy, into the community. They measure the performance of their agencies, focusing not on inputs but on *outcomes*. They are driven by their goals – their *missions* – not by their rules and regulations. They redefine their clients as *customers* and offer them choices – between schools, between training programs, between housing options. They *prevent* problems before they emerge, rather than simply offering services afterward. They put their energies into *earning* money, not simply spending it. They *decentralize* authority, embracing participatory management. They prefer *market* mechanisms to bureaucratic mechanisms. And they focus not simply on providing public services but on *catalyzing* all sectors – public, private and voluntary – into action to solve their community's problems. (Osborne and Gaebler, 1992: 19–20)

The chief target of 'entrepreneurial government' – that which it defines itself in opposition to – is the public service bureaucracy. The latter is represented as the enemy of 'good governance' for many reasons: for example, the 'bureaucratic model' is seen as unsuited to the dynamics of the 'global market place', the 'information age' and the 'knowledge-based economy', being too 'slow, inefficient and impersonal' to meet their imperatives (1992: 14–15).

Although advocates of entrepreneurial governance such as Osborne and Gaebler are critical of all forms of bureaucratic conduct, it is the perceived failure of bureaucracy to open up people's personal involvement and ideals – 'empowering' them – which comes in for some of the most severe criticism. According to Osborne and Gaebler (1992: 38), many employees in bureaucratic organizations 'feel trapped':

> Tied down by rules and regulations, numbed by monotonous tasks they know could be accomplished in half the time if they were allowed to use their minds, they live lives of quiet desperation. When they have the opportunity to work for an organization with a clear mission and minimal red tape . . . they are often re-born. When they are moved into the private sector, they often experience the same sense of liberation.

One can recognize a certain truth in their starting point – that bureaucratic organization can and often does create problems of 'motivation' for individuals, particularly those at lower levels of the hierarchy; however, they seem to neglect the fact that certain forms of organization have 'defects' as a result of delivering politically sanctioned 'virtues'. The rules and regulations against which Osborne and Gaebler rail were not invented with the sole purpose of inhibiting individual entrepreneurial activity but rather to prevent corruption and to ensure fairness, probity and reliability in the treatment of cases. Jettisoning rules and regulations in the pursuit of entrepreneurial innovation will not eradicate problems but simply change them. Rather than offering a 'permanent win/win' situation in opposition to a bureaucratic 'no win' situation, entrepreneurial forms of conduct exhibit both 'virtues' and 'defects'. The question is whether on balance the 'defects' associated with ordered, cautious, reliable administration are more widely acceptable than those associated with a more creative, risky, entrepreneurial style (du Gay, 1994; Jordan, 1994).

As Raymond Plant (1992), for example, has argued, in the public sector, which is part of government and which should therefore be subject to the rule of law, organizations are concerned with such things as equity and treating like cases in a like manner. These are not values primarily served by commercial enterprises and there is no *prima facie* reason why they should be. However, they are central to government and the rule of law in liberal democratic regimes. Thus, there is a clear danger here that the introduction of entrepreneurial principles into public-sector organizations so that they can function 'like a business' might undermine these basic principles of public provision and this serves to highlight the fact that in liberal democratic societies there is good reason to assume that markets have political and moral limits and that 'plotting some of the boundaries of markets will also involve putting enterprise in its legitimate place' (Plant, 1992: 86).

While the entrepreneur might reply that without 'enterprising up' public-sector organizations the liberties and equalities that citizens take for granted might become unaffordable, this argument assumes that the generalization of an enterprise form to the conduct of public administration, for example, will simply make the public sector 'work better' and not affect its integrity and identity as a particular form of life. However, as I argued above, it is extremely problematic to assume that the identity of a domain of activity can remain the same when its basic organizing principles are fundamentally altered. In other words, this argument neglects the fact that making public-sector organizations function like private enterprises redefines the nature of their endeavour and hence their very identity.

As Max Weber (1968: 1404), for example, argued long ago, the ethos of governing the conduct of the 'bureaucrat' (or public-sector manager, if you will), the 'entrepreneur' and the 'politician' are not identical. In addressing the different kinds of responsibility that these 'persons' have for their actions, Weber insisted upon the irreducibility of different spheres of ethical life and on the consequent necessity of applying different ethical protocols to them:

> An official who receives a directive he considers wrong can and is supposed to object to it. If his superior insists on its execution, it is his duty and even his honor to carry it out as if it corresponded to his innermost conviction and to demonstrate in this fashion that his sense of duty stands above his personal preference . . . This is the ethos of office. A political leader acting in this way would deserve contempt. He will often be compelled to make compromises, that means, to sacrifice the less to the more important . . . 'To be above Parties' – in truth, to remain outside the struggle for power – is the official's role, while this struggle for personal power, and the resulting political responsibility, is the lifeblood of the politician as well as the *entrepreneur*. (emphasis added)

By demanding – in the name of the 'market', the 'customer' or whatever – that the ethical conduct of the public administrator be judged according to the ethos of the entrepreneur, the discourse of enterprise in fact requires public-sector bureaucrats to assume the role of business persons.

Such 'boundary crossings' form an essential component of many of the public-sector reforms currently taking place across liberal democratic societies. In Britain, for example, the introduction of entrepreneurial norms and techniques into the Civil Service as a result of the 'Next Steps' initiative seems in danger of undermining the public service ethos. Top civil servants, it would appear, are increasingly being encouraged to adopt a 'can do' style of conduct characterized by 'decisiveness and an ability to get things done, rather than the more traditional approach which lays greater emphasis on analysis of options and recommendations for action based upon that analysis' (Royal Institute of Public Administration, 1987). As Richard Chapman (1991b: 3) has argued with regard to these reforms, 'the emphasis on enterprise, initiative, and a more business-like style of management . . . seems oddly at variance with the expectations of officials working in a bureaucracy.'

The central mechanism of Next Steps – the replacement of a 'unified' civil service by a host of 'autonomous' agencies – is explicitly represented as a means of 'enterprising up' the public sector. The 'new' agencies, it is argued, are structured to enable civil servants to 'obtain a sense of ownership and personal identification with the product' (Goldsworthy, 1991: 6). In other words, rather than seeking to moderate the perfectly understandable enthusiasms of public officials for particular projects and policies the agency system seems designed to incite them.

> Staff, we are told, now often think of themselves as belonging to a particular department or agency, not to a wider civil service. They work in units that, far from displaying a team spirit with a common ethos, compete with each other . . . [E]fforts are now made to stimulate feelings of enterprise and initiative in them and there can be no doubt that these have resulted in a fundamental change from an ethos . . . which contributed to the identity of the civil service. (Chapman, 1991b: 3)

The advocates of these reforms seem unable to imagine that business management and public administration are not identical in every respect. While there is a sense in which the state and the business concern are both rational 'enterprises' – deliberately and explicitly directed towards advancing goals and objectives in an efficient and effective manner – public administration differs from business management primarily because of the constraints imposed from the *political* environment within which the management processes are conducted. As Neville Johnson (1983: 193–4), among others, has argued

> Undoubtedly, the official in public service is . . . engaged extensively in the use and deployment of resources taken away from the people he or she serves and returned to them as benefits and entitlements legitimated by the system of government. It is clear that in these circumstances he or she bears a responsibility for the efficient use of resources and to this end must be ready and able to use such methods of management as will offer the best prospect of optimal performance. But the function of officials *cannot be exhaustively defined in terms of achieving results efficiently.* There is also a duty to observe the varied limits imposed on action by public bodies and to satisfy the political imperatives of public service – loyalty to those who are politically responsible, responsiveness to parliamentary and public opinion, sensitivity to the complexity of the public interest, honesty in the formulation of advice, and so on. It is out of these commitments that a professional ethic was fashioned in the public services. Even if this has weakened in recent years we cannot afford to dispense with it. This is because a system of representative government does require officials to act as the custodians of the procedural values it embodies. The contemporary concern with efficient management, with performance, and with securing results, should not be allowed to obscure this fact. *The pursuit of better management in government, important though it is, has to recognize the political limits to which it is subject.* (emphasis added)

Simply representing public-service bureaucracy in economic terms as an inefficient form of organization fails to take account of the crucial ethical and political role of the bureau in liberal democratic societies. If bureaucracy is to be reduced or abandoned and an entrepreneurial style of management adopted, then it must be recognized that while 'economic efficiency' might be improved in the short term, the longer-term costs associated with this apparent improvement may well include fairness, probity, complex equality and other crucial qualitative features of liberal democratic government. As Chapman (1991a: 17) argues

> When attention is focused on public sector management as distinct from management in other contexts, a distinctively bureaucratic type of organisation, with accountability both hierarchically and to elected representatives, may mean that far from being inefficient it is in fact the most suitable type of organization . . . Consequently, regarding bureaucracy as an inefficient type of organization may reflect a superficial understanding of bureaucracy and, perhaps, a blinkered appreciation of public sector management. Bureaucracy may be more expensive than other types of organization, but that is not surprising when democracy is not necessarily the cheapest form of government.

We are in no danger of forgetting the disasters and dangers to which bureaucracies are prone if we remind ourselves every now and again of the threats – including those posed by an unbridled entrepreneurialism – against which they offer protection.

### Concluding remarks

> We are taught that corporations have a soul, which is the most terrifying news in the world.
>
> (Gilles Deleuze, 1992)

As we have seen, a crucial feature of the discourse of enterprise is its assumption that ostensibly different organizations – hospitals, banks, charities, government departments – will have to adopt and develop broadly similar norms and techniques of conduct, for without so doing they will lack the capacity to pursue their preferred projects. The urgency with which such claims are deployed gives the very definite impression that *there is no alternative*. As Kanter (1990: 356) so forcefully declares, organizations 'must move . . . to post-entrepreneurial flexibility . . . or stagnate – thereby cancelling by default any commitments they have made'.

While such insistent singularity has obvious attractions – for one thing it offers the sort of easily graspable and communicable *Weltanschauung* that can act as a catalyst for change – it neglects the fact, as we have seen, that the generalization of an enterprise form to all forms of conduct may of itself serve to incapacitate an organization's ability to pursue its preferred projects by redefining its identity and hence what the nature of its project actually is. As the example of public-service bureaucracy indicates, different forms of life contain valuable, but often mutually unrealizable, conceptions of self-realization. To make different forms of life conform or adhere to similar norms and techniques of conduct is less likely to make those forms of life 'work better' than it is to deprive them of the props that must be in place if they are to be possessed of any distinct identity or persuasive rationale.

The more that previously distinct 'spheres' of existence become commensurable through the logic of 'enterprise', the more likely it seems to be that the possession of particular entrepreneurial attributes and capacities can be converted into general success: 'a triumphant parade through all the spheres' (Walzer, 1994: 38). This may seem unduly pessimistic and yet such developments are not as rare as they could be. If they were, perhaps, there would have been more public disquiet concerning the appointment of the former head of a cable television company – with no experience whatsoever of public sector management – to be chief executive of the prison service in the UK. While such a move could be and indeed was represented as pluralist and egalitarian in spirit – opening up the 'restrictive' labour markets of the public bureaux to anyone with the requisite talent – it is perhaps better seen as evidence of the UK government's complete indifference to the boundaries and barriers separating respective spheres of life and its determination to privilege a particular conception of the person – as entrepreneur – over all others.

While their advocates may believe that emerging entrepreneurial forms of government and the blurring of spheres that they engender are the source of an increasing egalitarianism and a deepening pluralism, I have tried to indicate that the conceptions of equality and pluralism that they deploy are remarkably thin.

The equality they promote is, in Walzer's terminology, simple not complex, being premised upon the triumph of one good over all others: enterprise. As Walzer (1994: 38) himself has argued, simple equality is the hallmark of unjust societies. Justice requires the defence of difference – different goods distributed for different reasons among different groups of people – and enterprise, as we have seen, flattens difference by making distinct spheres commensurable through the medium of the market mechanism.

Similarly, their pluralism is premised upon a vision of human wholeness. The pluralization of the centre that Donzelot (1991) refers to, for example, involves the devolution of the problems of the state so that individuals and collectivities become implicated in the task of solving them. However, as we have seen, the price of this involvement is the requirement that they conduct themselves in accordance with a particular model of action – that of the enterprise form. This latter mode of action obviously draws upon certain human capacities but it certainly does not exhaust them. Indeed, what sort of 'pluralization' process is it which presupposes a single ethical hierarchy with the entrepreneur at its apex? Such a process seems remarkably one-dimensional and frighteningly thin.

The pluralism and equality that enterprise promises and delivers can seem like an unalloyed good when seen in a certain light. By traversing established barriers between different spheres of existence, levelling the hierarchies of value they incorporate and by redefining individuals as entrepreneurs of their own lives, enterprise appears to offer the possibility of spreading the satisfaction of ruling more widely throughout the social fabric. This has ensured it some contemporary popularity on both the Right and the Left of the political spectrum. For the Right, 'spheres' means unnecessary regulation: that which inhibits individual freedom and responsibility as well as economic efficiency. On the Left, particularly the cultural Left, talk of barriers and boundaries is inimical to cherished romantic values such as freedom from normative compulsion. No wonder then that the simple egalitarian and pluralist claims of enterprise have met with continuing success, chiming as they do with crucial elements of contemporary Right- and Left-wing populism.

The possibility that different spheres of life give rise to different conceptions and comportments of the person is anathema to those predisposed to think that a common form of ethical life exists in the capacities of the individual human subject, whether as neo-conservatives we identify this figure with the 'entrepreneur of the self' or as cultural radicals we project these capacities onto 'embracing multiplicity and provisionality'. In their different ways they urge us to the same course of action: we should reject the 'exclusionary' discourses and practices that presently delimit our perceptions and abrogate our freedom of action. On the one hand, this is advocated in order that we can better become what we are – responsible, autonomous, risk-taking, free-choosing individual entrepreneurs of ourselves. Because a human being is considered to be continuously engaged in a project to shape his or her life as an autonomous choosing individual driven by the desire to optimize the worth of his or her own existence, life for that person is represented as a single basically undifferentiated arena for the pursuit of that endeavour. Multiple ethical selves constituted across the spheres give way to a singular conception of a human life as 'enterprise of the self'.

On the other hand, boundary crossing is advocated by the cultural Left in order that we might become more flexible and multidirectional in our mode of being and thus do justice to everything we have recently learned about the historicity of our situatedness; we should classify less and be forever open as befits a creature 'always in process'.

At least with the former conception of personhood one always knows where one is because everything is amenable to one singular rationale – enterprise. The latter conception is, however, simply impossible. As Stanley Fish (1994: 251) has argued, this form of 'indeterminate negativity' – understood as a refusal to be pinned down in any context – cannot be lived, and it cannot be lived because it 'demands from a wholly situated creature a mode of action or thought . . . that is free from the entanglements of situations and the lines of demarcation they declare; it demands that a consciousness that has shape only by virtue of the distinctions and boundary lines that are its content float free of these lines and boundaries and remain forever unsettled.'

The unsettling of various boundaries and barriers that enterprise performs – between work and leisure, production and consumption – could explain some of the tacit support it has received from cultural radicals, assuming as perhaps they do that it will allow increased opportunities for individuals to perform 'multiplicity and provisionality'. For Chantal Mouffe (1994: 5), among others, this tacit support is harmful because 'it impedes the constitution of distinctive political identities'. To make meaningful choices there have to be clearly differentiated alternatives. Increasingly, however, enterprise flattens difference.

In Walzer's 'spheres', success in one setting is not automatically convertible into a general success – a triumphant parade throughout the spheres. In a sense, one is always starting again as one moves across the spheres. In the world of enterprise, one is never finished with anything because one is always at it – the family, the corporation, the educational system being, in Gilles Deleuze's (1992: 5) phrase, 'metastable states coexisting in one and the same modulation, like a universal system of deformation'. As distinct spheres, with their particular conceptions and comportments of personhood, are converted into a continuous network with the entrepreneur at its centre, it is up to us to discover what we are being made to serve.

# Appendix: Research Details

The original empirical research presented in this book derives from a study into the construction of new forms of work-based subjectivity and identity in contemporary British retailing undertaken between December 1989 and January 1991. During that period over 100 semi-structured and unstructured individual interviews were conducted with a range of staff – from senior management to sales assistant level – in four multiple retail organizations. These interviews were combined with non-participant observation of a variety of formal organizational practices and informal shopfloor practices in a small number of stores located in the south-east of England.

### Company A

Company A is the main retail division of a corporation specializing in the production and marketing of health and beauty products. Company A has been the main contributor to overall group profits since at least 1986. At the end of March 1990, the chain comprised 1,051 outlets – divided into 'small' stores and 'large' stores – with a total staff (including area offices and head office) of 55,168. The chain is a market leader in many areas of its core business.

Research at A was conducted between April and July 1990. The research took place at the company's head office, at its Central London area office, its Central London training office, and in two stores in Central London, one large and one small. In all, 52 interviews were conducted with members of staff during that period. Five repeat interviews were conducted.

### Company B

Company B is the young women's wear division of a large fashion retailing corporation. During 1990–1, the company employed around 3,000 staff operating in 269 outlets of varying size nationwide. Research at B was conducted between August and November 1990. The research took place in B's head office and in six stores of differing size located in the south-east of England. Two of these stores were located in Central London. Interviews were conducted with 42 members of staff. Six repeat interviews were conducted.

## Company *C*

Company *C* produces and sells health and beauty products. Although the company operates more than 700 shops in 40 countries, with one-third of these located in the UK, it directly controls very few of the stores carrying its name. Most are franchised. In 1990, only 42 UK stores were run directly by the company. As a result the company doesn't employ many people itself – around 2,000 – the rest are employed through franchisees.

Research at company *C* was conducted in January and October 1990, and in January 1991. Three in-depth interviews were conducted with senior management staff responsible for the development and implementation of employee relations and human resource policy within the company.

## Company *D*

Company *D* is one of the UK's leading retailing organizations. Its variety store chain in the UK forms the core of the company's operations. The chain is distinctive in that it sells only 'own brand' products. Company *D* has around 300 stores and around 57,121 employees. Research at company *D* was conducted in May and October 1990. This research consisted of two in-depth interviews with senior management staff responsible for personnel and training policies.

# References

Abercrombie, N. and Warde, A. (eds) (1992) *Social Change in Britain*. Cambridge: Polity Press.

ACAS Work Research Unit (1991) 'B&Q: "Who cares wins"'. London: Advisory Conciliation and Arbitration Service, Case Study Report.

Allen, J. (1992a) 'Fordism and modern industry', in J. Allen, P. Braham and J. Lewis (eds), *The Political and Economic Forms of Modern Societies*. Cambridge: Polity Press. pp. 229–74.

Allen, J. (1992b) 'Services and the UK space economy', *Transactions of the Institute of British Geographers*, 17: 292–305.

Allen, J. and du Gay, P. (1994) 'Industry and the rest: the economic identity of services', *Work, Employment and Society*, 8(2): 255–71.

Anthony, P. (1977) *The Ideology of Work*. London: Tavistock.

Anthony, P. (1994) *Managing Culture*. Milton Keynes: Open University Press.

Argyris, C. (1957) *Personality and Organization*. New York: Harper and Row.

Armstrong, P. (1989) 'Limits and possibilities of HRM in an age of management accountancy', in J. Storey (ed.) *New Perspectives in Human Resources Management*. London: Routledge. pp. 154–66.

Baldamus, W. (1961) *Efficiency and Effort*. London: Tavistock.

Bamfield, J. (1980) 'The changing face of British retailing', *National Westminster Quarterly Review*, May: 33–45.

Bamfield, J. (1987) 'Competition and change in British retailing', *National Westminster Quarterly Review*, May: 15–29.

Barrett, M. (1991) *The Politics of Truth*. London: Verso.

Baudrillard, J. (1988) *Selected Writings*, ed. M. Poster. Cambridge: Polity Press.

Bauman, Z. (1987) *Legislators and Interpreters*. Cambridge: Polity Press.

Bauman, Z. (1988) 'Is there a postmodern sociology?', *Theory, Culture and Society*, 5(2–3): 217–37.

Becker, H.S. (1963) *Outsiders*. New York: The Free Press.

Becker, H.S. (1971) *Sociological Work*. London: Allen Lane.

Beechey, V. and Donald, J. (eds) (1986) *Subjectivity and Social Relations*. Milton Keynes: Open University Press.

Berger, P. (1964) 'Some general observations on the problem of work', in P. Berger (ed.), *The Human Shape of Work*. New York: Macmillan. pp. 211–41.

Bernstein, R.J. (1991) *The New Constellation*. Cambridge: Polity Press.

Beynon, H. (1992) 'The end of the industrial worker?' in N. Abercrombie and A. Warde (eds), *Social Change in Britain*. Cambridge: Polity Press. pp. 167–83.

Beynon, H. and Blackburn, R.M. (1972) *Perceptions of Work*. Cambridge: Cambridge University Press.

Blackwell, R.D. and Wayne Talarzyk, W. (1983) 'Lifestyle retailing: competitive strategies for the 1980s', *Journal of Retailing*, 59(4): 7–27.

Blauner, R. (1964) *Alienation and Freedom*. Chicago: University of Chicago Press.

Bluestone, B. and Huff Stevenson, M. (1981) 'Industrial transformation and the evolution of dual labour markets: the case of the retail trade in the United States', in F. Wilkinson (ed.), *The Dynamics of Labour Market Segmentation*. London: Academic Press. pp. 23–46.

Blumer, H. (1966) 'Sociological implications of the thought of George Herbert Mead', *American Journal of Sociology*, 71(5): 535–48.

Bonner, F. and du Gay, P. (1992) 'Representing the enterprising self: thirtysomething and contemporary consumer culture', *Theory, Culture and Society*, 9(2): 67–92.

Bottomore, T. and Rubel, M. (1963) *Karl Marx: Selected Writings in Sociology and Social Philosophy*. Harmondsworth: Penguin.

Bourdieu, P. (1984) *Distinction*, trans. R. Nice. London: Routledge.

Bourdieu, P. (1989) 'Social space and symbolic power', *Sociological Theory*, 7(1): 14–25.

Braverman, H. (1974) *Labour and Monopoly Capital*. New York: Monthly Review Press.

Brown, R. (1986) 'Occupational identity and career change', Paper delivered at the British Sociological Association Annual Conference, 1986.

Brown, R. and Brannen, P. (1970a) 'Social relations and social perspectives amongst shipbuilding workers – a preliminary statement. Part I', *Sociology*, 4(1): 71–84.

Brown, R. and Brannen, P. (1970b) 'Social relations and social perspectives amongst shipbuilding workers – a preliminary statement. Part II', *Sociology*, 4(2): 197–211.

Brown, R., Brannen, P., Cousins, J.M. and Samphier, M.L. (1972) 'The contours of solidarity: social stratification and industrial relations in shipbuilding', *British Journal of Industrial Relations*, 10(1): 12–41.

Bulmer, M. (1975) 'Introduction', in M. Bulmer (ed.), *Working-class Images of Society*. London: Routledge and Kegan Paul. pp. 3–15.

Burawoy, M. (1979) *Manufacturing Consent*. Chicago: University of Chicago Press.

Burawoy, M. (1985) *The Politics of Production*. London: Verso.

Burchell, G. (1993) 'Liberal government and techniques of the self', *Economy and Society*, 22(3): 266–82.

Burchell, G., Gordon, C. and Miller, P. (eds) (1991) *The Foucault Effect: Studies in Governmentality*. Brighton: Harvester Wheatsheaf.

Burkitt, I. (1991) 'Social selves: theories of the social formation of personality', *Current Sociology*, 39(3).

Burrell, G. and Morgan, G. (1979) *Sociological Paradigms and Organisational Analysis*. London: Heinemann.

Butler, J. (1993) *Bodies that Matter: on the Discursive Limits of Sex*. London: Routledge.

Campbell, C. (1987) *The Romantic Ethic and the Spirit of Modern Consumerism*. Oxford: Basil Blackwell.

de Certeau, M. (1984) *The Practice of Everyday Life*. London: University of California Press.

Chambers, I. (1986) *Popular Culture: the Metropolitan Experience*. London: Methuen.

Chapman, R.A. (1991a) 'Concepts and issues in public sector reform: the experience of the United Kingdom in the 1980s', *Public Policy and Administration*, 6(2): 1–19.

Chapman, R.A. (1991b) 'The end of the civil service?', *Teaching Public Administration*, 12(2): 11–15.

Child, J. (ed.) (1973) *Man and Organization*. London: Allen and Unwin.

Clarke, J. (1991) *New Times and Old Enemies*. London: Harper Collins.

Clarke, J., Critcher, C. and Johnson, R. (eds) (1979) *Working-class Culture*. London: Hutchinson.

Clutterbuck, D. and Crainer, S. (1988) *The Decline and Rise of British Industry*. London: W.H. Allen.

Confederation of British Industry (1988) *People – the Cutting Edge*. London: Confederation of British Industry.

Connolly, W. (1987) *Politics and Ambiguity*. Madison: University of Wisconsin Press.

Connolly, W. (1991) *Identity/Difference*. New York: Cornell University Press.

Corner, J. and Harvey, S. (eds) (1991) *Enterprise and Heritage*. London: Routledge.

Craig, C. and Wilkinson, F. (1985) 'Pay and employment in four retail trades', *Department of Employment Research Paper*, 51. London: Department of Employment.

Critcher, C. (1979) 'Sociology, cultural studies and the post-war working class', in J. Clarke, C. Critcher and R. Johnson (eds), *Working-class Culture*. London: Hutchinson. pp. 13–40.

Daniel, W.W. (1973) 'Understanding employee behaviour in its context', in J. Child (ed.), *Man and Organization*. London: Allen and Unwin.

Davies, L. and Cherns, A. (eds) (1975) *The Quality of Working Life*, 2 vols. New York: The Free Press.

Davies, R. and Howard, E. (1988) *The Changing Retail Environment*. London: Longman/ Oxford Institute of Retail Management.

Davies, S. (1990) 'Inserting gender into Burawoy's theory of the labour process', *Work, Employment and Society*, 4(3): 391–406.

Davis, H.H. (1979) *Beyond Class Images*. London: Croom Helm.

Deleuze, G. (1992) 'Postscript on the societies of control', October, 59: 3–7.

Donzelot, J. (1984) *L'Invention du social*. Paris: Éditions du Seuil.

Donzelot, J. (1991) 'The mobilization of society', in G. Burchell et al. (eds) *The Foucault Effect*. Brighton: Harvester Wheatsheaf. pp. 169–79.

Dowling, P. (1987) 'Asda's competitive advantage for the 1990s', in *Strategic Issues in Retailing*. Oxford: Institute of Retail Management Research Papers.

Dreyfus, H. and Rabinow, P. (1982) *Michel Foucault: Beyond Structuralism and Hermeneutics*. Brighton: Harvester Wheatsheaf.

Dubin, R. (1962) 'Industrial workers' worlds; a study of the central life interests of industrial workers', in A. Rose (ed.), *Human Behaviour and Social Processes*. London: Routledge and Kegan Paul. pp. 247–66.

Ducatel, K. and Blomley, N. (1990) 'Rethinking retail capital', *International Journal of Urban and Regional Research*, 19(2): 207–27.

Eagleton, T. (1991) *Ideology*. London: Verso.

Earl, M.J. (ed.) (1983) *Perspectives on Management*. Oxford: Oxford University Press.

Edgar, D. (1991) 'Are you being served?', *Marxism Today*, May: 28.

Edwards, R. (1979) *Contested Terrain*. London: Heinemann.

Elster, J. (1985) *Making Sense of Marx*. Cambridge: Cambridge University Press.

Euromonitor (1990) *Retail Trade UK 1989/1990*. London: Euromonitor.

Featherstone, M. (1982) 'The body in consumer culture', *Theory, Culture and Society*, 1(2).

Featherstone, M. (1987) 'Lifestyle and consumer culture', *Theory, Culture and Society*, 4(1): 55–70.

Featherstone, M. (1990) *Consumer Culture and Postmodernism*. London: Sage.

Fish, S. (1994) *There's No Such Thing as Free Speech . . . and it's a Good Thing Too*. Oxford: Oxford University Press.

Fiske, J. (1989) *Understanding Popular Culture*. London: Unwin Hyman.

Fitch, R. and Woudhuysen, J. (1987) 'The strategic significance of design', in E. McFadyen (ed.), *The Changing Face of British Retailing*. London: Newman Books.

Fitch-RS plc (1989) *Retail Insight* (spring). London: Fitch-RS plc.

Foucault, M. (1972) *The Archaeology of Knowledge*. London: Tavistock.

Foucault, M. (1977) *Discipline and Punish*. Harmondsworth: Penguin.

Foucault, M. (1980) *Power/Knowledge*. Brighton: Harvester Wheatsheaf.

Foucault, M. (1981) *The History of Sexuality*, vol. 1. Harmondsworth: Penguin.

Foucault, M. (1982) 'The subject and power', in H.L. Dreyfus and P. Rabinow (eds), *Michel Foucault: Beyond Structuralism and Hermeneutics*. Brighton: Harvester Wheatsheaf. pp. 208–26.

Foucault, M. (1984) 'On the genealogy of ethics: an overview of work in progress', in P. Rabinow (ed.) *The Foucault Reader*. Harmondsworth: Penguin. pp. 340–72.

Foucault, M. (1987) *The Use of Pleasure: the History of Sexuality*, vol. 2. Harmondsworth: Penguin.

Foucault, M. (1988a) 'Technologies of the self', in L.H. Martin, H. Gutman and P. Hutton (eds), *Technologies of the Self*. London: Tavistock.

Foucault, M. (1988b) 'The political technology of individuals', in L.H. Martin, H. Gutman and P. Hutton (eds) *Technologies of the Self*. London: Tavistock.

Foucault, M. (1988c) *The Care of the Self: the History of Sexuality*, vol. 3. Harmondsworth: Penguin.

Foucault, M. (1991) 'Governmentality', in G. Burchell, C. Gordon and P. Miller (eds), *The Foucault Effect: Studies in Governmentality*. Brighton: Harvester Wheatsheaf. pp. 87–104.

Fox, A. (1974) *Beyond Contract: Work, Power and Trust Relations*. London: Faber and Faber.

Fox, A. (1980) 'The meaning of work', in G. Esland and G. Salaman (eds) *The Politics of Work and Occupations*. Milton Keynes: Open University Press. pp. 139–91.

Freedland, M. (1994) 'Government by contract and public law', *Public Law*: 86–104.

Fuller, L. and Smith, V. (1991) 'Consumers' reports: management by customers in a new economy', *Work, Employment and Society*, 5(1): 1–16.

Gamble, A. (1988) *The Free Economy and the Strong State*. London: Macmillan.

Gardner, C. and Sheppard, J. (1989) *Consuming Passion: the Rise of Retail Culture*. London: Unwin Hyman.

Gaukroger, S. (1986) 'Romanticism and decommodification: Marx's conception of socialism', *Economy and Society*, 15(3): 287–333.

du Gay, P. (1991) 'Enterprise culture and the ideology of excellence', *New Formations*, 13: 45–61.

du Gay, P. (1994) 'Colossal immodesties and hopeful monsters: pluralism and organizational conduct', *Organization*, 1(1): 125–48.

du Gay, P. and Negus, K. (1994) 'The changing sites of sound: music retailing and the composition of consumers', *Media, Culture and Society*, 16(3): 395–413.

du Gay, P. and Salaman, G. (1992) 'The cult(ure) of the customer', *Journal of Management Studies*, 29(4): 616–33.

Giddens, A. (1979) *Central Problems in Social Theory*. London: Macmillan.

Giddens, A. (1991) *Modernity and Identity*. Cambridge: Polity Press.

Goffman, E. (1961) *Asylums*. New York: Anchor Books.

Gold, R. (1964) 'In the basement – the apartment building janitor', in P. Berger (ed.), *The Human Shape of Work*. New York: Macmillan. pp. 1–49.

Goldsworthy, D. (1991) *Setting up Next Steps: a Short Account of the Origins, Launch and Implementation of the Next Steps Project in the British Civil Service*. London: HMSO.

Goldthorpe, J.H., Lockwood, D., Bechhofer, F. and Platt, J. (1968) *The Affluent Worker: Industrial Attitudes and Behaviour*. Cambridge: Cambridge University Press.

Goldthorpe, J.H., Lockwood, D., Bechhofer, F. and Platt, J. (1969) *The Affluent Worker in the Class Structure*. Cambridge: Cambridge University Press.

Gordon, C. (1987) 'The soul of the citizen: Max Weber and Michel Foucault on rationality and government', in S. Whimster and S. Lash (eds), *Max Weber: Rationality and Modernity*. London: Allen and Unwin. pp. 293–316.

Gordon, C. (1991) 'Governmental rationality: an introduction', in G. Burchell, C. Gordon and P. Miller (eds), *The Foucault Effect: Studies in Governmentality*. Brighton: Harvester Wheatsheaf. pp. 1–51.

Gorz, A. (1965) 'Work and consumption', in P. Anderson and R. Blackburn (eds), *Towards Socialism*. Harmondsworth: Penguin.

Gorz, A. (1989) *Critique of Economic Reason*. London: Verso.

Gouldner, A. (1957) 'Cosmopolitans and locals', *Administrative Science Quarterly*, 2.

Grant, R.M. (1987) 'Manufacturer–retailer relations: the shifting balance of power', in G. Johnson (ed.), *Business Strategy and Retailing*. London: John Wiley. pp. 43–58.

Grossberg, L. (1988) 'Wandering audiences, nomadic critics', *Cultural Studies*, 2(3): 377–91.

Guest, D. (1990) 'Human resource management and the American dream', *Journal of Management Studies*, 27 September: 377–97.

Hacking, I. (1983) *Representing and Intervening*. Cambridge: Cambridge University Press.

Hacking, I. (1986) 'Making up people', in T.C. Heller et al. (eds), *Reconstructing Individualism*. Stanford: Stanford University Press. pp. 222–36.

Hall, S. (1984) 'The problem of ideology', in B. Matthews (ed.), *Marx 100 Years on*. London: Lawrence and Wishart.

Hall, S. (1988) *The Hard Road to Renewal*. London: Verso.

Hall, S. (1991) 'And not a shot fired', *Marxism Today*, December: 10–15.

Hall, S. (1992) 'The West and the rest: discourse and power', in S. Hall and B. Gieben (eds), *Formations of Modernity*. Cambridge: Polity Press. pp. 275–331.

Hall, S. and du Gay, P. (eds) (1995) *Questions of Cultural Identity*. London: Sage.

Haraway, D. (1990) 'A manifesto for cyborgs: science, technology and socialist feminism in the 1980s', in L. Nicholson (ed.), *Feminism/Postmodernism*. London: Routledge. pp. 190–233.

Hebdige, D. (1979) *Subculture: the Meaning of Style*. London: Methuen.

Hebdige, D. (1981) 'Object as image: the Italian scooter cycle', *Block*, 5: 44–64.

Hebdige, D. (1989) 'After the masses', *Marxism Today*, January: 48–53.

Heelas, P. (1992) 'The sacralization of the self and new age capitalism;, in N. Abercrombie and A. Warde (eds), *Social Change in Britain*. Cambridge: Polity Press. pp. 139–66.

Henriques, J., Hollway, W., Venn, C. and Walkerdine, V. (1984) *Changing the Subject*. London: Methuen.

Herzberg, F. (1968) *Work and the Nature of Man*. St Albans: Staples Press.

Hill, S. (1976) *The Dockers*. London: Heinemann.

Hill, S. (1991) 'How do you manage a flexible firm? The Total Quality model', *Work, Employment and Society*, 5(3): 397–415.

Hirst, P. and Woolley, P. (1982) *Social Relations and Human Attributes*. London: Tavistock.

Hochschild, A. (1983) *The Managed Heart*. Los Angeles: University of California Press.

Hollway, W. (1984) 'Fitting work: psychological assessment in organizations', in J. Henriques, W. Hollway, C. Venn and V. Walkerdine (eds), *Changing the Subject*. London: Methuen. pp. 26–59.

Hollway, W. (1991) *Work Psychology and Organizational Behaviour*. London: Sage.

Howard, R. (1985) *Brave New Workplace*. New York: Viking Penguin.

Hughes, E.C. (1971) *The Sociological Eye: Selected Papers*. Chicago: Aldine-Atherton.

Hunter, I. (1987) 'Setting limits to culture', *New Formations*, 4: 103–23.

Hunter, I. (1994) *Re-thinking the School*. Sydney: Allen and Unwin.

Hyman, R. (1987) 'Strategy or structure? Capital, labour and control', *Work, Employment and Society*, 1(1): 25–55.

Jameson, F. (1990) 'Clinging to the wreckage – a conversation with Stuart Hall', *Marxism Today*, September: 28–30.

Joas, H. (1987) 'Symbolic interactionism', in A. Giddens and J.H. Turner (eds), *Social Theory Today*. Cambridge: Polity Press. pp. 82–115.

Johnson, G. (ed.) (1987) *Business Strategy in Retailing*. London: John Wiley.

Johnson, N. (1983) 'Management in government', in M.J. Earl (ed.), *Perspectives on Management*. Oxford: Oxford University Press.

Jordan, G. (1994) 'Re-inventing government: but will it work?', *Public Administration*, 72: 271–9.

Kanter, R.M. (1990) *When Giants Learn to Dance*. London: Unwin Hyman.

Keat, R. (1990) 'Introduction', in R. Keat and N. Abercrombie (eds), *Enterprise Culture*. London: Routledge. pp. 3–10.

Keat, R. and Abercrombie, N. (1990) *Enterprise Culture*. London: Routledge.

Knee, D. and Walters, D. (1985) *Strategy in Retailing*. Oxford: Philip Allan.

Knights, D. (1990) 'Subjectivity, power and the labour process', in D. Knights and H. Willmott (eds), *Labour Process Theory*. London: Macmillan. pp. 297–335.

Knights, D. and Willmott, H. (1989) 'Power and subjectivity at work: from degradation to subjugation in social relations', *Sociology*, 23(4): 535–58.

Knights, D. and Willmott, H. (eds) (1990) *Labour Process Theory*. London: Macmillan.

Knights, D., Morgan, G. and Sturdy, A. (1991) 'Strategic management, financial services and information technology', Paper presented to the 10th Colloquium of the European Group for Organizational Studies (EGOS), Vienna, 15–17 July.

Lacan, J. (1987) 'Television', *October*, 40: 1–50.

Laclau, E. (1990) *New Reflections on the Revolution of our Time*. London: Verso.

Laclau, E. and Mouffe, C. (1985) *Hegemony and Socialist Strategy*. London: Verso.

Laclau, E. and Mouffe, C. (1987) 'Post-Marxism without apologies', *New Left Review*, 166: 79–106. Reprinted in E. Laclau (1990) *New Reflections on the Revolution of our Time*. London: Verso.

Lash, S. (1988) 'Discourse or figure? Postmodernism as a "regime of signification"', *Theory, Culture and Society*, 5(2–3): 311–36.

Lash, S. (1990) *Sociology of Postmodernism*. London: Routledge.

Lash, S. and Urry, J. (1987) *The End of Organized Capitalism*. Cambridge: Polity Press.

Lash, S. and Urry, J. (1993) *Economies of Signs and Space*. London: Sage.

Lefort, C. (1986) *The Political Forms of Modern Society*. Cambridge: Polity Press.

Legge, K. (1989) 'Human resource management: a critical analysis', in J. Storey (ed.), *New Perspectives in Human Resources Management*. London: Routledge. pp. 19–40.

Lewis, J.C. (1985) 'Technical change in retailing: its impact on employment and access', *Environment and Planning B: Planning and Design*, 12: 165–91.

Lockwood, D. (1975) 'Sources of variation in working class images of society', in G. Esland et al. (eds), *People and Work*. Edinburgh: Holmes/McDougal/Open University Press. pp. 197–208.

Lockwood, D. (1988) 'The weakest link in the chain? Some comments on the Marxist theory of action', in D. Rose (ed.), *Social Stratification and Economic Change*. London: Hutchinson. pp. 57–97.

Lyotard, J-F. (1984) *The Postmodern Condition*, trans. G. Bennington and G. Massumi. Minneapolis: University of Minnesota Press.

McGregor, D. (1960) *The Human Side of Enterprise*. New York: McGraw-Hill.

MacIntyre, A. (1985) *After Virtue*. London: Duckworth.

McRobbie, A. (1991) 'New times in cultural studies', *New Formations*, 13: 1–17.

Marchington, M. and Parker, P. (1990) *Changing Patterns of Employee Relations*. Brighton: Harvester Wheatsheaf.

Marcuse, H. (1964) *One-dimensional Man*. Harmondsworth: Penguin.

Marsden, D. and Richardson, R. (1994) 'Performing for pay? The effects of "merit pay" on motivation in the public service', *British Journal of Industrial Relations*, 32(2): 243–61.

Marshall, G. (1988) 'Some remarks on the study of working-class consciousness', in D. Rose (ed.), *Social Stratification and Economic Change*. London: Hutchinson. pp. 98–126.

Martin, P. and Nicholls, J. (1987) *Creating a Committed Workforce*. London: Institute of Personnel Management.

Mauss, M. (1979) *Sociology and Psychology*. London: Routledge and Kegan Paul.

Mayo, E. (1933) *The Human Problems of an Industrial Civilisation*. New York: Macmillan.

Mayo, E. (1949) *The Social Problems of an Industrial Civilisation*. London: Routledge and Kegan Paul.

Mercer, K. (1991) 'Welcome to the jungle', in J. Rutherford (ed.), *Identity*. London: Lawrence and Wishart. pp. 43–71.

Miller, D. (1987) *Material Culture and Mass Consumption*. Oxford: Basil Blackwell.

Miller, P. and O'Leary, T. (1989) 'The entrepreneurial order', Paper presented to the 5th Annual UMIST/Aston Conference on the Organization and Control of the Labour Process.

Miller, P. and O'Leary, T. (1993) 'Accounting expertise and the politics of the product: economic citizenship and modes of corporate governance', *Accounting, Organizations and Society*, 18(2/3): 187–206.

Miller, P. and Rose, N. (1988) 'The Tavistock Programme: the government of subjectivity and social life', *Sociology* 22(2): 171–92.

Miller, P. and Rose, N. (1990) 'Governing economic life', *Economy and Society*, 19(1): 1–31.

Mills, C.W. (1953) *White Collar*. New York: Oxford University Press.

Mills, C.W. (1963) 'Situated actions and vocabularies of motive', in C.W. Mills, *Power, Politics and People*. New York: Oxford University Press. pp. 439–52.

Milward, N., Stevens, M., Smart, D. and Howes, W.R. (1992) *Workplace Industrial Relations in Transition*. Aldershot: Dartmouth.

Minson, J. (1985) *Genealogies of Morals*. London: Macmillan.

Moorhouse, H.F. (1984) 'American automobiles and workers' dreams', in K. Thompson (ed.), *Work, Employment and Unemployment*. Milton Keynes: Open University Press. pp. 247–60.

Moorhouse, H. (1989) 'Models of work, models of leisure', in C. Rojek (ed.), *Leisure for Leisure*. London: Routledge. pp. 15–35.

Morley, D. (1992) 'The geography of television: ideology, domesticity and community', Paper presented to the Open University Seminar Series 'Culture and Communication', May.

Morris, M. (1988) 'Banality in cultural studies', *Discourse*, 10: 2–29.

Mort, F. (1989) 'The writing on the wall', *New Statesman and Society*, 12 May: 40–1.

Mouffe, C. (1991) 'Pluralism and modern democracy: around Carl Schmitt', *New Formations*, 14: 1–16.

Mouffe, C. (1994) *The Return of the Political*. London: Verso.

Mulgan, G. (1994) *Politics in an Anti-political Age*. Cambridge: Polity Press.

Murray, R. (1988a) 'From Fordism to flexibility: the place of retailing', Paper presented at a Symposium on the Micro-electronics Revolution and Regional Development, Labour Organisation and the Future of the Post-industrialising Societies, Milan, April.

Murray, R. (1988b) 'Life after Henry (Ford)', *Marxism Today*, October.

Nava, M. (1987) 'Consumerism and its contradictions', *Cultural Studies*, 1(2): 204–10.

Newby, H. (1977) *The Deferential Worker*. London: Allen Lane.

Noyelle, T. (1987) *Beyond Industrial Dualism*. Boulder, Colorado: Westview Press.

Noyelle, T. (ed.) (1990) *Skills, Wages and Productivity in the Service Sector*. Boulder, Colorado: Westview.

Ogbonna, E. and Wilkinson, B. (1988) 'Corporate strategy and corporate culture: the management of change in the UK supermarket industry', *Personnel Review*, 17(6): 10–14.

Ogbonna, E. and Wilkinson, B. (1990) 'Corporate strategy and corporate culture: the view from the checkout', *Personnel Review*, 19(4): 9–15.

Ollman, B. (1971) *Alienation*. Cambridge: Cambridge University Press.

Osborne, D. and Gaebler, T. (1992) *Re-inventing Government*. Reading, Mass.: Addison Wesley.

Ouchi, W. (1981) *Theory Z*. Reading, Mass.: Addison Wesley.

Pateman, C. (1989) *The Disorder of Women*. Cambridge: Polity Press.

Peters, T. (1987) *Thriving on Chaos*. Basingstoke, Macmillan.

Peters, T. (1992) *Liberation Management*. Basingstoke: Macmillan.

Peters, T. and Waterman, R.H. (1982) *In Search of Excellence*. New York: Harper and Row.

Pinchot, G. (1985) *Intrapreneuring: Why You Don't Have to Leave the Corporation to Become an Entrepreneur*. New York: Harper and Row.

Plant, R. (1992) 'Enterprise in its place: the moral limits of markets', in P. Heelas and P. Morris (eds), *The Values of the Enterprise Culture: the Moral Debate*. London: Routledge.

Pond, C. (1977) *Trouble in Store*. London: Low Pay Unit.

Robertson, R. (1980) 'Aspects of identity and authority in sociological theory', in R. Robertson and B. Holzner (eds), *Identity and Authority*. Oxford: Basil Blackwell. pp. 218–65.

Robins, K. (1991) 'Tradition or translation: national culture in its global context', in J. Corner and S. Harvey (eds), *Enterprise and Heritage*. London: Routledge. pp. 21–44.

Robinson, O. (1988) 'The changing labour market: growth of part-time employment and labour market segmentation in Britain', in S. Walby (ed.), *Gender Segregation at Work*. Milton Keynes: Open University Press.

Robinson, O. and Wallace, J. (1974) 'Part-time employment and low pay in retail distribution in Britain', *Industrial Relations Journal*, 5(1): 38–54.

Rock, P. (1979) *The Making of Symbolic Interactionism*. London: Macmillan.

Roethlisberger, F.J. and Dickson, W.J. (1939) *Management and the Worker*. Cambridge, Mass.: Harvard University Press.

Rorty, A. (1988) *Mind in Action*. Boston: Beacon Press.

Rorty, R. (1982) *Consequences of Pragmatism*. Brighton: Harvester Wheatsheaf.

Rorty, R. (1991) *Objectivity, Relativism and Truth*. Cambridge: Cambridge University Press.

Rosaldo, R. (1993) *Culture and Truth*. London: Routledge.

Rose, M. (1988) *Industrial Behaviour*. Harmondsworth: Penguin.

Rose, N. (1989) 'Governing the enterprising self', Paper presented at a Conference on the Values of the Enterprise Culture, University of Lancaster, September. Also published in P. Heelas and P. Morris (eds), *The Values of the Enterprise Culture: the Moral Debate*. London: Routledge. pp. 141–64.

Rose, N. (1990) *Governing the Soul: the Shaping of the Private Self*. London: Routledge.

Rose, N. (1993) 'Government, authority and expertise in advanced liberalism', *Economy and Society*, 22(3): 283–99.

Rose, N. (forthcoming) 'Identity, genealogy, history', in S. Hall and P. du Gay (eds), *Questions of Cultural Identity*. London: Sage.

Roy, D. (1969) 'Making out: a counter-system of workers' control of work situations and relationships', in T. Burns (ed.), *Industrial Man*. London: Allen Lane. pp. 359–79.

Roy, D. (1973) 'Banana time: job satisfaction and informal interaction', in G. Salaman and K. Thompson (eds), *People and Organisations*. London: Longman. pp. 205–22.

Royal Institute of Public Administration Working Group Report (1987) *Top Jobs in Whitehall: Appointments and Promotions in the Senior Civil Service*. London: RIPA.

Rubery, J., Tarling, R. and Wilkinson, F. (1987) 'Flexibility, marketing and the organization of production', *Labour and Society*, 12(1): 131–51.

Rushdie, S. (1991) *Imaginary Homelands*. London: Granta.

Sabel, C. (1982) *Work and Politics*. Cambridge: Cambridge University Press.

Sabel, C. (1991) 'Moebius strip organizations and open labour markets: some consequences of the reintegration of conception and execution in a volatile economy', in P. Bourdieu and J.S. Coleman (eds) *Social Theory for a Changing Society*. Boulder, Colorado: Westview Press. pp. 23–54.

Salaman, G. (1974) *Community and Occupation*. Cambridge: Cambridge University Press.

Salaman, G. (1986) *Working*. Chichester: Ellis Horwood/Tavistock.

Segal-Horn, S. (1987) 'The retail environment in the UK', in G. Johnson (ed.), *Business Strategy and Retailing*. London: John Wiley. pp. 13–33.

Silver, J. (1987) 'The ideology of excellence: management and neo-conservatism', *Studies in Political Economy*, 24: 105–29.

Smith, P. (1988) *Discerning the Subject*. Minneapolis: University of Minnesota Press.

Smith, S. (1988) 'How much change at the store? The impact of new technologies and labour processes on managers and staffs in retail distribution', in D. Knights and H. Willmott (eds), *New Technology and the Labour Process*. London: Macmillan. pp. 143–62.

Sparks, L. (1987) 'Employment in retailing: trends and issues', in G. Johnson (ed.), *Business Strategy and Retailing*. London: John Wiley.

Sparks, L. (1989) 'The retail sector', in P. Jones (ed.), *Management in Service Industries*. London: Pitman.

Stallybrass, P. and White, A. (1986) *The Politics and Poetics of Transgression*. London: Methuen.

Storey, J. (1985) 'The means of management control', *Sociology*, 19(2): 193–211.

Storey, J. (ed.) (1989) *New Perspectives in Human Resource Management*. London: Routledge.

Storey, J. and Sisson, J. (1989) 'Looking to the future', in J. Storey (ed.), *New Perspectives in Human Resource Management*. London: Routledge. pp. 167–83.

Strauss, A. (1969) *Mirrors and Masks*. San Francisco: The Sociology Press.

Stryker, S. (1980) *Symbolic Interactionism*. California: Benjamin/Cummings Publishing.

Taylor, C. (1989) *Sources of the Self*. Cambridge: Cambridge University Press.

Thompson, P. (1990) 'Crawling from the wreckage: the labour process and the politics of production', in D. Knights and H. Willmott (eds), *Labour Process Theory*. London: Macmillan. pp. 95–124.

Thompson, P. and McHugh, D. (1990) *Work Organizations: a Critical Introduction*. London: Macmillan.

Townley, B. (1989) 'Selection and appraisal: reconstituting social relations?', in J. Storey (ed.), *New Perspectives in Human Resource Management*. London: Routledge. pp. 92–108.

Townley, B. (1994) *Re-framing Human Resource Management*. London: Sage.

Turner, B. (1986) 'Sociological aspects of organizational symbolism', *Organization Studies*, 7: 101–15.

Urry, J. (1990) 'Work, production and social relations', *Work Employment and Society*, 4(2): 271–80.

Veblen, T. (1957) *The Theory of the Leisure Class*. London: George Allen and Unwin.

Walsh, T. (1988) 'Segmentation and flexibility: part-time and temporary work in the retail and hotel trades'. Paper presented at the Conference on Questions of Restructuring Work and Employment, University of Warwick, Industrial Relations Research Unit, July.

Walters, D. and Knee, D. (1985) 'Competing successfully in a dynamic world', *Retail and Distribution Management*, March/April: 11–17.

Walzer, M. (1983) *Spheres of Justice*. Oxford: Basil Blackwell.

Walzer, M. (1984) 'Liberalism and the art of separation', *Political Theory*, 12(3): 315–30.

Walzer, M. (1994) *Thick and Thin: Moral Argument at Home and Abroad*. Notre Dame, Indiana: University of Notre Dame Press.

Warde, A. (1992) 'Notes on the relationship between production and consumption', in R. Burrows and C. Marsh (eds), *Consumption and Class: Divisions and Change*. Basingstoke: Macmillan.

Weber, M. (1968) *Economy and Society*, 3 vols. New York: Bedminster.

Westergaard, J. (1970) 'The re-discovery of the cash-nexus', in R. Miliband and J. Saville (eds), *The Socialist Register*. London: Merlin. pp. 111–38.

White, D. (1987) 'The role of advertising in developing retail strategy', in *Strategic Issues in Retailing*. Oxford Institute of Retail Management Research Papers.

Williams, R. (1977) *Marxism and Literature*. Oxford: Oxford University Press.

Williamson, J. (1986) 'The problems of being popular', *New Socialist*, 41: 14–15.

Williamson, J. (1991) Article in the *Guardian*, 4 July: 28.

Willis, P. (1978) *Profane Culture*. London: Routledge and Kegan Paul.

Willis, P. (1990) *Common Culture: Symbolic Work at Play in the Everyday Cultures of the Young*. Milton Keynes: Open University Press.

Wood, S. (1989) 'New wave management?', *Work, Employment and Society*, 3(3): 379–402.

Wright, P. (1987) 'Excellence'. *London Review of Books*, May: 8–11.

Yudice, G. (1989) 'Marginality and the ethics of survival', in A. Ross (eds), *Universal Abandon?* Edinburgh: Edinburgh University Press. pp. 214–36.

Zizek, S. (1989) *The Sublime Object of Ideology*. London: Verso.

# Index